THE ETHICS OF WITNESSING

CULTURAL EXPRESSIONS OF WORLD WAR II

INTERWAR PRELUDES, RESPONSES, MEMORY

PHYLLIS LASSNER, SERIES EDITOR

The Ethics of Witnessing

The Holocaust in Polish Writers' Diaries from Warsaw, 1939–1945

Rachel Feldhay Brenner

NORTHWESTERN UNIVERSITY PRESS | EVANSTON, ILLINOIS

Northwestern University Press
www.nupress.northwestern.edu

Printed in the United States of America

10   9   8   7   6   5   4   3   2   1

Library of Congress Cataloging-in-Publication Data

Brenner, Rachel Feldhay, 1946– author.
  The ethics of witnessing : the Holocaust in Polish writers' diaries from Warsaw,
1939–1945 / Rachel Feldhay Brenner.
      pages cm. — (Cultural expressions of World War II)
    ISBN 978-0-8101-2975-7 (cloth : alk. paper)
    1. Holocaust, Jewish (1939–1945) — Poland — Warsaw — Personal narratives —
History and criticism. 2. Holocaust, Jewish (1939–1945), in literature. 3. Authors,
Polish — 20th century — Diaries. 4. Warsaw (Poland) — Intellectual life — 20th
century. 5. Dabrowska, Maria, 1889–1965 — Criticism and interpretation.
6. Iwaszkiewicz, Jaroslaw, 1894–1980 — Criticism and interpretation. 7. Wylezynska,
Aura — Criticism and interpretation. 8. Nalkowska, Zofia, 1884–1954 — Criticism
and interpretation. 9. Rembek, Stanislaw — Criticism and interpretation. I. Title.
II. Series: Cultural expressions of World War II.
DS134.64.B74 2014
891.85 — dc23

                                                            2014001058

For my grandsons, Eli and Levy

May you be always open-minded and curious about the world

Contents

Acknowledgments

On this page, which marks the completion of this book, I wish to express my gratitude for the good fortune to have had the exceptional support and confidence of friends, scholars, and institutions throughout the long process of writing. First, I would like to thank the University of Wisconsin-Madison and the College of Letters and Science, whose generous support has aided my research for many years. My tenure as a senior scholar at the Institute for Research in the Humanities under Professor Susan Friedman's leadership was invaluable in conceptualizing and crystallizing considerable parts of the book. I remain grateful for that enriching experience.

This book was conceived during my Sosland Foundation Fellowship at the Center for Advanced Holocaust Studies in the United States Holocaust Memorial Museum, and I would like to thank the center and its staff, especially Michlean Amir and Aleksandra Borecka, for the archival materials and ideas they contributed to the project.

I am profoundly indebted to my friends in Poland for their support. Dr. Alina Molisak most generously introduced me to libraries and archives in Warsaw in the first stages of my research; Professor Lucyna Aleksandrowicz-Pędich supported the book by giving it a public forum at her university. Professor Barbara Engelking gave me of her time and attention, and Professor Sławomir Buryła supplied me with invaluable information and sources. My dear friends Professors Shoshana Ronen and Stanisław Obirek offered me their encouragement and support.

My project was supported by wonderful friends on this continent as well. I am deeply indebted to Professors Anthony Polonsky and Berel Lang, whose gracious encouragement and interest in my work sustained me in moments of doubt; it is a debt of gratitude I will never be able to repay. I am thankful to my friend and editor Dr. Debra Hershkowitz for making this book so much better. Her intellectual engagement with the subject matter was of enormous value to the project.

I would like to thank Northwestern University Press, and especially Professor Phyllis Lassner, the editor of the Cultural Expressions series, whose friendship and confidence in the project made this book possible.

As always, I am grateful to my children, Guy and Shelly, for their patience and love.

The Ethics of Witnessing

The Holocaust and the Problem of Empathy: Polish Christian Diarists Look at the Ghetto

Looking at the burning Ghetto in April 1943, the prominent Polish writer Jarosław Iwaszkiewicz noted in his diary, with horror and despair, that

> there die artists such as Roman Kramsztyk, such close, old friends as Olek Landau, parents of friends such as Pawełek Hertz, Józik Rajnfeld, and we can do nothing. We helplessly watch the dark smoke that rises from their houses, from their bodies. This is extremely difficult to comprehend and to live through. We don't try to understand; we just go on.[1]

On April 22, 1943, Maria Dąbrowska, Iwaszkiewicz's contemporary and fellow writer, offered a laconic, emotionally disengaged observation of the same event in her diary: "We saw billows of smoke above the Ghetto, where apparently the fighting still continues."

Iwaszkiewicz and Dąbrowska were among five notable Polish writers who stayed in Warsaw or its vicinity during the war. They, along with Zofia Nałkowska, Aurelia Wyleżynśńska, and Stanisław Rembek, kept diaries in which they recorded the Occupation and the unfolding Jewish genocide. Theirs are the only wartime diaries known to have been kept by writers in that city.[2] The Holocaust challenged the very foundations of these liberal intellectuals' formative, humanist Weltanschauung. Staunch believers in humanity's enlightened progress, they were now confronted with a world which no longer endorsed the humanistic universals of human dignity and the sanctity of human life, a world in which the capacity for empathy, which enables human beings to recognize each other's mental and emotional sameness, had been shattered.[3]

Despite their firm commitment to humanism, the Warsaw diarists did not display a uniform response to the Jewish genocide, whose evolution — the establishment of the Ghetto, the deportations in 1942, and the Uprising and liquidation of the Ghetto in 1943 — they all saw, heard, and smelled. Their reactions ranged from deliberate evasion of the victims' plight, to paralyzing dismay at the unfolding horror, to active participation in altruistic rescue operations. These varied responses shed light on the moral and psychological effect of witnessing. Whereas the unopposed racist ideology which led to the extermination of part of the human race shattered the ethical legacy of the Enlightenment on a worldwide scale, the immediacy of the degradation and death of the Warsaw victims of the Final Solution tested the steadfastness of the diarists' humanistic selves. I will suggest that the diarists' contemporaneous responses to the Jewish genocide deepen our understanding of the ethical, mental, and emotional challenges that face any witness of terror.

The Warsaw diarists' ethical crisis must be understood within the larger historical narrative of the diaries, namely, the increasingly oppressive German occupation of Poland. For the Poles, the physical deprivations and terror inflicted on the general population by the occupiers, combined with the reality of the Jewish genocide, created an environment of uncertainty, danger, and brutality that affected the basic ethics of all social interaction. The German occupation was especially ruthless in Warsaw, where the aim was to destroy the center of Polish culture along with Poland's intelligentsia.[4] It was commonly believed that "once the Germans finish the Jews off, the Poles will be next in line." While this grim prediction did not reflect actual German plans, which destined the Poles not for extermination but for slave labor, it gained credence due to the horrifying conditions of the occupation. While we must recognize, respect, and, above all, remember Polish rescuers of Jews,[5] the majority of Poles, demoralized by the rule of terror, had very few qualms about the extermination of the Jews, and many acquiesced in the Nazi plan of the Final Solution.[6] In Barbara Engelking-Boni's words, "The many Poles who actually saved Jews . . . did so in the face of general indifference among most Poles to the fate of the Jews."[7] Gabriel Finder corroborates this position, arguing that "Polish indifference to the fate of

Jews magnified their isolation, making it easier for the Germans to persecute, seize, and deport them, and much harder for the small number of Poles, relatively speaking, who wished to extend a helping hand or hide them."[8]

Already in 1944, Emanuel Ringelblum delivered a devastating indictment of the Polish attitude to the Holocaust. Writing after the destruction of the Warsaw Ghetto, Ringelblum tried to present an objective historical perspective of Polish-Jewish relationships during the war. He acknowledged that some Poles were sympathetic to the Jews, but the general answer to his questions "What did the Poles do when millions of Polish Jews were led to the stake? . . . What did our neighbors do the moment when the invader, armed from head to foot, attacked the most defenseless people of all, the Jews?" reaffirmed the prevailing anti-Semitic Polish response to the Jews' plight.[9] Even earlier, in 1943, Czesław Miłosz had commemorated this attitude in his poem "Campo di Fiori," in which Poles watch the burning Ghetto while riding the carousel set up for Easter in Krasinskich Square (Plac Krasińskich) near the Ghetto wall.[10] And in a 1940 report, "Solution of the Jewish Question," Jan Karski observed that

> [the Polish] attitude toward the Jews is overwhelmingly severe, often without pity. A large percentage of them are benefiting from the rights that the new situation gives them. . . . It brings them, to a certain extent, nearer to the Germans. . . . Although the Polish nation loathes the Germans mortally this question [i.e., the Jewish Question] is creating something akin to a narrow bridge upon which the Germans and a large portion of Polish society are finding agreement.[11]

Contemporary discussion of the problem of the Polish population's general disregard for Jewish suffering was instigated by Jan Błoński's seminal 1987 essay "The Poor Poles Look at the Ghetto."[12] Błoński used Miłosz's other 1943 poem, "A Poor Christian Looks at the Ghetto," written in Warsaw when the Ghetto was burning, to diagnose the Poles' repressed guilt for not having shown solidarity with the victimized Jews and for having acquiesced with the genocide on Polish territory.[13] As Błoński saw it, the Poles, having been shaped by xenophobic nationalism and pervasive anti-Semitism before the war,[14] did little to oppose the murder of the Jews during it. Indeed, the prewar years of Poland's independence were marked by intensifying anti-Semitic propaganda and discrimination. Following the death of Józef Piłsudski, the authoritarian but revered ruler of Poland, in 1935, nationalistic right-wing elements, supported by the Catholic Church, ramped up their anti-Semitic propaganda, which promoted Jewish emigration, boycotts of Jewish businesses, and expulsion of Jewish students from the universities.[15] In contrast, the opposition of left-wing intellectuals to anti-Semitism, and especially to the persecutions of Jewish students at the universities, represented a contrary sociopolitical drive to develop Polish society in the spirit of scientific progress, humanistic values, and democratic ideas.

Błoński claimed that Miłosz's poem represented Poland's repressed past, and that in order to purge the stigma of having desecrated their land with genocide, Poles must "face up to our duty of viewing our past truthfully," which would amount to a straightforward, honest acknowledgment of the transgressions committed against the Jewish people. Błoński's provocative essay sparked off discordant Polish-Jewish debates, which have often erupted into acrimonious exchanges. The controversy continues to rage. Błoński's assessment has been disputed by those who claim that an exceptional humanitarian attitude existed among wartime Poles toward the Jews, or that only an insignificant number of Poles actually assisted the implementation of the Final Solution in Poland, or that the immense suffering of ethnic Poles under the Occupation is comparable to that of the Jews, while Jewish and Polish Holocaust scholars have attempted to refute such denials of Polish moral failure.[16]

Błoński's call for expiation was certainly of great merit. However, his anachronistic interpretation of Miłosz's poem in support of a psychoanalytical solution to lingering Polish postwar trauma, through an acknowledgment of the repressed past, obfuscated the poem's more immediate message. Miłosz's use of the present tense in the poem's title, the date of the poem's composition, and the poem's Warsaw setting all capture the liquidation of the Ghetto as it happens, and emphasize the impact of Jewish genocide on the Christian self-identity of the witnessing Poles.

Miłosz's focus on the immediacy of the eyewitness's experience raises the question of what the "poor Christian" on the "Aryan side" of Warsaw would actually have seen when he looked at the Ghetto walls. Certainly he could see, as many did, the infamous carousel set up in Krasinskich Square. And, as Dąbrowska's diary note indicates, it was impossible not to see the clouds of smoke rising over Warsaw from behind the Ghetto wall. However, the mass auto-da-fé could not be seen. As Iwaszkiewicz observed with dismay, the burning bodies behind the wall could only be imagined. Miłosz's poem thus records the Christian speaker's imagined picture of the invisible horror and the transforming effect of this unseen image.

After having described the collapsed material world, where "Bees build around red liver, Ants build around black bone," Miłosz's poetic narrator notices that

> Slowly, boring a tunnel, a guardian mole makes his way
> With a small red lamp fastened to his forehead.
> He touches burned bodies, counts them, pushes on.
> He distinguishes human ashes by their luminous vapour,
> The ashes of each man by a different part of the spectrum.

The "guardian mole" is making a grotesque inventory of the unidentifiable dead: he counts the charred bones and organs, and sifts through the ashes.[17] The total annihilation of the Jews has devastating implications for the "poor Christian's" Christian self-identity:

> I am afraid, so afraid of the guardian mole,
> He has swollen eyelids, like a Patriarch
> Who has sat much in the light of candles
> Reading the great book of the species.
> What will I tell him, I, a Jew of the New Testament,
> Waiting two thousand years for the second coming of Jesus?
>
> And he will count me among the helpers of death:
> The uncircumcised.

The "great book of the species," the Torah,[18] whose story of Creation established the dominion of the human race over other species, has become obsolete; in the apocalyptic reality of human extermination, ants and bees have become the superior species, appropriating burned human organs and ashes for their quotidian needs. Thus the annihilation of the Jews has abolished the natural order of the species. But the genocidal reality of the war has also eliminated the natural order of human existence by placing the human race in the realm of death: the silent complicity of the Christian witness with the immolation of the Jews in the Ghetto signifies the death of the religious foundations of the Christian faith. It erases the narrator's identity as "a Jew of the New Testament" by severing the affinity of Christians with Jesus, the Jew.[19] The Final Solution, aimed at all Jews, puts an end to the centuries-long wait for the return of the circumcised Messiah. The murder of the Jews by his fellow Christians implicates Miłosz's Christian witness in the Redeemer's irrevocable immolation, which terminates the promise of the second coming and, ironically, impoverishes the "poor Christian" by robbing him of Jesus's message of love, grace, and spiritual salvation.

Miłosz's Christian's sense of complicity resulted in "metaphysical guilt," a feeling by no means foreign to the Warsaw diarists. Nałkowska's despair at the sight of the liquidation of the Ghetto echoed Iwaszkiewicz's torment at his helplessness upon seeing the smoke arising from his Jewish friends' burning bodies. On April 29, 1943, Nałkowska wrote,

> I am next to it [i.e., the burning Ghetto], and I still live! . . . How could I have been forced into this, when just to be next to it, just to be alive, means to acquiesce with it? This is infamy, not only torment. This is horrendous shame, not just compassion. All the efforts to bear it, not to go insane, to somehow sustain one's self in the midst of this horror evoke guilt.

Wyleżyńska's self-inflicted guilt produced a frightening vision, when on the third night of the Uprising (April 21, 1943), she imagined the ghosts of the Jews she was rescuing blaming her for their unavoidable deaths: "At my bedhead settle phantoms of people who are still alive. [They were] those who stayed outside the battlefield [i.e., the Ghetto], but who belonged there. They will torment me as the emissaries of those who were perishing." In contrast, Dąbrowska and Rembek evaded the pain of witnessing the Jewish suffering by reaffirming their prewar anti-Jewish prejudices. Clinging to nationalistic propaganda which proclaimed the special historical destiny of the ethnic Poles, Dąbrowska and Rembek privileged Polish suffering over that of the Jews, but neither endorsed Polish participation in the genocide, which Rembek strongly indicted in his postwar fiction.

It should be noted that none of the Warsaw diarists were free from what I call "anti-Semitic socialization." Though adhering to the ideals of progress and equality, they were all nonetheless conditioned by an increasingly xenophobic social climate, which highlighted and denounced the "otherness" of Jews. I would therefore like to warn against an anachronistic judgment of these writers' often unself-conscious anti-Semitic tendencies. In today's Western ideological climate of forcefully promoted pluralism and racial blindness, the writers' condescending, often mocking, and dismissive attitude toward Jews would not have been tolerated. Polish prewar anti-Semitism, however, confronts us with a complex and by no means monolithic phenomenon, and the wide range of Polish behavior toward Jews during the Holocaust requires nuanced consideration rather than unequivocal condemnation. Indeed, the diarists' wartime recordings of their responses to the meticulously planned and executed Final Solution show that their prewar anti-Semitic mindset did not necessarily foretell a lack of moral integrity in the extreme situation of the Final Solution, and it certainly did not presage consent to the victimization of the Jews.[20]

The emotional and ethical impact of the Jewish genocide on Polish witnesses has not been the subject of scholarly investigation.[21] Research on the non-Jewish response to the Jewish extermination has mainly focused on Polish acquiescence with the Holocaust and on testimonies of Polish rescuers.[22] However, most research on contemporaneous responses to the Holocaust has focused exclusively on Jewish diaries, chronicles, and letters.[23] This research has shown that Jewish writing at the time was motivated primarily by a desire to leave a historical testimony of the horror, though they also wrote to alert the world or to call for revenge or to provide future legal evidence.[24] Very little attention has been given to the victims' emotional and mental efforts to maintain their moral values and faith in humanistic ideals. In my study of personal accounts of Jewish intelligentsia from the Holocaust, I examined the victims' methods of coping with the traumatic collapse of their faith in the enlightened humanistic creed which they embraced and considered their own.[25] With regard to the Polish intellectuals discussed here, scant attention has been given to the diaristic responses of Dąbrowska, Nałkowska, and Iwaszkiewicz. The principal objective of the often contentious investigations of their responses to the Jewish destruction has been to evaluate the extent of the diarists' anti-Semitic proclivities.[26] These studies consider the diarists' direct responses to the Jewish genocide along the lines of the Polish-Jewish controversies that arose in response to Błoński's essay.

The diaries themselves, however, resist such partial, ideologically informed appraisals. A close reading of the texts reveals complex patterns in the diarists' mental and emotional struggles to protect their eroding faith in humanist ideals and beliefs. Each diary searched, in its own way, for means to cope with what Iwaszkiewicz aptly named "świat na Opacz," a play on words meaning "an upside-down world."[27]

The diarists' wartime struggle for a semblance of normalcy in a world which no longer made sense needs to be considered against the background of their prewar ideological formation. Polish sovereignty shaped these writers as worldly men and women of letters and as Polish citizens. The interwar world made it possible to integrate their cosmopolitan and national Weltanschauungs. They all traveled extensively in western Europe, which allowed them to acquire European languages and keep abreast with Western cultural trends; their interest in literature, the arts, and music affiliated them closely with the European intellectual scene, by which they were all deeply influenced. But their attraction to the progressive, culturally, and scientifically advanced West did not detract from their proud self-identification as patriotic Poles. They were keenly interested in Poland's cultural, social, and economic progress. For all of them, the reestablishment of the Polish state confirmed Poland's special position among the nations. This heroic national myth, shaped by the Romantic Polish poets such as Mickiewicz, Słowacki, and Krasiński in response to the Partitions of Poland, designated Poland as "Christ of the nations" with a messianic destiny.[28] Thus Dąbrowska saw the Polish people as the model of universal human friendship for the Western world, and Iwaszkiewicz envisioned Poland as the bulwark of Western civilization against the "barbaric" East. In the interwar period, the patriotic ethos of Poland became increasingly ethnically exclusive, and therefore antagonistic to minorities, especially the Jews. But even as

Endecja, the nationalistic right-wing National Democratic movement, characterized by powerful anti-Semitic xenophobia, was gaining power in interwar Poland, the diarists remained steadfast adherents to the humanistic ideals of equal rights, human dignity, solidarity, and individual freedom. They hoped that the miraculously reconstituted Polish state would measure up to the political, social, and economic models of the West and would become a respected member in the family of progressive democracies.

These writers belonged to the Polish intellectual elite and they knew each other well. Understandably, their relationships were occasionally competitive: they read each other's new works, saw each other's stage productions, and reviewed each other's accomplishments in the press, often expressing more critical opinions in their diaries. During the Occupation, the writers mentioned each other in their wartime diaries. Wyleżyńska used to see Nałkowska in the Literary Kitchen (Kuchnia Literacka), a meeting place offering cheaper meals for writers and artists and a forum for prohibited teaching. Wyleżyńska also wrote quite critically about Dąbrowska, who refused her support to a young Polish intellectual. In her diary, Nałkowska mentioned her hospital visits with ailing Dąbrowska, while Dąbrowska recorded meeting Nałkowska at literary and social gatherings, and paying her respects when Nałkowska's mother died. The perennially destitute Rembek visited Iwaszkiewicz and commented enviously on his affluence; Iwaszkiewicz, who extended hospitality and support to many impoverished Warsaw artists and writers, as well as to fugitive Jews, at his family estate of Stawisko, wrote about meeting Nałkowska and Dąbrowska at writers' gatherings. Nałkowska documented her wartime correspondence with Iwaszkiewicz about the financial help she received from him. Three of the writers, Dąbrowska, Nałkowska, and Iwaszkiewicz, remained friends after the war; for lack of choice, they signed on with the communist party line and often served on the same committees. And, as attested by their diaries, they did not refrain from gossip, commenting on each other's looks, tastes, and relationships.

While their fictional writing drew upon Western literary, psychological, and philosophical thought, the writers also adopted the tradition of diary writing, producing extensive and, in the cases of Iwaszkiewicz, Dąbrowska, and Nałkowska, lifelong diaries. Iwaszkiewicz started his diaristic recordings in 1911 during his Kiev gymnasium years; there are no recordings left from his apparently lost diaries of the 1920s except for important fragments from 1921. He resumed his diary on the eve of the breakout of World War II, which he continued until his death in 1980. He also produced multiple volumes of memoirs and reminiscences, the most significant of which was *The Book of My Reminiscences*, written from 1941 to 1943. Dąbrowska started her *Diaries* in 1914, upon her return to Poland from her studies abroad at the beginning of World War I, and with the exception of the World War II years, when her notations became more sporadic, she wrote almost daily up to the moment of her death in 1965. Nałkowska, whose desire to eternalize the moment drove her to record her life in the fullest detail, produced the longest and most prolific diaries in the Polish history of letters; these diaries extend from 1899 to a few days before her death in 1954, when a stroke interrupted her writing. In addition to his *Diary of the Occupation*, Rembek also wrote diaries during the Polish-Bolshevik war (1918–21), and continued sporadically until 1937; he also produced a short journal during the September 1939 German invasion of Poland and the siege of Warsaw. Only Wyleżyńska confined her diaristic writing to the war years, but her rationale for starting her diary at the outset of the war — as a declaration of her independence in the face of the Occupation, and as an opportunity for unsparing self-examination — reflected all the diarists' prewar trust in the ideas of the Enlightenment.

The diary as an autonomous act of self-education originated in the French tradition of *le journal intime*. Alain Girard saw the emergence of the personal diary in France at the end of the eighteenth century as a result of the evolving concept of the individual, complemented by the growing scientific interest in the investigation of human nature.[29] As Peter Boener observed, the popularity of "diary writing in the beginning of this [twentieth] century" was indeed due to "the earlier *Journaux intimes* and their promotion as masterworks of self-analysis."[30] The phenomenon of self-writing for self-understanding and for social self-actualization arose from the modern conceptualization of the human subject: the Romantic idea of the "centrality and uniqueness" of the person[31] coalesced with the Enlightenment concept of *Bildung*, which evoked the responsibility of a lifelong process of socialization through disciplined character formation. In this sense, self-writing was seen as a trajectory of self-evolution toward an autonomous, rational, and moral social self.[32]

The Warsaw writers espoused the tradition of *le journal intime*. While they were familiar with a wide range of diaristic and autobiographical writings of prominent European writers, including Tolstoy, Stendhal, Proust, Amiel, and Rousseau, their diaristic comments show that particular *journaux* commanded their individual attention. Both Iwaszkiewicz and Wyleżyńska were avid readers of the journals of André Gide; Dąbrowska spent years translating the diaries of Samuel Pepys; Nałkowska made clear that her decision to start a diary was influenced by the diaries of Marie Bashkirtseff.[33] Getting to know a diaristic life account of a distant and unacquainted individual was possible due to the self-evident fact that *les journaux intimes* were published and therefore accessible to general readership. Initially intended as the author's private and secret recordings, diaries soon entered the public sphere, and in the nineteenth century became a popular genre.[34] The phenomenon of diary publishing indicated that the diarist was eager to reveal her personal life story to unknown readers. But while the reader was socially unknown to the diarist, the latter's willingness to share her unstructured, idiosyncratic flow of spontaneously jotted down occurrences and private thoughts signaled a familiarity with the reader's mindset. The desire to publish her evolving life story communicated the diarist's awareness of the intended reader's "horizon of expectations,"[35] namely, the cultural and ethical orientation of the recipient of the text, which her story could meet. Thus the willingness to share the story of her daily existence with strangers implied the diarist's assumption of an extent of the reader's sympathetic reception. The nineteenth- and early twentieth-century diarists clearly felt mental and emotional affinity with the readership they were addressing with their private life stories.

The sense of anxiety, uncertainty, and oftentimes dread that characterized the Warsaw diarists' preoccupation with the fate of their diaries indicates a breakdown of the trusting diarist-reader relationships. Personal writing was forbidden under the German Occupation and keeping diaries therefore put the authors in great danger.[36] The frequent pseudonyms, acronyms, renaming of persons and of places, and cryptic notations attest to their constant apprehension that the diaries could be seized at any moment and provide sensitive information to the Gestapo.

Beside the constant fear of the physical destruction of the notebooks, followed by unavoidable terrifying personal hardship, the diarists felt overwhelmed by the events they were recording and therefore concerned about their ability to present a believable record of the apocalyptic horrors of the war, and especially of the Holocaust, to future readers.

The reality of the Final Solution also transformed the perception of the diary as genre vis-à-vis its future readers. Nineteenth- and early twentieth-century diaries narrated a reality of ordinary lives familiar enough to assure intelligible reception. In contrast, the witnesses of the Holocaust could not entertain the hope that their wartime reality would in any way be related to their future readers' ordinary lives. As their responses to the burning Ghetto show, the diarists were describing events which, as some of them acknowledged, drove them to insanity and despair, events which they were struggling to grasp and integrate into their life experience.

The Warsaw diarists' deep and sometimes debilitating sense of alienation in the present-day world of the Occupation and the Holocaust contrasted sharply with the sense of compatibility of the nineteenth-century individual with the world. Such a sense of social congeniality can be traced back to the ethical Zeitgeist of the eighteenth-century Enlightenment, and its transformative "human universal" that "human beings command our respect." This principle, which was inseparable from the concept of "a universal, natural right to life," has become, in Charles Taylor's view, "central to our [modern] moral thinking,"[37] and was central to the prewar thinking of all the diarists. It explained the popularity of the diary genre, which illustrated the relevance of an individual life shaped and reshaped by everyday physical, emotional, and mental experiences. The reader's attraction to the author's personal life story engendered a social encounter whereby author and reader explored, in the spirit of Bildung, the social and moral potential of human beings.

Such constructive social interaction was possible thanks to the inherent human capacities for independent rational thinking and for affective identification with another human being, claimed perhaps most famously by the Enlightenment thinkers Immanuel Kant and Adam Smith. Kant postulated that the individual could actualize his rational potential by heeding other "independent thinkers," who "will disseminate the spirit of the rational appreciation of both their own worth and every man's vocation for thinking for himself."[38] Smith posited that every human being has the imaginative capacity to understand others, "and feel not altogether unlike them," because the power of "reason, principle, conscience" teaches him that "he is no better than his neighbour."[39] A consciousness that every member of society has an autonomous rational existence and, at the same time, is capable of learning from others and of cultivating interpersonal ties leads to the modern moral idea of equal worth of all persons and, therefore, of the equal right to life and respect of all human beings. Such a perception of the individual envisioned a society grounded in human sameness rather than in differentiations of class, religion, blood relations, or ethnic origins. In the Enlightenment tradition, society is conceived as a fellowship of rationally thinking autonomous subjects who interact with one another on the basis of the sameness of their shared human mental and affective qualities.

The notion that human interaction was possible thanks to the sameness of autonomous human beings made it possible to identify and develop the concept of empathy. Empathy, Karsten R. Stueber says, is "the ability to understand other persons as minded creatures . . . [which] has to be conceived of as the psychological foundation of our ability to be social animals and to become full members of society."[40] According to Edith Stein, meaningful social encounters are possible because "empathy is the experience of foreign consciousness . . . which an 'I' has of another 'I.'" The similarities of human consciousness mean that "the 'you' is another 'I.'"[41] Thus empathic reciprocity, which makes it possible to see ourselves imaginatively through the eyes of another, allows us not only to understand ourselves better as subjects, but also to deepen our imaginative understanding of the mental and affective processes of other subjects.

Even before it was formally identified and scientifically examined, the capacity for empathy was an important factor in shaping the modern perception of society as a congregation of fellow human beings. As Lynn Hunt sees it, the emerging awareness of the capacity of human beings to understand each other empathically promoted the conceptualization of human rights in the age of the Enlightenment. Hunt proposes that "reading novels created a sense of equality and empathy" and "the readers came to see others — people they did not know personally — as like them, as having the same kind of emotions." She attributes the "recognition that others feel and think as we do, that our inner feelings are alike in some fundamental fashion" to the popularity of the eighteenth-century novel, and especially the epistolary novel. The make-believe authenticity of the fictional correspondents "heightened the [reader's] sense of identification" with the characters.[42] I would add that the epistolary plot enhanced the empathic reading of the novel because it facilitated the process of transference. The reader was encountering characters that responded empathically to each other by literally reading each other in conformity with the familiar social convention of letter writing.

Like the novel, the diary was also a text intended for publication and therefore directed at an empathic reader, who shared the diarist's worldview. Unlike the novel, however, the empathic reception of the diary did not require transference from the fictional into the real, due to the diary's unfeigned authenticity. In this sense, the seriousness of the Warsaw writers' engagement with diaristic writing communicated not only a formal imitation of the Western tradition of *le journal intime*, but also an identification with the lifestyle, cultural orientation, and intellectual Weltanschauung of the Western writers whose diaries they were reading. Indeed, the climate of political and social stability in interwar, independent Poland made it possible for Polish writers to affirm cultural same-mindedness with their Western counterparts. The avant-garde Skamander group of modernist poets, which was founded by, among others, Iwaszkiewicz and two poets of Jewish origins, Tuwim and Słonimski, is a case in point. The group's foundation in 1918, coinciding with Poland's independence, reflected the identification of the young generation of Polish artists with the Western modernist movement, while the extraordinary talent and outstanding oeuvre that the group produced demonstrated Polish achievements on the modernist scene. Despite the increasing nationalism and anti-Semitism in prewar Poland, the membership of the Skamander project showed adherence to the Western Enlightenment's "human universal" of common respect, and its empathic recognition that as a fellow artist, regardless of ethnic origins, "the 'you' was another 'I.'"

There are, of course, numerous interpretations of the concept of empathy. C. Daniel Bateson has identified eight possible definitions of empathy arising from a social-neuroscientific standpoint.[43] Empathy has also been perceived in terms of "theory theory," which understands the capacity of "mind-reading" as analogy and inference, and of "simulation theory," which ascribes empathy to the human capacities for imitation and simulation.[44] Other definitions of empathy, especially in children, encompass mimicry, conditioning, and direct association.[45] While the various interpretations of empathy overlap, this study will privilege the phenomenological perception of empathy, which focuses on intersubjectivity.[46] This approach, which deals with living beings, incorporates the capacities for mimicry, imitation, and simulation. More importantly, I have found that a phenomenological grounding of empathy in the human capacity to interact with the world of living human subjects helps illuminate the crisis of the empathic consciousness in an age of the genocide.

The Occupation severed the empathic horizon that Polish intellectuals thought had been established with the West. The Enlightenment's universals of human rights, human dignity, and the sanctity of human life, along with the social concept of *Bildung*, disintegrated in the reality of the Occupation and the Holocaust. This reality of terror, evolving genocide, and a prohibition of any contact with the outside world put an end to the prewar affinity with the European cultural community. Iwaszkiewicz's and Wyleżyńska's reactions in 1943 to the Western intellectuals that they used to emulate provide a telling example of the Polish diarists' loss of any sense of commonality with the Western enlightened mindset.

In a poem in Iwaszkiewicz's wartime cycle *Dark Pathways*, completed in 1943, a French poet and "an old athlete" who paces in the sunspotted "boulevards of Paris" is addressed with a rhetorical, yet painful question: "Can you smell the burning Ghetto . . . and see the faces of the fallen young poets?" While the French poet remains blissfully unaware of the Warsaw horrors in sunny Paris, the Polish poet is well aware that the horrors of war have transformed him and that his poetry will never be the same. From now on, he will sense "the joy of a new dish mixed with ashes."[47] As in Miłosz's poem, the experience of the burning Ghetto transformed the world picture of the witnessing speaker: the ashes and the smell of burned Jewish bodies have irrevocably invaded and branded the hopeful horizons of faith and creativity. Iwaszkiewicz sees the intellectual giants, the "athletes" he used to emulate, through the lens of suffering he has witnessed, and has become conscious of their empathic detachment.

This sense of empathic disconnection emerges conspicuously in one of Wyleżyńska's observations of July 1943. She recalled that Gide used to be her "spiritual alter ego," her mentor whom she trusted unconditionally, and that his diary was her "Bible." However, overwhelmed by the recent liquidation of the Ghetto, the Jewish fugitives seeking shelter from extermination, and the spreading demoralization of the Polish society, Wyleżyńska found she could "no longer feed on confidence, faith in the future, and good advice for humanity," and expressed her disappointment in her former master: "What is André Gide thinking now, as he watches the fall of humanity? I believed in his wisdom as I did in my own experience" (July 24 and 25, 1943).

While the Warsaw diarists expressed their sense of abandonment by the Western intellectual world, Western intellectuals, including Gide, were distraught over the terror that destroyed enlightened Europe. They deplored the madness of the world and were dismayed at the collapse of humanist progress. Gide, who was able to foresee the approaching disaster, had already noted in 1937: "I see nothing but distress, disorder and madness everywhere. . . . In what absurd mess is humanity sinking and, how and where to escape?" In 1940 he chose to evade the increasing madness, making a decision to escape into diaristic silence: "I shall continue to cover the pages of this notebook as if nothing were happening."[48] In June 1940, watching the fall of Europe just before the Blitz, Virginia Woolf recognized, with desperation, the emptiness of the cultural lexis that had shaped her: "Those familiar circumlocutions . . . which have for so many years given back echo and so thickened my identity are all wide and wild as the desert now. . . . We pour to the edge of the precipice." She did leap into the precipice, taking her life by drowning herself on March 28, 1942.[49] Looking at the ravaged Europe of 1943, Albert Camus recognized that "there is a stage in suffering, or in any emotion or passion, when it belongs to what is most personal and inexpressible in man and there is a stage when it belongs to art." However, he contended that in the present-day reality, suffering had become so incomprehensible that "art can never do anything with it."[50]

It is, of course, possible to explain the Warsaw diarists' disillusion with European intellectuals by the seclusion of occupied Warsaw from the rest of world. At the same time, it is impossible to discount the traumatic concreteness of the diarists' wartime experience. However little they knew about the outside world, the unbearable closeness of the Ghetto in the center of their city intensified their conviction that their experience of witnessing placed them outside the ethical and intellectual horizon of their Western counterparts. Consequently, the sense of foreignness with regard to their Western mentors reflected their sense of ethical-psychological aloneness; the unprecedented situation of the Holocaust had made the ethical, cultural, and literary sources and models they could draw upon in prewar situations suddenly devoid of meaning.

This sense of an empathic void was further exacerbated by the diarists' growing dissonance with their own community. Some of the diarists were observing the "fall of humanity" not only with regard to the German rule of terror, but perhaps even more painfully with regard to their fellow Poles. While they were involved, some more actively than others, with the Polish resistance, and while they painted a compassionate and sympathetic picture of the hardships sustained by the Warsaw population, the diarists also described the Polish persecutions of the Jews seeking refuge on the "Aryan side" of Warsaw. And while in their depictions of the miseries of the Occupation the diarists demonstrated solidarity with the oppressed Polish population, the widespread Polish compliance with and profiteering from the Jewish genocide in their city made the diarists aware of being at odds with their compatriots. The diarists could no longer share a "horizon of expectations" even with their fellow Poles because with regard to the Jews, the majority of Poles shared the horizon of expectations with the Germans.

Disconnected from European and Polish empathic horizons, the witnessing diarists found themselves in the position of primarily bearing witness to their humanistic selves. They could no longer depend on Western models of the Enlightenment tradition, nor could they hope for the fulfillment of Poland's special mission to the world which the great Polish poets, Mickiewicz, Słowacki, and Krasiński, had prophesized. The compliance of the Poles with the Final Solution forced them to examine their moral cores. In this sense, the issue of the plight of the Jews became a crucial test for the Warsaw writers' moral integrity, which required that they remain loyal to their humanistic Weltanschauung. Steadfast insistence on the humanity of the Jews, and more specifically, on the unbroken "horizon of expectations" with the victims, would have attested to the witnesses' own humanity. However, the reality shaped by the genocide confronted the diarists with an insolvable moral dilemma. Condemned to death, the Jews resembled trapped animals frantically seeking ways to survive. In this sense, the Jews indeed became the grotesque, contempt-evoking creatures of German propaganda, who had lost human dignity. How was it possible to maintain the empathic horizon with the Jews by insisting on their human dignity and autonomy when the reality of the Final Solution transformed them into hunted creatures doomed to extinction?

As we shall see, both Dąbrowska and Rembek evaded the issue by clinging absurdly and against all evidence to their prewar perception of Jews. Their diaries remain almost completely indifferent about the Ghetto, the deportations, and even the Ghetto Uprising. This insensitivity reflects their adherence to prewar Polish nationalist ideology which presented Jews as exploiters and victimizers of the Polish people, and as a threat to Poland's progress. Thus on May 27, 1944, Dąbrowska wrote, "Oh, my God, how I shudder lest the Bolshevik-British victory hands Poland once again into the hands of the Jews . . . that black crowd which will tear everything again from our hands. I shudder and don't want to live." In February 1941, Rembek wrote about the consequences of the disappearance of the Jews as a result of resettlement to the Ghetto, "The streets are empty without Jews, but their absence has had a positive impact on the town's economic life. Anyway, a number of them have already returned on various pretexts." The ability to conjure up such misperceptions attests to the remarkable degree to which formative ideological beliefs may affect the ethics of witnessing. Dąbrowska's and Rembek's willful denial of the reality of Jewish mass murder effectively eliminated the ethical problem of empathic identification with the victims.

Maintaining an empathic attitude toward the degraded Jews, robbed of all dignity and desperate to survive, proved problematic even for the other, altruistically oriented diarists. On February 23, 1941, Iwaszkiewicz described taking a tram through the Ghetto and seeing enormous black crowds of people everywhere, horribly pale beggars on the pavements, corpses covered with newspapers lying in the streets, and smuggled packages of food thrown out of the tram and grabbed wildly by people who disappear, and declared that it was a sight of a world of death from which he could not recover.[51] On July 29, 1942, Wyleżyńska wrote, "The surroundings of Warsaw are full of unfortunate fugitives, who flee from place to place hoping for a safe hideout. But there is no safety anywhere, and their situation can improve only if they find strength in themselves." And on January 27, 1943, Nałkowska wrote, "I was wondering about them [i.e., the Jewish victims]. 'A senseless fate,' wrote [Bruno Schulz]." She confessed to being unable "to understand this fate and his attitude toward it," and she admitted to have "wondered why they remained in their corner until the last moment, why they didn't seek wide open spaces."

The tone of pity that underlines these shocked but rather scornful characterizations of the victims' passivity indicates the diarists' shared crisis of empathy. The Jews die in the streets, desperately seek safety in the countryside, run in panic or remain in their corner — they do not act, do not oppose their "senseless fate." The diarists' admission of their failure to comprehend the attitude of the victims reflects their inability to identify empathically with the experience of the victims. Ironically, the diarists' formative faith in human dignity, autonomy, and human fellowship precluded their comprehension of the victims' world. The edict of the Final Solution placed the victims on the horizon of death, the implacability of which erased autonomy, rational decision making, and a sense of commonality with those on the horizon of the living. In this sense, the Final Solution vanquished the legacy of the Enlightenment, because it eliminated the same-mindedness of human subjects. In other words, it ruled out the capacity to recognize the "you" as another "I." Paradoxically, the rescue operations mounted by some of the diarists for the sake of the victims could not mend their loss of respect for the victims. The courageous actions of rescue were motivated by altruism, which necessarily constituted an unequal relationship between the benefactor and the needy. Equally, the annulment of the right to life for one human group created an asymmetry which revealed the failure of humanistic ethics.

The fact that the Jewish genocide marked the end of empathy was not lost on the diarists. Iwaszkiewicz searched among the Poles for signs of decent behavior not just toward the Jews but also toward fellow Poles in order to convince himself of the viability of humanism. Wyleżyńska concluded that the world of the Jews was beyond her comprehension and that her "imperative obligation" lay in extending concrete help to the victims.

Two of the diarists attempted to revalidate humanistic values in their postwar fiction. In *Medallions*, her 1946 collection of short stories, Nałkowska attempted to restore respect to the victim. The pieces in this slim volume, considered a masterpiece of Holocaust literature, consist mainly of survivors' testimonies. As an authorial narrator, Nałkowska restricts herself to the role of listener and recorder of the victim's story. By immersing herself in the world of the genocide from the perspective of the victim, Nałkowska attempts to understand that which escaped her in wartime, when the overwhelming horror of the physical destruction and the "metaphysical guilt" dismantled the language of communication between witness and victim. In her postwar reckoning, Nałkowska sought a new mode of communication which would enable her to redefine the values of autonomy and respect in a time of genocidal terror.

An even more surprising attempt to mend the collapsed ethics during the Holocaust is Rembek's 1947 novel, *The Sentence of Franciszek Kłos*, based on authentic war situations that he recorded in his diary. In the diary, Rembek strove to diminish the Jewish tragedy by adhering to his patriotic convictions and anti-Jewish biases, yet in the novel, Rembek reiterates Miłosz's view of the Holocaust, whereby the complicity of Polish Christians with the destruction of the Jews amounts to the destruction of Christian ethics. Rembek's narrative introduces the character of a priest who tries — in vain — to stop his parishioners from hunting and killing Jewish fugitives from the Ghetto, reminding them that "Jesus himself was of that nation, as well as the Holy Mother and all the Apostles. . . . Jesus loved his people as a human being."[52] The evocation of Jesus as a Jew and as a human being restores the Jews to the community of living human beings, which would reinstate the empathic interaction of all human beings. The failure of the priest to repair his congregation's ethics ends the novel with a foreboding warning of the irrevocable domination of evil over the world. While the message is horrific, its authorial source mitigates its horror. As we shall see, a consideration of the anti-Semitic proclivities of the author leaves us with a measure of cautious hope that humanistic ethics may not be completely dead after all.

Not dead perhaps, but irreversibly damaged. This book focuses on the implications of the Holocaust for the ethical constitution of the witnessing world. It explores how a license to murder one part of humanity transformed the essence of social interaction for humanity at large. As the five diaries show, the edict of the Final Solution inflicted an irreparable injury on the Enlightenment vision of humanity, which promoted progression toward the realization of the human potential for human fellowship. Never again will the human right to life be looked on as an immutable axiomatic tenet. As an examination of each of the diaries will show, the assessment of the imperfection of the human moral constitution has replaced the ideal of empathic human solidarity. The humanistic legacy of the Holocaust lies in the realization of the undeniable vulnerability of a modern civilization grounded in humanistic values. This vulnerability signals the danger of complicit witnessing that Miłosz saw as the termination of the hope for redemption. In this sense, the legacy of the diaries is a consciousness of the moral weakness of humanism. The diaries teach us about the ease with which solidarity based on the empathic sameness of all human beings can be abolished.

CHAPTER 2

Jarosław Iwaszkiewicz: The Holocaust and the Struggle for Humanism

The conduct of Jarosław Iwaszkiewicz (1894–1980) toward the victims of the German Occupation was beyond reproach. The State of Israel and Yad Vashem posthumously awarded Anna and Jarosław Iwaszkiewicz the medal of the Righteous Among the Nations in 1987. The award citation states that the couple hid Jews on their Stawisko estate, helped others find hiding places, and returned money paid for an unrealized prewar real estate transaction to Jewish buyers who were incarcerated in the Ghetto. Anna Iwaszkiewicz risked her freedom, if not her life, when she entered the Ghetto to undo the transaction. The couple also obtained, often with great difficulty, false documents for Jews to enable them to pass as Poles on the "Aryan side."[1] They gave shelter to hundreds of destitute fugitives after the Warsaw Uprising in 1944. Thanks to Anna's inheritance of the estate, the Iwaszkiewiczs were relatively affluent, and also extended hospitality and monetary assistance to Polish friends, relatives, and acquaintances, as well as generously supporting fellow writers and artists; Nałkowska and Dąbrowska benefited from their support, and Rembek also visited Stawisko.[2]

Iwaszkiewicz was steeped in European humanism and its culture. His behavior during the war and his reactions to wartime events must be seen through the lens of his European Weltanschauung. How deep and steadfast did his ideological beliefs, grounded in the tradition of the Enlightenment, prove to be under the Occupation? Was Iwaszkiewicz capable of maintaining his faith in humanity's moral nature while witnessing the horror of the Jewish extermination? To what extent was he able to reconcile his patriotic identification with his fellow Poles and the moral disintegration of Polish society under the German Occupation? A close look at Iwaszkiewicz's three autobiographical texts traces his evolving ethical worldview as he sought to reaffirm his humanistic picture of the world during a time of dehumanization and genocide.[3]

Toward Europe: Youthful Hopes and Ambitions

Iwaszkiewicz's extensive knowledge of European philosophers, musicians, writers, and of European languages informed his intensely Eurocentric ideological orientation. He was born in 1894 in the village of Kalnik in the Ukraine. After completing his high school studies in Kiev, and serving with a Polish battalion in World War I, he moved to Warsaw in 1918. There he joined a mixed group of Christian and Jewish intellectuals and artists who became known as Skamandrites (Skamandryci) after the avant-garde literary journal *Skamander,* to which they contributed their earliest works. Ardent admirers of western European culture and its modernistic trends, they became famous for the public readings of their avant-garde poems in the café Picador.

Iwaszkiewicz first expressed his attachment to Europe in his 1921 poem "Europa." In this poem, which introduces the collection of poems *Return to Europe* (1931), Iwaszkiewicz declared his unequivocal love for Europe, whose welcome was like "the touch of a native land . . . like a mother's unrestrained joy on the return of her son from faraway places."[4] In his study of Iwaszkiewicz's affinity with Europe, Piotr Drobniak argues that Iwaszkiewicz's extensive prewar travels in Europe — he participated in the meetings of the European International Intellectual Union and Pen Club in the 1920s and 1930s — inspired his vision of a unified Europe, whose various cultures would eventually coalesce into a multicultural whole.[5] This idea of European cultural unification is especially important in view of Iwaszkiewicz's persistent aspiration to have Poland qualify as a member in the family of western European nations. While acknowledging that Poland's unhappy history of partitions was a hindrance to its cultural and intellectual progress, he nonetheless saw his country as making important contributions to European culture through its artists and poets, such as Mickiewicz and Kochanowski.[6]

For Iwaszkiewicz, therefore, western Europe was the model of cultural, ethical, and aesthetic excellence which he followed and emulated. To understand the way in which European Weltanschauung inspired his *Bildung*, namely, his self-education in the spirit of the European cultural and aesthetic tradition, it is important to consider his initial self-presentation to his readers. In 1921, the year in which he wrote "Europa," Iwaszkiewicz also wrote a short memoir, "Fragments from Diaries" ("Fragmenty z pamiętników"). The memoir, which tells about his childhood, school years, and brief service in the Austrian army, starts with a short exposition for the reader. Here Iwaszkiewicz explains that the narrative consists of those "fragments" which demonstrate his artistic ability to depict "the touch and colors" of his experiences. The author tells the reader "not to expect a memoir such as Goethe's *Dichtung und Warheit* or Rousseau's *Les confessions*," insisting that his story will be different.[7] The references to such great writers highlight Iwaszkiewicz's desire to find his own style, but the invocation of these giants of European art in comparison with his own writing attests to the extent of the writer's youthful ambition, and reveals a remarkable measure of naive hubris. This conjecture is reinforced when Iwaszkiewicz mentions that his memoir may find its way to Ferdynand Hoesick, the famous biographer of two great Polish artists, the poet Juliusz Słowacki and the composer Frédéric Chopin.[8]

The rich array of references to great Polish, French, and German artists in the introduction to the memoir suggests that Iwaszkiewicz wished to appear as a highbrow intellectual author who expected a highly cultured reader. Indeed, the memoir presents a narrative of high school friendships with young people who, without exception, shared attraction to European culture. To a large extent, it is a story of profound discussions and sweeping passions informed by readings of Wilde, Turgenev, and Słowacki, musical performances of Chopin and Wagner, translations of Horace, and the songs of Jules Massenet.[9] The memoir confirms Iwaszkiewicz's erudition in European culture, and reaffirms his ambition to follow in the footsteps of the greatest European artists. Like Joyce's youthful Stephen Dedalus, young Iwaszkiewicz painted his portrait as an artist ready to "conquer the world." He was poised to achieve greatness with which he intended to transcend the limits of his native Poland and, at the same time, to inscribe Poland into the consciousness of Europe.

Wartime Recollections of Artistic and Humanistic Growth

Whereas in his 1921 memoir the young Iwaszkiewicz envisioned his future, in the wartime memoir *The Book of My Reminiscences* (*Książka moich wspomnień*) (written in 1941–43, added to in 1956, and published in 1957), the mature writer turned to his past. In the twenty years that separated him from his literary beginnings, Iwaszkiewicz had realized many of his youthful ambitions. A prolific writer, poet, playwright, and translator, he had gained recognition not only in Poland but also in Europe. His diplomatic service in Copenhagen and Brussels in the 1930s enhanced his public stature and contributed to his renown in the intellectual circles in Europe. Under ordinary circumstances, it would have been quite natural for the celebrated writer to give an account of his successful life to the public. But the war was not an ordinary circumstance.

Iwaszkiewicz's introduction to *The Book* underscores his need to recall the past in a time of the upheaval that disconnected him from his prewar life: "We seem to be separated from the past by cataclysmic events which turn even recent times into distant history."[10] Indeed, the critic Andrzej Zawada describes the memoir as "a cycle of essays which depicts the childhood and the youth of the writer, his Skamander literary beginnings, intellectual friendships, his introduction to Poland, to Europe, and to life."[11] What is the underlying rationale of such an extensive memoir? Even though it was written in the midst of the war, except for the brief comment regarding "cataclysmic events," the memoir does not mention the war at all. According to Zawada, the memoir "depicts the tragic and irreversible ending of the cultural formations" of the Enlightenment, yet Zawada asserts that Iwaszkiewicz presents the world of his youth as the "ideal order" and the present upheaval as merely a temporary disruption of that order.[12]

Zawada misreads the position Iwaszkiewicz assumed in the text when he claims that Iwaszkiewicz placed the past world in the center of his memoir and himself as its mourner and restorer. To simultaneously see the memoir as both a lament over the death of European culture and as an expression of belief in the temporary nature of that cultural upheaval is incongruous to say the least. In contrast, I would argue that when Iwaszkiewicz places himself in the center of the memoir, he is seeking confirmation that his moral integrity has not been compromised with the disappearance of his prewar world. In other words, *The Book* represents the memoirist's search for an answer to the question of whether ideologically he was still the same person he was in the world of his past, despite the cataclysmic reality which has destroyed that world. Witnessing a history that collapsed the humanistic foundations of society, the writer was afraid he had lost the integrity of his prewar humanistic ethical self. In this sense, *The Book*'s undertaking to recall the formative years may be seen as Iwaszkiewicz's attempt to reconnect with the severed past in order to reaffirm its values. The expectation seems to be that a self-revision as a growing person and as a writer would provide reassurance of the durability of his moral integrity in a time of terror.

Indeed, in the introduction to *The Book of My Reminiscences*, Iwaszkiewicz outlines his course of action. The memoir will "tell how the outer world, with all its beauty, ugliness, tragedy, and joy affected my soul as a child, a youth, and a man. [It will show] how I prepared to accomplish the three goals which I set for myself at the dawn of my life: to be able to perceive, to understand, and to express this world in the most exact way possible."[13] Thus Iwaszkiewicz sums up his *ars poetica*. Artistic growth entails reciprocal relationships with the world. While the world shapes the artist throughout his life, the artist articulates his accumulating knowledge of the world in the language of art. The autonomy of the artist lies in communicating his vision of the world through his own particular form of self-expression. In this sense, *The Book* is a reaffirmation of the artistic identity of the author: under the duress of the Occupation, he exercises his autonomy by representing the destroyed world as he experienced it.

Iwaszkiewicz clearly spells out his intention to reaffirm his particular artistic signature. As in his 1921 memoir, he defines his artistic purposes in *The Book* within the context of the European tradition. Thus, he does not aim at an impersonal, factual chronicle of past events, like that of François Guizot's *Mémoires pour servir à l'histoire de mon temps*, nor will he engage in psychoanalytical, confessional introspection, as is popular in modern autobiography. Instead, Iwaszkiewich promises a life narrative which will privilege *Warheit* (truth) over *Dichtung* (poetry). His claim of truthful representation of the lost world, however, does not mean a striving for objectivity. Indeed, as the author declares: "I wish to offer a handful of recollections, images, and captions that will be a very personal echo of the events of this exceptional era in which I happened to live."[14] Through a deliberate selection of topics and events, he intends to tell about the lost world from his subjective personal perspective. Even in the reality of terror, which strove to erase the individuality of the oppressed, Iwaszkiewicz's insistence on commemorating his personal experiences reflects his continuing adherence to the humanistic assertion of the autonomy and uniqueness of the individual human being.

Why should Iwaszkiewicz focus on these particular recollections of prewar history at this particular historical moment? What "personal echo" of the past should reverberate in the reality of horror? The answer emerges in the very last sentences of the memoir. Iwaszkiewicz concludes with a reiteration of the humanistic idea of the world, when he expresses his "gratitude to people who liked, loved, or hated me — but who, each and every one of them, enriched, even if only by a single particle, my growing humanism."[15] This final statement, written in a reality of overwhelming social moral disintegration, communicates a threefold reaffirmation of the values of humanism, of the importance of social interaction in the humanistic development of the individual, and, on a personal level, of the writer's autonomy, which enables him to claim the importance of humanism in an inhumanely brutal present. When juxtaposed with the introduction, the closing statement of the memoir illuminates *The Book*'s trajectory of self-rediscovery. In the introduction, the author proposed to focus on his growth as an artist. The conclusion, however, demonstrates the memoirist's newly discovered awareness that the process of learning, understanding, and expressing the world through art was inseparable from the evolution of his humanism. His re-vision of the past brought forth the consciousness that his growth as an artist was interfused with his moral growth as a humane person.

The central chapter of *The Book*, "The Portrait of the Artist in His Youth" ("Portret artysty w młodości"), illustrates the inextricable connection between the artist and the person. Iwaszkiewicz begins the chapter with a rather comical self-portrayal:

> On November 14, 1918, a strange creature landed in the Warsaw Vienna Train Station. . . . I was starting a new life in a new atmosphere. . . . I was standing on the Warsaw pavement with my huge valise filled with books, deeply convinced that here

I would begin an easy literary life. . . . Though I knew what I wanted . . . I did not know how to take the first step.[16]

Indeed, he almost instantly becomes involved in the avant-garde literary life in Warsaw as a founding member of the Skamander group. Their famous literary events at the Picador café led to very close, though complex, relationships among the members of the group. The most prominent among them, such as Tuwim, Słonimski, and Grydzewski, who became Iwaszkiewicz's very close friends, were of Jewish origins.

These friendships were not just professional; they played a very important role in the private sphere of the Iwaszkiewicz family. In her diary, Anna Iwaszkiewicz refers to individuals, such as Kramsztyk, Słonimski, Tuwim, Grydzewski, and the Mieczysławskis, in practically every entry. Her accounts of their visits, artistic accomplishments, problems, love affairs, quarrels, and reconciliations communicate Anna's unreserved acceptance of these individuals as family friends who became an integral part of her life narrative, both figuratively and literally. The extent of the intimacy of these friendships is perhaps most evident in Anna's entry of March 17, 1924:

> Yesterday, for the first time since the birth of the little one [Maria Iwaszkiewicz], I saw the boys, that is, Tolek [nickname of Słonimski] and Gryc [nickname of Grydzewski, the founder and the editor of *Skamander*]. . . . As always, we talked a lot of nonsense . . . because everybody was in a happy mood. There were also many jokes on the subject of paternity and maternity. Grycuś [a further degree of endearment of the nickname Gryc] examined the baby with amusing gravity. (A later note: As the editor, he feels a measure of obligation to care for the wives of the Skamandrites, and now for the children!) Tolek declared he liked children only from the age of fourteen and fifteen, and therefore did not go to see her.[17]

Jarosław Iwaszkiewicz's wartime diary entry for August 12, 1939, just before the war, illustrates the extent of his personal attachment to Tuwim. Iwaszkiewicz's intimate understanding of the poet as an artist, as well as his sympathetic view of Tuwim's endurance of increasing anti-Semitism, demonstrate Iwaszkiewicz's deep feelings for Tuwim:

A few days ago, by chance, I met Tuwim in Zakopane. The girls [Iwaszkiewicz's daughters], who had not met him, were enchanted. . . . Undoubtedly, he possesses radiant and striking characteristics of greatness . . . the greatness of nobility, of goodness, and of purity. . . . He is a man for whom there is only one thing: poetry. . . . This is the source of his naïveté, anxiety, and bitterness, that he finds human nastiness so hard to take. But in truth, he seems to be haunted; at every step, he suffers the most incredible slights . . . but it will all pass.[18]

Iwaszkiewicz's comment shows his sensitivity to the anti-Semitic slurs to which Jewish men and women of letters and arts were subjected. Their "Polishness" was constantly questioned. For instance, in 1940, Prof. Karol Estreicher wrote that Słonimski's "origin disqualifies him as a good Pole and as a Polish poet." In 1943 the poet Tadeusz Gajcy argued that poets like Słonimski, Tuwim, and Leśmian were alien to the Polish culture in an article poignantly entitled "We No Longer Need (Them)" ("Już nie potrzebujemy").[19] At the same time, Iwaszkiewicz was astutely aware of the extraordinary contributions of the Jewish writers and poets to the Polish culture.[20] The continuation of these friendships after the war attests to the strength and sincerity of Iwaszkiewicz's relationships with his Jewish friends.[21]

Iwaszkiewicz's sensitivity and open-mindedness can be traced back to his origins in Kalnik. As Marek Rodziwien notes, this little Ukrainian town was at the intersection of cultures, religions, and languages. It was a place where synagogues existed alongside churches, where Jews mixed with Russians, Ukrainians, Germans, and Poles, and the multiethnic community, with its broad intellectual interests and educational depth, displayed a high level of tolerance.[22] In *The Book*, Iwaszkiewicz recalls how "the small, colorful Jewish homes, the big buildings erected by Polish aristocrats [Potocki] over the past two hundred years, the new, small Orthodox Byzantine (Ukrainian) Church . . . the Old City with its spectacular bell towers of the old Orthodox Church . . . created a very beautiful whole."[23]

This is not to say that Iwaszkiewicz was completely bias-free with regard to the Jews. Quite often he would succumb to the convention of a derisive and derogatory way of referring to Jews. This aspect of Iwaszkiewicz's social orientation emerges especially in the writer's letters to his wife Anna in the 1920s. The letters were replete with condescending and often quite negative observations about Jewish friends and acquaintances. Iwaszkiewicz referred to the Jews as "impossible" and "ubiquitous," and when telling Anna about a gathering in Paris, he humorously yet sarcastically complained *"c'est triste d'être seul parmi les juifs"* ("it is sad to be the only [Christian] among Jews"). At the same time, the Jewish origins of his friends never affected Iwaszkiewicz's judgment of their artistic achievements. So, for instance, he adored Arthur Rubinstein's music and was deeply moved by the pianist's love for Poland. An even clearer example of his critical impartiality and integrity emerges in a letter in which following the customary disparaging comments, such as "everywhere Jews, only Jews," he mentions a newly published "magical" poem by Tuwim, adding that "it's been a long time since I liked anything as much."[24]

In *The Book*, Iwaszkiewicz makes an oblique, apologetic reference to his biased pronouncements and attributes them to his maliciousness and envy; he claims that his resentment reflected his sense of inferiority vis-à-vis his friends who, he felt, did not appreciate him enough as a writer.[25] The mention of rivalry points to the complexity of the prewar relationships among the Skamandrites. It seems, however, that envy and rivalry only partly explain the Polish writer's negative comments about Jews, the abundance of which in the letters signals deeply ingrained ways of thinking, while the fact that they were made in private correspondence indicates that he was conscious of their impropriety.

I would ascribe this ambivalence to an emotional discord between an adherence to the values of humanism and the influence of "anti-Semitic socialization." His enlightened worldview made Iwaszkiewicz look beyond his friends' Jewish origins and see them as greatly talented artists, and, further, to condemn anti-Jewish practices. However, the prevalent anti-Semitic atmosphere in Poland shaped the way in which he perceived the Jewish people at large. A similar bias against Jews as a group emerges in Anna Iwaszkiewicz's personal writings as well. Iwaszkiewicz's stereotypes about the ubiquity of Jews reecho in Anna's diary. In the September 10, 1923, entry, in which she praised Kramsztyk as "our" best contemporary portrait painter, and noted that Słonimski's new novel was as interesting as the work of Jules Verne, Anna also complained that socializing with too many Jews at a time depresses her. She claimed that the "otherness" of the Jews, as demonstrated in their behavior and their way of talking, could not be obliterated and the gap between them and the Poles could not be undone. Then, reinforcing the stereotype, she claimed that Słonimski, whom she mentioned many times as a close friend and a wonderful poet, was different because he did not conform to the typical Jewish behavior.[26]

As we shall see, with the reality of the Holocaust, Iwaszkiewicz's pre-war bias against Jews disappeared completely during the war. Furthermore, as Iwaszkiewicz's and his wife's acts of rescue indicated, the Jews entered completely into their "world of obligation."[27] Unlike the majority of the Poles, who excluded Jews from their sphere of responsibility, the Iwaszkiewiczs related to Jews in a spirit of the humanistic value of moral responsibility for all fellow human beings. Ironically, to maintain his moral integrity during the Occupation, Iwaszkiewicz had to engage in a moral and emotional struggle with a different bias. It was the struggle with the positive view of his fellow Poles, which he realized could not be sustained in view of the general Polish moral disintegration. Yet his patriotic loyalty and his compassion for the Poles made it extremely difficult for him to acknowledge and to condemn their betrayal of humanistic values with regard to their Jewish fellow human beings.

Facing the Terror: The Humanistic Self in the Reality of Genocide

For Iwaszkiewicz, the significance of his friendships with Jewish artists did not diminish, even when the world in which those friendships were conceived ceased to exist. Interestingly, the tragic circumstances of the Occupation and the genocide, which separated him from his friends, seemed to intensify his feelings of friendship. In his wartime diary, *Notes 1939–1945* (*Notatki 1939–1945*), which Iwaszkiewicz prepared for publication in 1945, he waxes nostalgic about the Skamander era in the entry for November 29, 1943, "Picador's Twenty-Fifth Anniversary" ("Dwudziesta Piąta Rocznica Picadora"). He wonders whether Tuwim, Wierzyński, Lechoń, Słonimski, and other fellow Skamandrites, now scattered all over the world, remember the anniversary, and uses the opportunity to review and reevaluate the friendships forged in the Picador era: "How many things have always divided us and still do—and yet, how many [more] things still connect us? We have been linked by this remote day . . . remote but memorable, alive, still coursing with our blood through our veins."[28] The striking metaphor of blood and veins, which does not distinguish between the Jewish and non-Jewish Skamandrites, highlights the indispensability of these relationships to Iwaszkiewicz's emotional well-being, as well as his humanistic belief in the similarity of human beings which transcends his anti-Semitic socialization.

When surrounded by the complex yet stimulating social environment in which he shared artistic and humanistic horizons with his friends, Iwaszkiewicz trusted himself and the world. He and his fellow artists believed that art could have a positive impact on Polish culture. But as he remarks in *Notes*, "Twenty-five years ago I had much more self-confidence than I do today — this is certain."[29] The present-day reality of terror shattered every confidence in progress and turned the world into a dangerous, unpredictable place which could not be trusted. Indeed, writing in August 1939, on the brink of the war, he complained "Everything that represents European culture has been disappearing at a frighteningly fast pace in our society," and deplored the futility of his own "minimal 'culture,' which is wilting in [Poland's] primitive, barbaric society."[30] Furthermore, Iwaszkiewicz was aware that this increasing barbarism estranged him from his fellow Poles and marked his social uselessness as an artist steeped in the European cultural tradition. On the second day of the war, under the bombardments, Iwaszkiewicz notes his dejection at of the ruin of the country, which has just started to rebuild itself, and despairs over the disappearance of moral values in the time of war, which, he predicts, will be dominated by the struggle for material existence.[31]

Just before the Warsaw Uprising, Iwaszkiewicz presents a telling example of the demoralization of the society, which has been misinterpreting its mindless violence as heroism. In the entry for July 21, 1944, entitled "Young Poets" ("Młodzi Poeci"), Iwaszkiewicz tells how the thoughtless militancy of his compatriots almost cost him his life: he narrowly escaped an execution by young poets, emissaries of the underground, for his alleged and totally unfounded collaboration with the Germans. The young poets used to visit Iwaszkiewicz, bringing him their poems for his evaluation. At the same time, they were spying on him and his family. Iwaszkiewicz meditated bitterly on the mentality of aggression, which seemed to have become the customary mode of social interaction. "I don't understand it," he comments. "They had guns, so they needed to fire them . . . it didn't matter at whom; the main thing was to shoot somebody."[32]

In truth, he did not blame the young poets, but rather the Zeitgeist of unwarranted and unnecessary belligerence that caused worthwhile young people, including promising young poets and artists, to risk and very often lose their lives. Iwaszkiewicz doubted the necessity of heroic acts, such as those of two young poets who were executed for having defiantly disobeyed the prohibition of the Gestapo and placed a wreath at the foot of the Copernicus statue in the center of Warsaw. At the same time, he also realized that his position, which opposed violence and upheld the preservation of human life, estranged him from his fellow Poles, who predominantly considered risking their lives in ineffective and often unjustified criminal acts of violence and defiance as honorable and heroic.[33]

Iwaszkiewicz's reluctance to endorse the militant atmosphere of occupied Warsaw, where multiple politically diverse underground groups operated, can be traced back to his childhood and his memory of the devastating results of his father's participation in the failed 1863 Polish insurrection against Russian rule over partitioned Poland. In contrast with other diarists, such as Dąbrowska and Rembek, who held a romantic view of the insurrection as an illustration of uniquely Polish valor and patriotism, Iwaszkiewicz remembered, "My father's life was broken because of the 1863 rebellion." His father's and uncles' decision to join the uprising bore grave, deeply detrimental consequences for the family. While Jarosław's uncles were banished or incarcerated in Russian prisons, his father was barred from university studies. Consequently, he made a modest living as an accountant and could not provide for his son's education. Young Iwaszkiewicz had to finance his schooling by tutoring the sons of rich gentry, an occupation he very much disliked and found humiliating.[34]

Iwaszkiewicz's refusal to romanticize Poland's history of failed insurrections was characteristic of the "pessimistic" Kraków school of historiography, which emerged in the wake of the 1863 defeat. In contrast with the Warsaw school, which sought to maintain the romantic legacy of Polish heroism and the myth of the messianic "chosenness" of the

Polish people, the Kraków school saw the 1863 insurrection as a national calamity which it blamed on the Poles' disastrous lack of political judgment.[35] While we do not know whether Iwaszkiewicz was aware of these political trends in Polish historical studies, his unabashedly short and unenthusiastic account of his World War I military service, when he fought on the Austrian side to reinstitute Polish independence, in *The Book* echoed the rational and practical mindset of the Kraków school.

The fact that Iwaszkiewicz recounted the story of his service during the Occupation, when the Poles were once again engaged in a struggle for independence, did not seem to affect Iwaszkiewicz's account, which is devoid of any romanticism:

> [In 1918], I decided, together with Kozłowski, to join the third Polish Corps, which was being formed in Winnica. There we met many friends and peers . . . who were preparing to become officers in the Polish army. . . . We moved to Sutyski on the Boh, in the magical Podolski countryside. The moment I saw the reflection of the sunset in the waters of the Boh . . . was very significant for me. The impression was comparable to the description of "Les clochers de Martinville" in the first volume of Proust. The genius French writer was able to recreate the elusive moment of the birth of artistic consciousness as it emerged through the contemplation of various objects . . . whose true essence remained hidden behind their sensual forms. In Sutyski . . . I had yet another "revelation." I became familiar with the poem *King-Spirit* [*Król-Duch*] and for a long time it remained the dearest work to me of all romantic literature. . . . We would sit for hours with Słowacki's book, studying this dark, complex, and wonderfully poetic work from cover to cover. . . . In Gniewanie, we were surrounded [by the peasant divisions] and were saved from a sad end by the Austrians. Our stay in Uładówka was completely pointless. It was a beautiful spring, we were not participating in military exercises, and guard duty among the blossoming cherry trees was like taking a nature hike; that's why I wrote so many poems at that time. Desertions were permitted. . . . [so] we abandoned our weeks-long war games and returned to Kijów."[36]

Upon his realization of the uselessness of his military service, Iwaszkiewicz abandoned his unit. His desertion clearly communicated his rejection of romantic heroism. In fact, he was quite clear about his lack of military patriotism: "My attitude to military service was by no means tragic. Despite the pressure, I used to deal with it simply by saying, 'I don't feel like it right now,' and I did not have any qualms about doing so, despite the fact that I was frequently reproached for it."[37] While he remained indifferent to military action, which he sarcastically trivialized as "war games," Iwaszkiewicz discovered his identity as a writer; during his service he became conscious of his poetic calling. The view of the river Boh in sunset was magical not only because of its beauty, but also because, as the association with Proust indicated, it possessed the magic of literary inspiration. Like Proust's art, the landscape left its imprint on Iwaszkiewicz's artistic self. His passion for art took control of him even in life-threatening situations. While the war raged — his unit was surrounded and had to be saved by the Austrian army — Iwaszkiewicz was writing poetry.

Not only did Iwaszkiewicz display a balanced, non-sentimental approach to military matters, but his attitude toward literature was also marked by a reasoned appreciation of the aesthetic. The conciseness of his explanation of Proust's genius also characterized his admiration for Słowacki's romantic masterpiece, *King Spirit*. While he was inspired by the literary greatness of Słowacki's poem, he certainly had no desire to heed its romantic-patriotic message of heroic martyrdom for Poland. Clearly Iwaszkiewicz did not subscribe to the general veneration of the Romantic poets such as Słowacki and Mickiewicz — which, for instance, shaped Dąbrowska's partriotism — as prophets of Poland's messianic role among the nations. Instead, his discovery of his literary calling opened him to the universality of humanism. His praise for both Proust, the French Jewish writer, and Słowacki, the Polish poet par excellence, revealed his unbiased position toward artists as individuals who shared a passion and a talent for art.

As noted, Iwaszkiewicz did not compromise his anti-militaristic stance under the Occupation; while remaining critical of the tragic loss of lives in military actions, he sought to affirm his humanistic autonomy by acting to save lives. In contrast with the prevailing patriotic attitude which saw daring and life-risking operations as proper ways to defy the German rule, Iwaszkiewicz and his wife sought to defy the occupier through extending help to Poles and rescuing Jews.

Iwaszkiewicz was also preoccupied with the ethical aspects inherent in the resistance of terror, which challenged his humanistic convictions. A tram ride through the Ghetto in 1941 became a traumatic experience: the frenetically rushing crowds, the corpses in the street covered with newspapers, the terrible destitution, the density, stench, and squalor make him shiver at the thought that this is where his friends and their parents must live. It was an alien world, the sight of which affected him physically, prompting horror which he could not shake off.[38] In 1943, Iwaszkiewicz described the devastating impact of the heavy clouds of smoke rising from the Ghetto in the wake of the Uprising. He imagines the burning bodies of lifelong close friends and lists their names with unconcealed pain: Roman Kramsztyk, Olek Landau, Paweł Hertz, and Józik Rajnfeld.[39] He was dismayed by the reaction of his compatriots: "A carousel, swings, and a roller coaster have been placed in Krasinskich Square, and a loud barrel-organ is blaring. And two steps from there, behind the Ghetto walls, sounds of battle can be heard, and the smoke of the burning houses spreads into the streets." Iwaszkiewicz gathered these facts from Anna, who ventured into Warsaw in search of a hiding place for an old Jewish couple despite the danger that such an undertaking entailed at that time. As Iwaszkiewicz recorded, Anna returned empty-handed because she could not find Poles willing to offer a hiding place to the Jews. Both Iwaszkiewiczs were emotionally shattered by the fact that in the city life was continuing as usual while horrific atrocities were being committed in the Ghetto.[40]

Both the Jewish situation and the behavior of the Poles tested Iwaszkiewicz's faith in the steadfastness of humanism and its values of self-dignity, respect for others, and the sanctity of human life. The degradation of the Jews in the streets of the Ghetto, the immolation of Jewish bodies behind the Ghetto walls, and the dependency of Jewish fugitives destroyed any common horizon of expectations grounded in the empathic premise of the sameness of human beings. At the same time, the general acquiescence of the Poles with Jewish destruction, their general refusal to grant refuge to Jewish fugitives, their emotional numbness, illustrated by the carousel in front of the burning Ghetto, and their blackmailing and betrayal of the Jews demonstrated a moral degradation which undermined Iwaszkiewicz's sense of empathic affinity with the Poles. The very fiber of humanism seemed to have dissolved.

Iwaszkiewicz raises this point in the introductory section of *Notes*, entitled "Clarification" ("Objaśnienie") and dated 1945:

> Poetry readings and concert attendance — and often a chat over vodka — were not only forms of escapism, but also a search for better, more substantive aspects of human beings, a search which would end, more often than not, in complete disillusionment. If it is possible, if only for a moment, to discern in these notes a measure of humanity in that time of inhumanity, the goal of this publication will be fulfilled.[41]

Ironically, despite its ostensible intention to clarify, "Clarification" betrays ambivalence. On the one hand, Iwaszkiewicz admits that neither social interaction nor collective artistic experience helped him to reassert humanistic values, and expresses despondency over society's moral eclipse; on the other hand, he seems unable to accept this general loss of humanistic values. He therefore passes the challenge on to his readers, asking them to search *Notes* for a reaffirmation of humanism in wartime Warsaw.

Two discrete episodes particularly communicate the relevance of humanistic ideals in *Notes*. Both focus on the responses of the Poles to the Jewish plight. The first episode, "Surgery" ("Operacja"), is a story of the triumph of humanism. When Kramsztyk's daughter Joanna, in hiding at Stawisko, gets sick and needs surgery, Anna Iwaszkiewicz is reluctant to turn to her relative, the only doctor she knows who could help, fearing that the man, who has the reputation of a fierce anti-Semite, will refuse and denounce the young Jewish girl to the Gestapo. Iwaszkiewicz reports to have countered, "Yes, but he is a doctor and a human being." His more optimistic view proved correct. Although the doctor's own son was arrested and executed by the Gestapo at precisely that time, he kept his word and took care of the patient as he promised.[42] This story clearly demonstrates the integrity of the Polish doctor's professional ethics, and therefore proves that despite deeply engrained prejudices, the ultimate humanistic value of the right to life, and therefore the injunction to save life, has prevailed even under the rule of terror. In this episode, Iwaszkiewicz has triumphantly reaffirmed the empathic horizon between the Jews and the Poles.

The other episode, "Andrzejewski's Reading" ("Czytanie Andrzejewskiego"), raises fundamental issues which signal the ethical limits of the diarist himself. Andrzejewski wrote the story "Holy Week" ("Wielki Tydzień") immediately after the Ghetto Uprising, and read it to a group of distinguished writers, including Iwaszkiewicz, Dąbrowska, and Nałkowska, in June 1943. Written in the realistic genre, the story reaffirms humanism, through its Polish author's direct confrontation with and condemnation of Polish anti-Semitism. Andrzejewski describes the infamous carousel in front of the Ghetto and the glee of the revelers as the Jews burn, as well as the blackmail and extortion of Jews on the "Aryan side," and the widespread, visceral anti-Semitism of the time. The story's subplot presents some redemptive Polish behavior — a Polish underground fighter goes to help the Jewish fighters in the Ghetto, and one of the female characters expresses Christian pity for the Jews and makes efforts to help the protagonist, which prove futile. However, the story ends with a complete severance of empathic sentiments when the protagonist is forced to return to the burning Ghetto after being denied refuge by the Poles and threatened with denunciation to the Gestapo.

Iwaszkiewicz's reaction to Andrzejewski's story reveals the remarkable extent of his ambivalence over the behavior of the Poles toward the Jews. The fact that he never refers to the redemptive subplot attests to his awareness of the authenticity of the main plot as well as his own preoccupation with the issues that it raises. He vehemently repudiates the story, which, as he emphasizes, "left a disquieting impression." Yet his irate reaction barely conceals his response of dismay, shame, and guilt. Indeed, Iwaszkiewicz is quite explicit about the reasons for the unsettling impression made by the story when he points to the sense of the collective guilt of the listeners: "This is a very well written story which raises one of our most important issues, a fundamental moral problem for each of us."[43]

While Iwaszkiewicz is capable of acknowledging his shame and concern at the moral failure of Polish society, he nonetheless seems incapable of responding to it in a rational manner. The emotionally devastating impact of the story impels Iwaszkiewicz to deny the truthfulness of the story's moral picture of his people. First, he wishes to disprove the story by describing the risks he and especially his wife took when trying to find a hiding place for the old Jewish couple. However, the incongruity of his argument—the risks the Iwaszkiewiczs took were mainly due to the absence of other Polish offers to hide Jews and put them in danger of being denounced to the Gestapo by fellow Poles—confronts him with the realization that his own experience merely corroborates the authenticity of Andrzejewski's story.

Despite the fact that the mindless murder in cold blood of the Polish protagonist of Andrzejewski's story by Polish thugs reaffirmed Iwaszkiewicz's own observation of the general decline into senseless violence, which he denounced in "Young Poets," Iwaskiewicz remained incapable of accepting the story's horrific moral indictment of Polish society. Iwaszkiewicz chose to focus instead on aesthetics. He questions the appropriateness of a literary representation of the liquidation of the Ghetto, arguing that transmuting the destruction into a work of art "while the ashes of the Ghetto have not yet cooled off"[44] raises the ethical issue of disrespect for the victims. To express the horror of such a catastrophe, Iwaszkiewicz postulates, we need a new aesthetic, that is, a new language of art, which does not exist at this moment. Perhaps, he proposes, from a more distanced postwar perspective, such a language might be conceived.

In his search for a new language, Iwaszkiewicz diverts himself from the "disquieting" issue of the moral response of Poles raised by Andrzejewski's story. His concern about language centers on the proper depiction of the horrific suffering of the Jews burning in the Ghetto rather than on a language which would depict the Polish population's horrific response to this suffering. By asking the rhetorical question, "How is it possible to create a form of art which would not serve as a reflection of reality, but rather as its equivalent?" Iwaszkiewicz takes refuge in the problem of poetics in order to avoid Andrzejewski's poetic confrontation with the Poles' empathic failure to recognize the suffering of other human beings. Iwaszkiewicz's desire to evade the issue is clearly spelled in his concluding statement of his discussion of "Holy Week": "At this moment we should not worry about it. It's good enough just to be alive."[45]

Another Return to Europe

In poem 108 of *Dark Pathways* (*Ciemne Ścieżki*), a collection of poems Iwaszkiewicz wrote during wartime and completed in 1943,[46] Iwaszkiewicz struggles with the undeniable loss of an empathic horizon of mutual respect and cultural sharing which had existed between young Polish poets like himself and the intellectual giants of Europe before the war. Ironically, the cause of that loss was the disintegration of the empathic horizon between Poles and Jews. The horror of Warsaw destroyed the possibility of cultural and ethical commonality with the humanistic tradition of the Enlightenment. In poem 108, Iwaszkiewicz turns to his beloved French poet Paul Valéry, to whom he had dedicated his 1931 collection of poems, *Return to Europe.*[47] Iwaszkiewicz had addressed the French poet as "*boski*" ("divine") and declared, with awe and admiration:

> In your direction, O Paul we [the Poles] raise our eyes
> With a question and with envy,
> There where the Seine in its eternal currents rolls. But you
>   probably
> Cannot understand . . .
> That before a new labor heals the heart,
> A new Polish people cannot arise.[48]

The longevity, the peace and quiet of France, as represented by the majestically flowing Seine, produced divine artists like Paul Valéry, whom newly independent Poland watched enviously and from whom she sought guidance in national self-renewal in the spirit of French civilization.

In Iwaszkiewicz's wartime poem 108 in *Dark Pathways*, the references to France invoke the Polish poet's prewar love and admiration for European culture. The content and the tone, however, mark a drastic change in attitude toward the country that once was the object of Iwaszkiewicz's envy:

> One does not easily forget life,
> Nor does one turn away from tombstones and crosses.
> Can you smell the burning Ghetto,
> You, who stroll along the boulevards of Paris?
>
> Pacing over the stains of the sun like an old athlete,
> You don't know the taste of fresh July honey,
> But when you sleep, can you see emerging from hiding
> The faces of the young fallen poets?

As for me, every noon, when I sit down at the table,
Tired from work, nourished by hope,
I, full of flowers which laugh in June,
Feel joy in a new dish mixed with ashes.[49]

In the prewar evocation of Europe, the French poet, a product and model of European culture, was the addressee of the question about the possibility of Poland's spiritual and cultural horizon with Europe. In contrast, the questions addressed to the "old athlete" by the wartime poet who has witnessed the Holocaust are misplaced; the smell of the burning Ghetto and the faces of Warsaw's dead young poets could not enter the mind of the stroller of sunny Parisian avenues. The athlete — perhaps an oblique reference to Valéry's conviction that Greece and Rome had given birth to European culture[50] — is old. His age implies that European civilization, which drew its inspiration from the beauty, agility, and prowess of antiquity, is incapable of confronting the horrific twentieth-century reality of Europe. The history of European civilization has not provided the old athlete with a point of reference to the contemporary horrors of the Occupation. The empathic horizon of mutual understanding has been severed, and consequently the French poet can no longer be expected to answer the questions posed by the Polish poet.

Now Iwaszkiewicz, who has experienced the unimaginable, carries the task of perpetuating a civilization tainted with horror. His poetry, which sings of the beauty and joy of June flowers and of the sweetness of July honey, must also speak of the terror and suffering whose memory he keeps alive day and night, in every poem and in every dream. The indelible taste of ashes mixed into his creative joy brings forth in Iwaszkiewicz a realization of his responsibility to remember the tragedy, which has infiltrated his self. His body has been pervaded by the smell of the burning Ghetto, whereas the faces of the dead have invaded his mind. He has become hostage to the graves of the executed young poets and the ashes of the burned bodies of his Jewish friends. The component of horror that pervaded his life and work detached him from the humanistic Weltanschauung of Europe and the Enlightenment. It introduced a new language of art, which, as Iwaszkiewicz sees it, forever remained beyond the grasp of Valéry the European poet, and which therefore excluded the possibility of his empathic comprehension of the Polish poet-witness of genocidal reality.

CHAPTER 3

Maria Dąbrowska: Witnessing the Holocaust Through the Ideological Lens of Nationalism

Like Iwaszkiewicz, the reaction of Maria Dąbrowska (1889–1965) to the Holocaust was shaped by a deeply embedded ideological world picture. Iwaszkiewicz's early dissociation from the prevailing national romantic ethos of Polish uncommon military valor and heroic patriotism determined his humanistic-cosmopolitan ideology of tolerance and inclusion in the Enlightenment tradition of human fellowship. While he saw the Holocaust as humanity's descent into barbarism, his dismay and grief over Jewish suffering and his engagement in saving Jewish lives, as well as helping his Polish compatriots, reflected his belief in the viability of the humanistic creed in a time of terror. In contrast with Iwaszkiewicz's universal humanistic outlook, Dąbrowska's early espousal of the nationalistic-romantic ideology of Polish special destiny enabled her to keep practically silent about the Jewish genocide. Dąbrowska sought to adapt the Western model in the reality of the Polish ethnic Christian nation-state. The perception of the humanistic values through the prism of Polish national interests engendered anti-Semitic sentiments; Dąbrowska saw Polish Jews as rivals and exploiters who hindered the intellectual and economic potential of ethnic Poles. Her biased attitude toward Jews did not disappear during the Holocaust, nor did it diminish toward the Jewish survivors in postwar Poland.

Maria Dąbrowska, née Szumska, was born in 1889 in Russow, near the city of Kalisz, into a family of impoverished gentry. She maintained a lifelong emotional attachment to her birthplace; she saw the countryside as the true Poland, and continually reimagined it in her literary work, which was grounded in Polish rural and small town life. Dąbrowska's parents, Polish patriots — her father fought in the 1863 insurrection — who supported the Polish boycott of Russian education, sent Maria to a Polish girls' high school in Warsaw. There, young Maria witnessed the failed Revolution of 1905, and her teachers, all ardent Polish patriots, introduced her to the theories of socialism and Marxism. This formative experience in Warsaw influenced greatly her lifelong patriotic passion and her socialist orientation.[1]

Dąbrowska spent her student years abroad, in Lausanne and Brussels, where she studied natural sciences. There she met with the Polish émigré groups, which reinforced her nationalistic ideological orientation. In 1912 she married Marian Dąbrowski (1882–1925), a revolutionary socialist and fighter for Polish independence; she also met Edward Abramowski (1868–1918), a philosopher who promulgated moral, evolutionary socialism. After Dąbrowski's death, she began a lifelong relationship with Stach (Stanisław) Stempowski, a prominent and well-respected intellectual, who collaborated with her on her work and was instrumental in building her social image. Dąbrowska was a prolific journalist, and after her husband's death she also embarked on a literary career starting with the novel *People from Yonder* in 1926. Her masterpiece, *Night and Days*, published in installments between 1932 and 1934, became a landmark of Polish national literature. At the same time, she embraced social activism, seeking to improve the living conditions of the working classes, especially through peasant reforms, and came to be seen as a fearless advocate for the downtrodden.

Like other members of the left-wing intellectual elite, Dąbrowska despised the rabidly anti-Semitic Endecja movement. Her 1936 newspaper article "Annual Shame" was of particular importance in shaping her image as a defender of the oppressed.[2] Responding to increasing anti-Semitism at Polish universities, she denounced the persecution of the Jewish students. This public pronouncement, which, as we shall see, was in fact also a camouflaged statement about Jewish superiority over the Poles, was considered an act of courage and highly admired not only by Jews but also by the left-wing intelligentsia, and gained her the reputation of a "moral authority."[3]

Dąbrowska was not alone in her criticism of the anti-Semitic excesses at the universities. A collection of articles by socialist activists, journalists, politicians, and university professors, *The Poles About the Jews*

(*Polacy o Żydach*), was published in 1937, at the height of anti-Jewish hostilities. The articles argued that the persecution of Jewish students at the universities was a serious setback to Poland's reputation as a civilized, enlightened country. For instance, one of the contributors, Adam Próchnik, claimed that the pogroms were despicable "not only because of the harm to the Jews," but also because they caused "irreparable harm" to the Polish youth. "Is it possible," he asked, "that a generation that was guided by the ideals of social independence and justice would be followed by a generation which is content with beating Jews?" With dramatic rhetoric, Próchnik demanded: "Confront the youth with the noble ideals of freedom and justice. Tell them to rebuild the world, to destroy the bad and to create the good."[4] Despite such strong pronouncements by other left-wing activists, Dąbrowska nevertheless became and remained the standard-bearer of social justice in the public eye. This adulatory image did not change until her death in 1965, even though in the postwar period her literary career faded. Tadeusz Drewnowski, the foremost scholar of Dąbrowska and the first editor of her *Diaries*, noted, "Indeed, everything was falling apart, being rebuilt, and changing. The cataclysm of the war was over, as was the revolution, and there were immense migrations and transitions happening, yet Dąbrowska remained the national [moral] authority in the widest sense of the word."[5]

The sterling moral reputation of Dąbrowska's public persona explains the shock and disappointment which greeted the undeniably anti-Semitic self-portrait emerging from her posthumously published *Diaries* (*Dzienniki*). Dąbrowska started keeping a diary in 1914 when she was twenty-five, and continued to write almost daily, with the exceptions of the months she spent in Lwów after the German invasion in 1939 and during her emotional breakdowns during the war. Dąbrowska restricted the publication of the complete diaries, which are over 50,000 pages long, for forty years after her death.[6] Drewnowski published an abridged, five-volume edition in 1988, and in 2009 PAN published a limited number of copies of the complete text.[7] Dąbrowska's raison d'être for the diaries was to become "even after my death, the witness of my time" (May 10, 1950).[8] Her need to shape her posthumous reputation explains her compulsive recording. Indeed, later in life, Dąbrowska was preoccupied with typing her handwritten diaries. This raised the possibility that she had altered the original recordings. Aware of the problem, Drewnowski identified 150 spots of comparison by topic areas, and reached the conclusion that "the authorial typescript did not weaken the authenticity of the diaries."[9]

The authenticity of the *Diaries* not only affirmed Dąbrowska's lifelong anti-Semitic outlook, but also demonstrated that the Holocaust did not change her convictions about Jews. Even upon rereading the diaries with an eye on future publication, she clearly did not feel it was necessary to amend the anti-Jewish comments. In the postwar diaries, as Drewnowski observed, her "preoccupation with Jews increased to the point of obsession."[10] With considerable and understandable unease, critics have sought rationalizations for Dąbrowska's anti-Semitism. Drewnowski attributes them to a loss of astuteness and emphasizes her continuing friendships with Jews after the war.[11] Andrzej Mencwel inaccurately claims that she directed anti-Semitic comments mainly at postwar Jewish communists, whom she considered anti-Polish.[12] Grażyna Borkowska looks at Dąbrowska's anti-Semitism from a "psychological perspective" and ascribes it to the writer's growing aversion to the world at large.[13]

While Dąbrowska's interwar and postwar anti-Semitic comments caused consternation, the scarcity of references to the Holocaust, and especially to the Ghetto, in her wartime diaries was even more disturbing. Drewnowski points out that even in view of the prohibitions imposed by the Gestapo, the notations about the Ghetto were surprisingly brief.[14] Jan Gross sarcastically raises the question of the "silence about the fate of the Jews" in "one of the greatest contemporary Polish writers . . . who worked on behalf of the needy and the poor."[15] Indeed, Dąbrowska made only a few brief remarks about the Ghetto. On November 14, 1940, she mentioned the Ghetto in connection with the division of the city;[16] in April–May 1943, she wrote one sentence about the Uprising. Then she made three brief notations about the smoke of the burning Ghetto.[17] Dąbrowska's lack of response to the Jewish genocide represents a particular manner of "looking at the Ghetto," the liquidation of which could not remain unnoticed. Her silence about the tragedy of the Jews speaks loudly about her ideological worldview and her ethics.

The discrepancy between Dąbrowska's public condemnation of anti-Semitism and her anti-Semitic bias against Jews in her private writing highlights her nationalistic proclivities, which, as a widely known liberal, she could not readily divulge. On the one hand, Dąbrowska's social activities demonstrated her adherence to humanism, with its values of justice, equality, and the solidarity of humankind. On the other hand, she ardently espoused the messianic mission of Poland, shaped by the Christlike suffering of the Partitions and the traumatic defeats of the 1794, 1831, 1863, and 1905 uprisings, the last of which she witnessed in Warsaw. Between the wars, Dąbrowska's growing disappointment with Poland's inability to actualize its special destiny and join the enlightened progress of the Western world engendered a resentful, competitive attitude toward Polish Jews. This attitude did not disappear at the time of the Holocaust, and increased during the postwar years. Investigating Dąbrowska's national convictions will help us understand her remarkably restrained response to the mass murder of the Jews. Her response exemplifies the remarkable resilience of an exclusionary ideological Weltanschauung toward the sufferers of terror. Dąbrowska's silence demonstrates the human capacity to shape affective moral responses according to ideological credos. As Dąbrowska's case shows, ideologies make it possible for the witnesses of human — and humanistic — catastrophes to construct self-deceptive rationalizations which justify their emotional detachment.

Formative Ideologies and Their Ethical Implications

Dąbrowska's mentors were instrumental in shaping her nationalism. Her husband Marian Dąbrowski exposed her to revolutionary socialism. Dąbrowski, an activist in PPS-Frakcja Rewolucyjna (Polish Socialist Party–Revolutionary Faction), was the founder of the Brussels Filaret association.[18] The Filarets were a clandestine movement focused on the revolutionary struggle for Polish independence; their motto was "A free human being in a free Poland." Dąbrowska composed the resolution of the 1910 Filaret convention, glorifying the continuation of the struggle despite the odds: "Even if we don't deliver a free motherland to the next generation, it is our wish to deliver it in spirit, free and immortal."[19] This political pronouncement — Dąbrowska's first — attests not only to her patriotism, but also to its highly emotional, even theological, dimension. Indeed, she saw the émigré group's revolutionary work in terms of "a return to eternal sources . . . and holy ideals."[20]

Dąbrowska's other mentor, Edward Abramowski, represented a different ideological position. Initially a revolutionary Marxist and a cofounder of the PPS (Polish Socialist Party), Abramowski distanced himself from militant activities to develop a theoretical-philosophical grounding for a "moral revolution" which he believed must precede any political change. Abramowski became very popular in Polish intellectual socialist circles in the pre-independence period. He negated the concept of the state and talked about communes based on social responsibility. He claimed, "The political revolution will be a natural and necessary result of a moral revolution [which] argues that the creation of a new life . . . is possible here and now as an act of goodwill and sincere convictions. . . . The basis of the commune is brotherhood [and] mutual help."[21]

Dąbrowska embraced Abramowski's concepts of the "moral revolution" and cooperatism. In 1925 she published the laudatory monograph *Life and Work of Edward Abramowski* (*Życie i dzieło Edwarda Abramowskiego*) in which she sought to establish her affinity with Abramowski through the lens of her patriotic ideology. She situated Abramowski firmly in the tradition of the Polish revolutionary struggle for independence. Notably, her account of his life opens with his descent from Polish gentry and his family's involvement in the 1863 insurrection. She depicts him as a lover of the motherland and a fiery fighter for Polish independence and the brotherhood of all people. Abramowski emerges in Dąbrowska's account as a Polish prophetic visionary. She wrote, "It is as though Abramowski's whole ideology elucidated the ideology of each Pole and unveiled that which each of us, and all of us together, would like, with all our hearts, to offer the world as our singularly Polish achievement of Universal Brotherhood."[22] She emphasized his similarities with Józef Piłsudski, the Polish autocrat who, in the pre-state period, had struggled to revive the romantic traditions of insurrection.[23] Not incidentally, Dąbrowska also drew a comparison between Abramowski and Stefan Żeromski, the great Polish writer and supporter of the Filarets, who had commemorated the failed 1863 insurrection in his 1912 novel *The Faithful River* (*Wierna Rzeka*). Dąbrowska had herself written about the 1863 tragedy in her early short story "The 1863 Insurrection: A Welcome to War and Freedom" ("Powstanie 1863 roku: Powitanie wojny i swobody").[24]

Dąbrowska's association of the Filarets (through Żeromski) with Abramowski in a 1925 publication illustrates her conviction that the struggle for a free Poland had not yet truly ended and would only come with the fulfillment of its special mission. According to Mickiewicz, it was "the heroic destiny of Poland" to bring a redemptive message based on Christian ethics to the nations, whereas according to Abramowski, contrary to Dąbrowska, what the Polish nation will bring to the world was the model of "Universal Brotherhood."[25] Even though the historical circumstances differed — Mickiewicz's vision was shaped by post-Napoleonic Europe and the aftermath of a failed Polish insurrection, whereas Dąbrowska wrote of Abramowski's vision in the reality of an independent Poland — Poland's special moral destiny, as Dąbrowska observed with growing chagrin and bitterness, had not yet actualized.

Her disillusion was all the more acute because of the patriotic zeal of her youth, particularly during World War I. In her 1927 recollection of her voluntary service for Piłsudski's war effort, she painted a portrait of herself as a young woman full of hope for Poland's future. Her experience, as she remembered it, seemed to justify this hope:

> In mid-September 1914, Mrs. Kosmowska asked me if I would be willing to go to the countryside to establish a postal route which would deliver newspapers, documents, fliers, and news regarding the political and military activities of Józef Piłsudski to the [Warsaw] editorial office. . . . I found myself in an enormous area . . . between two armies pressing in upon each other. The incredible scarlet of the sun inundated everything . . . at dawn and at dusk. Even as the land basked in this conflagration, which was a sign of future bloodshed, it was calm and sweet. The people breathed just as calmly. Yet, despite appearances, everybody . . . was ready to join. . . . In Glinnek I found young people who had graduated from agricultural schools and who wished to make a change. There was a sense of exalted or even, one may say, positivist peasant romanticism. The youth embraced the task with the piety of believers. . . . I arrived in Kraków, from where the first shipment of [Piłsudski's] legionary materials was sent promptly.[26]

This testimony of Dąbrowska's war activities brings to mind Iwaszkiewicz's recollection of the countryside during his military service. But even though both writers expressed their admiration for the Polish landscape, the disparity between them could not be greater. While Iwaszkiewicz's war experience crystallized his aesthetic appreciation of the Polish landscape as an artist, Dąbrowska's war experience solidified her sense of belonging not only to the Polish land, but also to its people. Over a decade later she still remembered how the "burning" landscape, which signaled the imminent bloodshed of the war, did not affect the "sweetness" and the "calmness" of the countryside, which mirrored the gentleness and the dignity of its inhabitants. The shared breathing of the land and its inhabitants made them naturally inseparable: the land and the people constituted an indivisible whole. The oneness of the Polish countryside and its Polish peasant population seemed unbreakable, and not even the surrounding armies and imminent battle could separate them. The patriotic steadfastness and determination of the peasants made Dąbrowska aware of her own organic affiliation with the Polish countryside and its peasants, whom she now saw as the quintessential Poles.

Dąbrowska recalled immersing herself in the life of the rural communities she passed through on her mission. She associated their patriotic idealism with religious faith; the patriotism and dedication of the peasant youth to the common national cause invoked the "exalted piety of believers." These young people embodied the "peasant romanticism" spoken of by the poets Mickiewicz and Słowacki. They were "the Christ of Nations," ready to suffer for freedom in a heroic, if hopeless, struggle for independence. But for Dąbrowska the young people also represented "positivism," namely, the practical approach to economic and cultural progress intended to integrate independent Poland into the Western world. While Iwaszkiewicz's rational approach to the war echoed the "pessimistic" Kraków school of historiography, which defied the romantic-heroic myth and promoted economically sound politics, Dąbrowska's approach to the young peasants reflected the "optimistic" Warsaw school of historiography, which wished to conflate the romantic-heroic myth with a pragmatic Western-oriented development of Poland.

Despite Dąbrowska's patriotic exaltation, her idealization of the peasant, and her high hopes for Poland's future, she felt foreboding even as World War I drew to a close. On October 13, 1918, she wrote, "We live in a fairy tale, the most wonderful tale. I feel we are not grand enough to feel as happy as we should. We are not good enough to be worthy. O, let us be grand and good."[27] Dąbrowska's romanticism and moral expectations hardly concealed her concern as to whether the Poles would be capable of building a nation-state grounded in humanistic ethics. In this respect, she echoed the Polish intelligentsia, and certainly Iwaszkiewicz, who was well aware of Poland's cultural and economic backwardness compared to civilized western Europe.

History confirmed Dąbrowska's anxieties about Poland's future. The new state of Poland was not prepared to contend with Western markets, nor was it capable of establishing a sound educational system or a stable democracy. While the powerful gentry (*szlachta*) rejected agricultural reforms, their smaller estates could not be maintained. The situation was further aggravated by the economic crisis in the 1930s. The multinational population presented another problem. The new state was only two-thirds ethnically Polish; the rest of the population was Ukrainian, Belorussian, German, and Jewish. The Minorities Treaty, signed at Versailles in 1919 and intended to protect the rights of all minorities in the Polish state, was not implemented.[28] The Jews, who made up about 10 percent of the population, became the target of growing Polish nationalist extremism. Marshal Piłsudski's Sanacja [the movement of recovery], the popular name for the coalition of the Non-Party Block for Cooperation with the Government, which came to power in 1926, attempted to maintain the politics of tolerance,[29] but Endecja spread powerful propaganda about a Jewish conspiracy to take over the economic, professional, and cultural life of Poland.[30]

Endecja's platform promulgated a Polish nation-state whose citizens were of ethnic Polish descent and of Roman Catholic confession. Piłsudski's death in 1935, and fascist sentiments in Europe, intensified these xenophobic sentiments toward Jews. Anti-Semitic racism permeated many spheres of Polish life. In a May 9, 1926, article entitled "Two Questions" ("Dwa pytania") in the right-wing publication *Rozwój,* for example, the editor, Stanisław Pieńkowski, queried whether Jews believed in God and whether they were human. Having answered both questions in the negative, the author posited: "According to all historical and psychological evidence, Jews are a particular species of ape-men. The proof of the dovish heart of the white races [is] that on the basis of some physical similarity they are accepted as human beings." A November 7, 1931, *Rozwój* article, "We and Hitlerism" ("My a hitleryzm"), by Roman Dmowski, the founder of Endecja, urged the de-Judaization of

Poland "whether by Hitlerian, or by non-Hitlerian methods," and argued, "it does not matter, as long as the goal is achieved." The search for a solution to "the Jewish problem" even preoccupied the Polish church.[31] Ways to get rid of the Jews were openly and publicly explored, including emigration to Palestine or to Madagascar.[32]

While the general situation in independent Poland fell drastically short of Dąbrowska's prewar expectations, she could not subscribe to Endecja's crudely racist propaganda. Nonetheless, the increasing nationalism of Endecja confronted her with an ideological conundrum, which defined the split between her public and private persona with regard to the Jewish problem. On the one hand, racist demagoguery and the persecution of the Jewish minority were keeping Poland from entering the Western world, whose sociopolitical model was constructed on the concepts of fraternity, progress, and religious tolerance. On the other hand, Western political ethics, grounded in the democratic and civic rights and duties of all individuals, whatever their ethnicity, contradicted Poland's messianic mission, defined by common ethnic roots and a shared cultural and religious heritage.[33] Ironically, the exclusively Polish mission of inclusive Universal Brotherhood required the exclusion of Jewish citizens.

In terms of Polish interests, Endecja's struggle to ban Jews did not make sense. Jewish contributions to commerce, industry, and the arts played a vital role in the impoverished and unstable Polish state.[34] Whereas Endecja pictured Jews as an inferior race of "ape-men," Dąbrowska acknowledged the achievements of the Jews, who were spearheading Poland's progress into Western civilization. Ironically, the Jews were fulfilling the Polish intelligentsia's aspirations for the "Europeanization" of Poland. Moreover, Dąbrowska was aware that discrimination against the Jewish minority reflected badly on Poland.[35] Anti-Jewish propaganda hindered Poland's acceptance in the civilized world. As achievers and as victims, the Jews attested to the backwardness of the ethnic Polish population. Yet in ideological terms, Dąbrowska saw the Jews as being in competition with the Poles. That the Poles were losing this competition precluded any open-minded approval of the Jews' contributions to the nation, and, more fundamentally, called into question the special mission Dąbrowska envisioned for the Polish people.

While Dąbrowska's notion of what we would today call "political correctness" made her deny her anti-Semitism, she could not control the rhetoric of resentment which gave away the intensity of her competitive attitude toward the Jews. Her jealousy did not transcend this sense of inferiority; rather, it represents a mindset that Max Scheler, following Nietzsche, called *ressentiment*, "a lasting mental attitude caused by the impulse to detract and spite [the Other] who owns a good we covet [and who] is falsely considered to be the *cause* of our privation."[36] Ressentiment enables us to blame successful individuals for our own failure. Dąbrowska's growing ressentiment illuminates her ideological predicament which made it impossible for her to reconcile her conflicted ideological orientations; the "Jewish problem" presented her with irresolvable contradictions between nationalistic particularism and humanistic universalism. Her position between Endecja and the Jews in two incidents discussed in the next section exhibited a state of self-deception which, regardless of the horrific circumstances of the Jewish genocide, continued to fuel her competitive attitude toward the Jews.

Jewish Students, Jewish Doctors, and Anti-Semites

Dąbrowska became a "moral authority" in 1936 when she published the newspaper article "Annual Shame," in which she condemned the persecution of Jewish students. The anti-Semitic trend to exclude Jews from the universities began in the 1920s with the demand of *numerus clausus* on Jewish enrollment, and evolved into a call for *numerus nullus* in the 1930s. The restrictions included the "bench ghetto," assigned seats at the back of lecture halls to which Jewish students were relegated, as well as barring entrances to halls, and were sometimes enforced by physical violence. The majority of the faculty and student body acquiesced in the situation. The campaign was instigated by the church and by Endecja, and was carried out by the right-wing nationalist youth parties.[37]

"Annual Shame" was received with attacks from the right and with praise from the left. Despite the protest of other left-wing activists, professors, and public figures against the persecutions of Jewish students which appeared in the publication *Poles About Jews*, it was Dąbrowska's article which achieved fame in prewar progressive circles and continued to be taken as proof of the writer's principled defense of Jewish victims.[38] The entry in Dąbrowska's diary for November 4, 1936, however, revealed a less determined moral stance: "I've been revising the article about the anti-Jewish incidents all day. Why have I written it? I don't know. This is not my 'thing.' [But] anything unfamiliar is always tempting."[39] These are puzzling comments. Surely the anti-Jewish brawls at the universities were not "unfamiliar" to Dąbrowska. Surely journalistic writing was her "thing." Did the disavowal of her interest in the subject matter imply a resentful distance from the Jews which she wished to maintain? Did the private diaristic sphere of these comments imply her concern about her public standing, which she was afraid to compromise?

The rhetoric of the article gives credence to these conjectures. While Dąbrowska emphasized the superior education of the Jews and echoed the widespread belief in Jewish economic domination, she nevertheless attributed Jewish success to Polish lack of drive and absence of ambition. Her arguments distinguished Poles and Polish Jews as separate ethnic entities. At no point did she urge social integration of Jewish students into the Polish student body, nor did she encourage any social contacts between the groups. There was no expression of sympathy for the Jewish students, and she talked neither about the Jewish victims' physical suffering nor about their emotional hurt. Her main concern was that these brutal incidents were diminishing Poland's image as a progressive, education-oriented country:

> The majesty of that supreme value by which a nation inscribes itself into world civilization, the majesty of great innovative studies, has been affronted. These deeds are attempts to drive Poland back to the level of dark tribes which harbor in their primitive souls an animalistic hatred for the bright spirits who carry the light.

The few references to Jews in this long article reflect her lack of sympathy with the victims and reveal her own conviction of the negative effect of the Jews on Poland. Out of only seven actual mentions of Jews or anti-Semitism, the notion of the "Jewish problem" recurs four times. Dąbrowska argued that violence is the wrong way to resolve the problem. The solution lies in the transformation of the Polish mentality toward progress, especially in terms of education. "The educational establishment is to blame," she claimed, "for letting our youth enter the institutions of higher education mentally and morally unprepared and unable to match up to the Jewish students."

Dąbrowska reiterated these views privately in her diary on March 21, 1937: "These [persecutions of Jewish students at universities] are crimes committed not against the Jews, but against one's own nation."[40] Seeing anti-Semitism as damaging to the nation abstracted the Jews and their suffering; it presented them as a marker of Polish moral failure rather than as wronged individuals. The guilt of the injustice committed by her fellow Poles against innocent fellow citizens had no place in Dąbrowska's argument. Rather, she found the Polish anti-Semites guilty only of having tarnished the reputation of Poland.

Two years later, Dąbrowska's reluctance to engage in a defense of the Jews had intensified considerably. On October 29, 1938, she recorded that, as president of the Trade Union of Polish Writers (Związek Zawodowy Literatów Polskich; ZZLP), she was attacked by *Prosto z Mostu* (*As It Is*), a radical right-wing literary weekly and leading nationalist publication of the 1930s, over an incident concerning Jewish doctors. The incident took place in an incendiary historical context: a few days after Hitler's annexation of the Sudeten, a few days before Kristallnacht, and, in Poland, at the end of a ferociously anti-Jewish election campaign to the Polish Parliament (*Sejm*). Likely fueled by these events, the weekly's anti-Semitic ire was directed at the disproportionate number of Jews on the list of doctors who volunteered to treat Union members. The list appeared in the circular of the Union, signed by Dąbrowska, which, unbeknownst to her, included nine Jews and nine Poles.

Dąbrowska explains in her diary that the request for volunteer doctors was sent to nine Jewish doctors and to a much larger number of Polish doctors. With unconcealed exasperation, she notes, "Naturally *all* the Jewish doctors agreed and only nine non-Jewish doctors did. (Polish doctors don't read anything at all, so why should they care about treating writers.)"[41] She observed that the previous year, seven rural cooperative clinics had to close because only Jewish doctors offered voluntary services. Dąbrowska had no sympathy for the Polish doctors, whom she depicted as illiterate ignoramuses. Ironically, her irritation with the Poles contains a roundabout acknowledgment of the superiority of the Jews: "And then we are scandalized by Jewish supremacy. The stupidity of our people is repugnant." The condemnation of the Polish doctors reverberates with her criticism of the Polish students for not measuring up to their Jewish peers. As in "Annual Shame," where she expressed no appreciation of the

Jewish students' contribution to the Polish academia, she shows no appreciation for the Jewish doctors' selfless willingness to serve their country.

The disparity between Dąbrowska's official and personal responses to the situation is notable. In public, as she tells us, "I limited myself to demanding of the Board that no circulars bearing my signature be issued, and that something be done to increase the number of Polish doctors." In the private sphere of her diary, she clarified her position:

> I am not and have never been an anti-Semite. But I definitely would not wish: 1) to provoke the human beast that we have no power to destroy; 2) to pull strings for Jews; 3) to have my name publicized in connection with such banal and fundamentally repulsive matters. . . . But how shall I extricate myself from all this?

Dąbrowska's official response essentially amounts to an abdication of her authority as president of the Union, while her indictment of the Polish doctors and of Endecja remains on her diary pages. It may well be that the anti-Semitic "beast" has become too powerful to allow her to engage in a public struggle for the enlightenment of her fellow Poles. It is therefore possible to understand her declaration "I am not and have never been an anti-Semite" as a specific disavowal of Endecja's violent anti-Semitic activities. At the same time, her conviction that Jews were detrimental to Poland's mission precluded the possibility of sympathy with the victims of anti-Semitic discrimination.

The worsening situation of the Jews in Poland and in Europe at large did not change Dąbrowska's position. A few days later, on November 5, 1938, Dąbrowska wrote impulsively about her unhappiness with her noble public image: "I owe to Stach [Stempowski][42] a great portion of my so-called 'moral authority' which in return has caused me great dissatisfaction with my life. It made me old ten years too soon and unhappy, as if I were uncomfortably suspended with my head down."[43] The images of old age and of an upside-down position convey her visceral sense of the incongruity of her public image as defender of the Jews.

A short time later, she made her position toward the Jews and toward Polish anti-Semitism clear in her diary. On December 21, 1938, she wrote about Michał Rusinek's 1938 novel *The Land of Milk and Honey* (*Ziemia miodem płynąca*), which deals with the demoralization of Warsaw. Mentioning how the protagonist incites his friends to thrash (*prać*) the kikes (*żydłaków*), she remarked that such derogatory comments discredit Poland's good name, then adds in parentheses, "(Because what matters to me most is the Poles. The Jews will manage and will pay us back for everything with a vengeance.)" The parenthetical clarification signals Dąbrowska's need to reassure herself that her condemnation of the anti-Semitic behavior of the protagonist was not intended to defend the Jews. Her ressentiment emerges in the rationalization of her interest in Polish welfare rather than a concern about injustice toward the Jews. She exonerates the victimizer by claiming that Jews are immune to any hardship. This assertion releases her from any obligation toward the victim. Furthermore, she pictures Jews as enemies who are awaiting the opportunity to victimize Poles.

As we have already seen in the discussion of Iwaszkiewicz, biased views of the Jews were widely accepted in intelligentsia circles before the war. For Iwaszkiewicz and his wife, the horror of genocide superseded their bigotry and placed persecuted Jews within the sphere of their moral obligation. For Dąbrowska, a personal loss which made the genocide real defused the intensity of her nationalistic, xenophobic convictions, if only for a while.

Love and Despair in the Time of Genocide

Dąbrowska first met Stanisława Blumenfeldowa in January 1938 when she was lecturing in Lwów. Blumenfeldowa belonged to a prominent and wealthy Jewish family. Her uncle, Ostap Ortwin, was a prominent critic and writer; his tragic end in the Ghetto was later described in Adolf Rudnicki's short story "The Great Stefan Konecki" ("Wielki Stefan Konecki").[44] On her return from Lwów, Dąbrowska confessed in a letter to Stempowski that she did not like Blumenfeldowa, remarking that she would have become an anti-Semite had she stayed with her any longer. She claimed that Blumenfeldowa represented the aggression and self-promotion of the Jewish "race."

However, in the diary entry of January 17, 1938, about her visit, Dąbrowska presents a completely different picture. She acknowledged the good time she had with Lwów Jews, while allowing that "the Polonized Jews of Lwów are Polish in a much more unconstrained manner than Warsaw Jews, and they have a special kind of charm. . . . I met Ostap Ortwin . . . [who] does not look Jewish at all. Of this, too, only Lwów Jews are capable."[45] Clearly charmed by the family, she took pains to attenuate the "Jewishness" of its members, apparently in an attempt to rationalize her pleasure in Jewish company. With the outbreak of the war in September 1939, Dąbrowska and Stempowski escaped Warsaw to Lwów, where they stayed with the Blumenfelds until April, a period not documented in the *Diaries*. It was during this time that Dąbrowska fell in love with Blumenfeldowa. In November 1941, she went again to Lwów, already under German occupation, to see her beloved Stasia (diminutive of Stanisława). This was the last time she saw her. Blumenfeldowa most probably perished in the Lwów ghetto.

In contrast with Dąbrowska's consistent evasion of the genocide of Jews in Warsaw, Blumenfeldowa was constantly on the diarist's mind, and she mentioned her in practically every entry of her wartime diary, which is the shortest and the least systematic of the *Diaries*. Vacillating between hope and despair and constantly awaiting news, Dąbrowska was consumed with anxiety about her Stasia. Later on, she confessed that Stasia was one of the few people she ever truly loved (June 2, 1944).[46]

On June 27, 1943, Dąbrowska wrote in her diary:

> I have stopped making notes because of the nervous depression that has been tormenting me. . . . As a matter of fact, it has been only since May 12th [the day she learned the specifics about Blumenfeldowa's death] that I felt scared — scared of the sea of evil released by people and [scared] of [my] loss of faith in human beings. This faith was not reasoned out, nor was it "dialectical," as the socialists would have it; rather, it constituted the emotional substance of my nature.[47]

The diary does not specify how Blumenfeldowa died.

Dąbrowska only mustered her courage to face her lover's death years later, in an autobiographical story she wrote in the late 1940s. It also represents Dąbrowska's only attempt to confront emotionally the mass murder of the Jews. While taking a stroll on a snowy day, the story's male protagonist — a thinly disguised version of Dąbrowska herself — has a horrific vision of his lover "falling into an odious mass grave, crushed by lumps of earth even before she died." The pain almost makes the protagonist collapse in the snow and burst out crying.[48] The terror stirs a spontaneous wish to share, as closely as possible, the experience of his beloved. As this dramatic scene shows, Blumenfeldowa's death was an extremely traumatic event for Dąbrowska which dismantled her ideological defenses and compelled her to grasp the dehumanization of the Holocaust in a physical and emotional way.

The trauma reflected in the postwar story may explain Dąbrowska's dissociation from the horrific reality of the Ghetto as a psychic ploy to evade her fears about the fate of her lover. Her lack of response may also have reflected a desire to suppress the consciousness of Blumenfeldowa's Jewish origins. Indeed, Dąbrowska's representation of Blumenfeldowa as Maria Ersztynowa in her posthumously published novel *Adventures of a Thinking Person* (*Przygody człowieka myślącego*) diminished her lover's "Jewishness" by presenting her as a self-hating Jew.[49] During wartime, however, Dąbrowska could not deny Blumenfeldowa's Jewish ancestry and its implications. One of the few sentences in the diaries about the Ghetto Uprising seems to support this supposition. On May 12, 1943, Dąbrowska associates the burning Ghetto with her lover's horrific murder: "The sun [is] red from the smoke. Constant detonations, as if continuing mise-en-scène of her death."[50] The burning Ghetto becomes a haunting reenactment of Blumenfeldowa's death. The color of the sun hidden by the smoke, the sound of the explosions and the shootings, and undoubtedly the smell of the burning Ghetto infused the loss of her lover with concrete graphic and sensory dimensions. Yet Dąbrowska consistently avoided any mention of the Jews who were burning in the Ghetto, some of whom must have been her prewar friends and acquaintances.

Personal loss forced Dąbrowska to face, for a moment, the universal signification of the Holocaust. The genocide was a "sea of evil," which collapsed the basic mainstays of humanity. Her ideological assumptions had been shattered, forcing her to distinguish between inherent and learned perspectives of human beings. Her feeling of loss was deeper than socialism's dialectic reasoning; it undermined her being, revealing the futility of faith in progress, and leaving her helpless when confronted with human barbarism. Her inability to record her life in her diary during this time reflects the paralysis of despair: the assertion of individual autonomy reflected by the diaristic search for meaning has ceased to make sense. The dehumanizing death of her lover confronted Dąbrowska with the ultimate impotence of humanism and the Enlightenment.

The Power of Ideological Misperception

Dąbrowska's despair over human nature did not persist. Paradoxically, the collapse of the Enlightenment restored Dąbrowska's faith in humanism, and specifically, the humanism of the Polish nation. For Dąbrowska, the hardships of the war and the elimination of the Jews provided an opportunity for ethnic Poles to actualize the mission that Mickiewicz had termed the "heroic destiny of Poland."

On June 4, 1944, Dąbrowska made the following observation in her diary:

> This is the strange secret of the Occupation: that the destitution has not increased. On the contrary, not only has affluence risen, but it seems to be spreading more widely in society. From the stories of teachers, I conclude that today, despite everything, not fewer but rather more people are getting an education than in the time of independence. Quite simply, those who did not use to have the means to educate their children have them today. Many people attribute this to the disappearance of the Jews, and though it is terrible to admit (because of the inhuman way in which they have disappeared), I suppose it's true. Despite the concerns — how could Poland manage without Jews? — I think that without them, it would have blossomed like a flower.[51]

As Dąbrowska saw it, the Jews had hindered Polish progress in independent Poland. Their "disappearance" now allowed the Poles to actualize their intellectual and entrepreneurial potential; the "blossoming" Warsaw population demonstrated the extraordinary fortitude of the Polish people.

But Warsaw's situation at the time exposes Dąbrowska's counterfactual self-deception. It is true that under the Occupation some Poles prospered from the appropriation of Jewish property, the black market, and widespread smuggling. And on a positive note, an admirable network of clandestine schools was established. Nonetheless, Dąbrowska offered a distorted view of the economic situation, which contradicted her own reporting and, I would argue, trivialized the suffering of the Warsaw population. Dąbrowska's diaries, like the diaries of other Warsaw writers, consistently recorded not only the increasing economic difficulties, but also the author's own struggles. Thus, Dąbrowska envied Zofia Nałkowska, who was managing a small cigarette store. Yet, Nałkowska recorded the enormous hardships that managing the store entailed and the meager earnings it offered; at times she required assistance from Jarosław Iwaszkiewicz. The deprivations of the Occupation did not spare Iwaszkiewicz either, as can be seen by his descriptions of the pitiful meals that he and his wife often served to friends who sought refuge from destitute Warsaw at their Stawisko estate. Stanisław Rembek often tried — sometimes without success — to sell personal objects to feed his starving family. Aurelia Wyleżyńska talked about her dependence on food supplies from Wielgolas, her family estate in the countryside.

Dąbrowska's perception of Warsaw's affluence also did not reflect the actual socio-historical circumstances of the occupied city. The June 1944 entry marks a critical moment: Warsaw was a couple of months away from the Warsaw Uprising (August 1944); the city lived in terror of roundups, incarcerations, and executions. The Soviet army's advance westward was heralded by frequent air raids. Warsaw residents earned only a fraction of what they needed to survive, while food rationing kept them on the verge of starvation.[52] The Germans prohibited secondary and university education. Libraries and archives were destroyed, cultural activities were forbidden, and the Polish intelligentsia was decimated.[53] The brutality of the Occupation brought forth prevalent demoralization, manifest not only in hunting the hiding Jews, but also in a rampant crime rate among the Poles. German racist politics designated the Poles as *Untermenschen* and slaves, and the terror of the German rule reflected this classification.[54] Among the oppressed population, however, it was widely believed that the Germans were planning the extermination of the Poles. Dąbrowska found these fears plausible. On November 20, 1943, she noted, "Terrible rumors [are spreading] amongst the Warsaw population. Everybody talks about gas chambers and that the Germans want to murder us the way they've been murdering the Jews. As a matter of fact, they're already doing it."[55]

How is it possible to reconcile Dąbrowska's fears of forthcoming extermination with her exultant claims about the Poles' improving quality of life? Her references to the absence of Jews elucidate the contradiction. Although the November 1943 entry demonstrates that Dąbrowska knew about the death camps, and the June 1944 entry shows her awareness of the Jews' "disappearance," her focus was not on the Jewish tragedy but rather on the Polish situation. Some Poles altruistically responded to the Jewish plight, while at the other end of the spectrum were the *szmalcowniki,* individuals who blackmailed hiding Jews and their Polish rescuers, and often handed them over to the Gestapo.[56] Most Poles, however, were not concerned about the plight of the Jews. This indifference may have resulted from the ferocious anti-Semitic right-wing press throughout the war,[57] or it might be that the Poles were simply too preoccupied with their own survival.[58]

Dąbrowska's description of an economic and intellectual revival in Warsaw seems to represent yet another response to the Jewish genocide. She was determined to see the "blossoming" of the city without Jews, and despite the horrifying premonition of extermination, as a reaffirmation of the extraordinary potential of Polish society; at the same time, Warsaw's civilized coping with the situation proved Dąbrowska's lifelong conviction of the messianic "chosenness" of the Polish people.

In the prewar period, Dąbrowska indicted the Poles for not having measured up to the Jews, but she now saw extraordinary Polish achievements under the most trying circumstances. Her lifelong hopes for the Polish people as a model of solidarity and friendship for the European nations were finally being realized. In a kind of poetic justice, Mickiewicz's prophecy of Polish heroic destiny had been fulfilled. Indeed, years later Dąbrowska continued to celebrate the uniqueness of Polish heroism under the Occupation. "One knows for sure," she wrote on December 1, 1959, "that elsewhere nobody would have survived the Occupation by adhering exclusively to the norms of sublime suffering. But among us there was a general rejection of the invasion (and even of the defeat) and even this was a source of happiness and strength."[59] Here she is clearly referring to Polish defiance of the German invader in the defense of Warsaw in September 1939, to the Polish underground, unparalleled among occupied Europe,[60] and to the heroic Warsaw Uprising in August 1944. Dąbrowska herself collaborated with the underground efforts. Together with Stempowski, she worked for *Poland Fights* and *The Republic's Eastern Lands*, the publications of the underground organization Union of Armed Struggle.[61]

Dąbrowska's postwar diaries show that her ressentiment did not disappear; rather, it shifted to other areas of competition with the remnant of the Polish Jewish population. For instance, on May 18, 1947, having met Professor Ludwik Hirszfeld, an eminent immunologist who told her of his escape from the Ghetto and his terrifying experience of hiding during the Occupation, Dąbrowska complained, "There is no way to make them suffer even a little with us."[62] Dąbrowska wanted the suffering of the Poles to be recognized even by the victims of the Final Solution.

The resentment at the immensity of the Jewish tragedy emerges in Dąbrowska's later controversy with the Jewish survivors of Kalisz, which, as Drewnowski observes, shows "her incapability to cope with the climactic event of the Holocaust."[63] In 1960, the Kalish Memorial Book Committee in Tel-Aviv asked the famous writer for a contribution. In their letter of invitation, the committee expressed great disappointment that the extermination of the city's 26,000 Jewish citizens was not remembered in its recent anniversary celebration. The committee hoped that Dąbrowska could rectify this omission. Dąbrowska told the committee that she remembered very little from her childhood, and briefly summarized her recollections of the Jewish shops and some Jewish acquaintances of her grandmother. She mentioned the Jewish characters in her novels. The only Jewish Kalish intelligentsia that she remembered were the Brokmans, who moved to Warsaw and "somehow avoided the Ghetto" ("jakoś uchronili się przed zamknięciem w gettcie"). While Dąbrowska reported that Mrs. Brokman took care of and eventually buried her sister, Jadwiga, who died in the Warsaw Uprising, she expressed no feelings for Mrs. Brokman whatsoever.

Finally, referring to the committee's letter, which claimed that Jewish love for Poland remained unrequited, she wrote, "There was love and there was hatred on both sides. . . . We must talk about it without complexes. I am referring to the entirety of the history [of the Jews in Kalisz], not the bestiality of Hitlerism, which invalidated any normative human relationships."[64] The committee expressed disagreement with Dąbrowska's assessment of the prewar relations between Poles and Jews and voiced disappointment with her lack of sensitivity to the destruction of Kalish Jews. "It is difficult for an outsider," they wrote, "to comprehend the tragedy of the Holocaust, which destroyed the Jewish population of Poland."[65] Significantly, Dąbrowska's recollections of Jewish Kalish were not published in the Memory Book. Her diary notation of July 15, 1960, demonstrates that the committee's assessment of Dąbrowska's resentful attitude toward Jewish suffering in the Holocaust was correct: "[Working] on the letter to the Kalish Jews in Tel Aviv. Oh my God, what huge complexes! They will not be satisfied with anything less than us talking in every publication, and on every occasion, about the destruction of the Jews!"[66]

Communists, Intellectuals, Dead Fighters, and the Indelibility of Ressentiment

Dąbrowska perceived the postwar Polish communist regime imposed by the Soviet Union as an occupation, as did many other Poles. The inclusion of Poland in the Soviet bloc robbed the Polish people of their deserved freedom, arrested their progress, and conditioned them to lead a life of corruption. On September 15, 1950, she wrote, "I think about the camouflaged face of our nation. Nobody exposes his true face. . . . Governmental lies prompt the society to counterlie. The nation has been learning to live on its knees."[67] A few years later she claimed, "Government propaganda spreads heroic ethics and a suspect kind of idealism, while social ethics decline to scandalous lows. . . . Literally from day to day we are becoming a nation of hooligans, psychopaths, thugs, and robbers of public and private property" (November 28, 1954).[68] Dąbrowska directed her scathing criticism of the regime at Polish Jewish communists, who, as she saw it, dominated the ruling institutions.

Dąbrowska attributed unlimited political power to Jewish party members, which made them implacable prosecutors and persecutors of the Poles. In an entry on May 17, 1947, she deplored the injustice of the situation:

> The Public Security Office and the legal system are entirely in Jewish hands. In the past two years not even one Jew has had a political trial. The Jews judge and sentence Poles to execution. How could this situation not be spreading vicious anti-

Semitism? Who can suppose that the only good Poles and citizens who never deserve trial are Jews? How terrible is the fate of my unhappy motherland. Why does everyone, everyone around us only want to kill us?[69]

Dąbrowska had predicted Jewish revenge for Polish anti-Semitic persecutions. Now her ressentiment of the Jews who, as she believed, ruled Poland was so great that she was able to condone anti-Semitism as an understandable reaction. Poland as "unhappy motherland" recalls the Polish history of victimhood and of suffering at the hands of the Russians at the time of the partitions. In view of the long-standing hatred for the Russians, the collaboration of Polish Jews with the Soviet authorities was evidence of their disloyalty to Poland. Indeed, in the description of her train journey from Wrocław to Warsaw on November 5, 1949, Dąbrowska mentions that in the men's sleeping cars "one always meets a lot of Jews and Russians." She observes, "In their conversations with the Moskals [a pejorative term for Russians], the Jews are obsequious and submissive, not at all like communists, but rather like old time traders."[70] In order to achieve privilege and power, Jews were reenacting their prewar practices as shrewd manipulators and gain-seekers. Dąbrowska cannot hide her ressentiment of the reversal of Jewish fortunes from a persecuted minority in interwar Poland to the ruling elite in postwar Poland.

Even when a Jew acted boldly against communist propaganda—Adolf Rudnicki, the notable writer, publicly tore up copies of a journal that maligned writers for not being Marxist enough—Dąbrowska's ressentiment toward the Jews resurfaced. Dąbrowska claimed, "I extremely liked this repudiation of *Odrodzenie* in the State Council hall, and Rudnicki gained my sympathy for this gesture, which, it is true, only a Jew, and therefore 'a first class citizen,' can afford to make today" (March 3, 1950).[71]

Dąbrowska's response to Rudnicki reveals the complexity of her ressentiment. Whereas the cooperation of the Jewish communists with the Soviet regime signified a moral sellout to the enemy, Rudnicki's act affirmed his personal autonomy against the totalitarian regime. Seeking rationalization for his audacity in his superior position as a Jew reflects Dąbrowska's ressentiment for not having been able to stand up to the authorities as he did. This mixture of admiration and envy characterizes her postwar view of all Jewish intellectuals. Thus in the May 22, 1956, entry, which starts with a remark about having been for over a month "in exclusively Jewish company," she blames anti-Semitism on the Jews who have been "occupying all the 'key positions' in Polish life." Yet, she admits, "to be fair, if there is any free, creative thought around here, it is theirs. In this moment, they are the most courageous 'obstructors of the police order.' Even in conversations they are more interesting than ethnic Poles." The entry concludes with a revealing statement: "All this irritates people; it is as if somebody who is not one of us wanted to live our lives for us. . . . One wishes that these involuntary differentiations and emotional 'discriminations' would disappear."[72]

Significantly, the Jews' subversion of the hated regime does not erase the differentiations between "us" and "them." While Dąbrowska acknowledges Jewish contributions to Polish progress, she cannot overcome the emotional antagonism that the Jews as Jews evoke. Just as before the war Dąbrowska recognized Jewish contributions to the enlightened progress of Poland, yet resented the contributors, now, in a similar way, the Jews' contributions to the intellectual freedom and cultural autonomy of the Polish nation engender in Dąbrowska estrangement and annoyance. Ironically, Dąbrowska's consciousness of her discriminatory attitude toward the Jews does not liberate her from her prejudices; rather, it reaffirms the potency of its xenophobic effect.

On April 19, 1948, the date of the unveiling of the Monument to the Ghetto Heroes, Dąbrowska wrote, "I have nothing against Jewish heroes. But Warsaw still doesn't have a monument for its own insurgents, nor for the children who fought in the [Warsaw] Uprising."[73] Her emphasis on Warsaw's "own insurgents" communicates her ineluctable exclusion of the Ghetto Uprising from the Warsaw Uprising. This emphatic distinction between uprisings throws more light on the scarcity of references to the Ghetto Uprising in her war diary. It was not only that the fight of the Jews was not her fight; the heroism of the Jews detracted from the heroism of the Poles.

This conjecture about Dąbrowska's wartime silence concerning the Ghetto Uprising is strengthened by her position on commemorative plaques for Polish resistance fighters. Taking into consideration the Jews who fought in the underground, the committee wished to dedicate the plaques to "Polish citizens." By her own record of November 9, 1948, Dąbrowska told the committee,

> Warsaw already has the Monument to the Ghetto Heroes. . . .
> But the city has no monument in honor of the Poles. . . . As far
> as the objection that Jews were also dying there, first, if Jews
> happened to be killed in a public execution, it was completely
> exceptional. Jews died in other places and in a different man-
> ner. At any rate, Jews who fought in the Ghetto fought also for
> Poland and did not hide it; in fact, they appeared under Polish
> banners. If there happened to be a Jew who died in a public ex-
> ecution, he died there as a Pole and perhaps even as a Catholic.
> It will not be an insult to his memory if we include him under
> the inscription 'Poles.'[74]

Dąbrowska's emotional outburst was informed by her ideology. Her
allusion to the "manner" in which Jews died in death camps implies
Jewish passivity. To dismiss Jewish heroism, she attempts to co-opt both
the Ghetto Uprising fighters and the "rare" Jewish fighter in the Polish
underground. In her view, the former should be considered Poles and
the latter Catholic. The opportunism of this proposal signals a compulsion to maintain the exclusivity of "Polish heroic destiny." The suggested
"conversions" of the Jewish fighters into Poles and Catholics reveal the
depth of Dąbrowska's need to eliminate the Jews from the scene of Warsaw heroism. Her ressentiment did not enable her to share the glory of
the Polish resistance with the Jews. Her obliteration of the Jewish presence in the resistance stripped Polish Jews of their patriotism for Poland.
It also excluded them from Polish history.

The case of Maria Dąbrowska presents us with a complex and thought-
provoking demonstration of the function of ideologies in moral responses
to the suffering Other. Neither the horrific spectacle of the Ghetto burning, nor an awareness of gas chambers and mass extermination elicited
an empathic identification with the victims. The ideology of ethnic nationalism, combined with a patriotic faith in national "chosenness," prevented this lifelong advocate for human rights from having an emotional
response to the suffering of fellow human beings. The postwar continuation of Dąbrowska's prewar ressentiment highlights the continued absence of any impact of the Holocaust on her ethno-national perceptions.
The Holocaust seems not to have changed her attitude to the Jew as Other,

an outsider in the ethnic Polish nation. Dąbrowska's enduring sense of resentment against the Jewish minority reaffirms the power of ideology on the individual's emotional constitution. Dąbrowska's unchanged position should not be considered the norm. Nonetheless, Dąbrowska presents a cautionary example of the foreboding capability of nationalistic ideology to distort the meaning of humanistic ethics at the deepest emotional level in most tragic historical reality.

CHAPTER 4

Aurelia Wyleżyńska: Rethinking Art and Ethics in the Reality of the Holocaust

The wartime diary of Aurelia Wyleżyńska (1881–1944), scarcely mentioned in Polish research of the Holocaust,[1] is practically unknown to the general public. Wyleżyńska was a well-known literary figure in the prewar and wartime Warsaw intellectual milieu. Yet, of all the Warsaw war diaries discussed in this book, only Wyleżyńska's diary remains unpublished. This author of numerous prizewinning novels and biographies, of translations and journalistic writings, and above all, of an extraordinary wartime diary, has been all but forgotten.[2]

Wyleżyńska was born in 1881 in Podolia Governorate, at that time a province of the Russian Empire. From 1907 to 1911 she studied philosophy at the Jagiellonian University in Kraków, where she started her literary career, publishing essays and articles in popular magazines. After World War I, which she spent in Russia, she settled in Lwów, where she continued writing and was active in the Union of Professional Polish Writers. In 1924 she moved to Paris. She wrote for publications in Poland and was actively engaged in the Paris-based association Les Amis de la Pologne, gave lectures, and traveled extensively in Europe. Wyleżyńska returned to Poland in 1937 and settled in Warsaw. During the Occupation, she worked as a volunteer in a hospital, and was actively engaged in saving Jews. She also worked for the Polish underground and wrote articles and reviews for the clandestine press. Her patriotic determination to stay in Poland never faltered. Sometime in 1940, when the situation was getting worse, she decided to register as a permanent Warsaw resident and observed, "Finally the globetrotter has settled down, and will remain in this land to the end. Now I am solidly tied to my first motherland, though there was a time when the second [France] was the foundation of my identity." She was shot on the first day of the Warsaw Uprising, on August 1, 1944, and died on August 3.

The manuscript of Wyleżyńska's wartime diary, which was preserved by her sister Fela, is now in the National Library, Department of Rare Manuscripts, in Warsaw. The first section of the text, approximately 150 pages covering the period from September 27, 1939, to January 1, 1942, exists only in the original, which has been damaged; some pages are partly or completely illegible and, for the most part, it is impossible to decipher the dates of the entries. The remainder of the text, approximately 450 double-spaced pages covering January 2, 1942, to August 29, 1943, has been retyped; the dates are mostly legible. It seems likely that the final section of the diary has been lost.[3]

As a writer and a humanist, Wyleżyńska sought in her diary to assess the impact of German tyranny on the validity of humanistic ethics and on the relevance of art. The reality of the Occupation and the Holocaust disempowered existing norms of artistic representation, demanding new aesthetic modes not only to describe the sights and sounds of an un-imaginable world of horror, but also to explore psychological and moral responses. But for Wyleżyńska, aesthetics could not be separated from ethics. Her search for an appropriate language of art dovetailed with the question of the steadfastness of humanistic values in a time of terror. She was increasingly appalled by the brutality of German rule and by the hostile indifference of the majority of Polish society to Jewish suffering. Her decision to devote herself altruistically to rescuing Jews confronted her with unforeseen complications. While defying the Germans and evading Polish collaborators and blackmailers, she also became aware of the increasingly complex pattern of her interactions with the Jews she was trying to protect. In her diary, Wyleżyńska made a conscious effort to distance herself from her self, becoming an analytical teller of the story of her ethical and psychological transformation. Her descriptions of her rescue operations in her diary, as well as of people and events, form a remarkably insightful narrative of the altered meaning of ethics in a reality of genocide.

The Diary as Last Will and Testament

Wyleżyńska explicitly expressed her intention to make a formal testament twice. On February 7, 1943, she wrote,

> I delay making my will, even though it is worth doing, because the making of a will is a practical, not a poetic action. The first and most important point I wish to posit is the obligation of my heirs . . . to publish the diary posthumously, but with a sharp restriction: neither changes nor cuts are allowed.

Two months later, on April 7, she wrote,

> My testament . . . formulated in no poetic words . . . concerns the publication of the last child of my thoughts and feelings. From Horace to Pushkin, every writer wished to erect a monument for himself. . . . My desire is to publish this diary, whether in my lifetime or after my passing. I also wish to make clear the importance of the restriction that nobody dare to change, cross out, or concoct anything *ad usum*[4] of the family.

Clearly, Wyleżyńska attached great importance to her diary. Her reference to Horace and Pushkin, both of whom affirmed the monumental and eternal significance of poetry,[5] attests to her belief in the power of art. At the same time, her determination to have her diary published and thus to turn it into a bona fide book indicates her intention to write herself, so to speak, into a long tradition of publications of *les journaux intimes.* The wish to be published implies a desire to bring her story to the general public. While the other diarists — especially Dąbrowska, but also Nałkowska and Iwaszkiewicz — also planned publication of their diaries, Wyleżyńska's desire to share her diary with others was particularly intense. The dramatic perception of her diary as her "last child" and as her "monument" reflects its central place not just in her oeuvre but also in her life. Although Wyleżyńska was an accomplished and prolific writer, her metaphoric characterizations of the diary imply that she came to see it as having unique importance which obliterated all her other literary achievements. In fact, the stipulations she intended to put in her legally prepared testament do not mention her other works. As her "monument," the diary became her de facto testament, and in this sense, her life story would become her legacy to her future readers. This rhetorical aspect of the diary's self-referentiality as its author's "monument" and "testament" reinforces the importance of its message.

This importance is evident in Wyleżyńska's painstaking preparations for the diary's publication, which she recorded in detail. Despite the scarcity of paper, Wyleżyńska wrote the diary in two copies (April 4, 1942). Her sister retyped the handwritten pages, and Wyleżyńska hired a secretary to compare the two texts. When working on the two versions of the diary, she reports that she was particularly attentive to the organization and the explicitness of the ideas (January 26, 1943). Indeed, her concern for precision is evident in the multiple handwritten corrections on the typed pages. She paid close attention to the explication of the codes and shortcuts she used, as well as of her "verbal fantasies," to improve the diary's readability and clarity. Even though she was aware all along that the diary might "go to the garbage or be burned or destroyed," and despite having a serious heart condition and problems with her eyesight, she made a persistent effort to complete the task.

Wyleżyńska declared to have put her trust in the long-remembered phrase "you, not your oeuvre, will be buried." This second echo of Horace and Pushkin[6] attests to Wyleżyńska's insistence on her prewar Weltanschauung, which saw the signature of civilization and culture in poetic beauty. She was aware of the incongruity of this Weltanschauung in the reality of the Occupation. The Germans prohibited personal writing, the possession of typewriters was strictly forbidden, and printing and distributing materials was extremely dangerous. She knew the risk she was taking and the immense odds against the preservation of her work. Nevertheless, her work on the diary as an object of culture intended to be read by others made her feel reenergized and potent; as she claimed, it "reawakens my will to live" (April 11, 1943).

Yet Wyleżyńska's designation of her wartime diary as her "monument" was puzzling not only because its concrete physical existence was uncertain, but also because her references to the tradition of art, in her present-day reality, bordered on anachronistic. The phrase "from Horace to Pushkin" invokes the enormous scope of the humanistic tradition, which she literally watched being systematically destroyed, whereas the adage "you, not your work will be buried," recalls times when books were preserved and cherished as their authors' "monuments" rather than intentionally and consistently destroyed. Therefore, a question arises as to why the diarist attempted to justify her artistic production by contextualizing it within the tradition of the old masters. Furthermore, in view of the contemporary barbarism, whose ending she could not predict, how could she foresee a continuation of the prewar civilization of Horace and Pushkin, which would recognize her "monument"?

A closer look at the text reveals Wyleżyńska's own ambivalence: she was compelled to chronicle the present for the future despite her awareness that the cataclysmic present not only destroyed the past, but also called in question any vision of the future. On the one hand, she declared to have "imposed upon [herself] the role of the reporter of life today" (April 12, 1942), and found herself in a state of obsessive recording of events for "immortalization" (April 30, 1943). On the other hand, she was conscious of the uncertainty of the future reception of her diary as a chronicle. She saw herself writing for an indefinite reader in an indefinite future, a vague "somebody sometime" (February 21, 1940). Her material was intended for "authors who will tell it [i.e., the war story] — or maybe won't" (March 3, 1940). The story was destined for an unspecified "future reader" (September 23, 1942) or for "new talents" who have not yet been born (May 16, 1943). She sensed that the future was "deaf" (May 3, 1943) and remained "closed" (July 24, 1943) to the hopeless present. Despite her reluctance to acknowledge the collapse of the great tradition of the European aesthetic, Wyleżyńska was able to foresee the difficult, if not impossible, communication of her reality of unspeakable horror to the postwar generations of readers and artists.

The Diary as a Writer's Workshop

I would argue that Wyleżyńska's attempt to explain her desire for a "monument" in the spirit of the tradition of great poetry from Horace to Pushkin represents only a brief but instructive relapse into her prewar Weltanschauung. Eventually, her unavoidable recollections of humanistic civilization effected an equally unavoidable realization of the powerlessness of the tradition of aesthetic representation. Indeed, she frequently observed that neither the Spanish paintings of the passion of Christ nor Goya's *Los desastres de la guerra* possessed the capacity to depict the present-day situation (February 1 and August 6, 1942). The horror not only made the past artistic tradition obsolete, but it also silenced contemporary literary expression. Wyleżyńska observed, "The Poles have never been deprived of beauty in literature as they are today" (May 16, 1943). She claims that even at the most difficult times in Polish history, at the times of the insurrections and Russian oppression when free expression was impossible, Polish writers and poets wrote in codes, allegories, and symbols, persisting in their search for aesthetic means to produce moral guidance for sympathizers with the cause (May 16, 1943). Today, she lamented, "writers do not want to write" (May 16, 1943).

Wyleżyńska, however, sought to overcome this creative paralysis, persistently searching for modes of artistic representations of the reality she was chronicling so compulsively and, as she came to realize, so ineffectively. In this respect, her diary became *un atelier d'écriture* — a writing workshop which abounded in experimentations in genre and content appropriate for a fictional representation of the unprecedented reality of the Occupation and the genocide. Thus, for instance, she proposed novels, such as "People Behind the Fence," about Jews in the Ghetto, and noted ideas for film scripts, such as "Kraków, Montelupich Prison," about Polish prisoners fooling the Germans. She also outlined radio sketches, such as "Germans in the Polish Mansion," about German officers in the Polish countryside, and invented a great number of short scenes for films, such as "A Diamond in a Tooth," about conspiratorial underground activities.

This profusion of genres and ideas for literary representations of the Occupation and the genocide demonstrates the intensity of Wyleżyńska's desire not only to chronicle the present for posterity, but also to revive Polish literary and artistic creativity at large. Yet she was also becoming aware of the improbability of these attempts as she realized that the fantastic qualities of everyday existence had surpassed all artistic imagination: "Events are accumulating. . . . It is as if somebody were creating a film. . . . What only yesterday seemed like a figment of the imagination becomes today's reality" (April 24, 1942). Therefore, "we are learning new forms of life, because what often seems at first sight to be absurd turns out to be real" (April 15, 1943). In a reality which unfolds like a surreal horror film, she perceived the "need for a new vocabulary to depict what we experience, what we see, and what is happening." She confessed her inability to meet the linguistic needs of the present: "The former language is too pale, and therefore when using some past expression, I often put it in quotation marks. I realize that it is a template of a previous situation which is inapplicable today. . . . What we need is renewal, renewal" (September 28, 1942).

Wyleżyńska's acute sensitivity to her inadequacy to find a language which would adequately chronicle the surrounding reality of horror seems at odds with her emphatic designation of her diary as the "monument" which will assure her future "immortality." Why, then, would she want the diary, rather than her other, already published and highly acclaimed books, to become her signature on the landscape of the literary tradition? On one level it is possible to see this inconsistency as a rhetorical strategy. Her linguistic powerlessness to chronicle the genocide enhanced the incomprehensibility of the event. The indescribability of the situation communicated its apocalyptic, otherworldly nature. From this perspective, the diary can be considered a landmark, or a "monument," because its acknowledgment of the limits of imagination to represent the "new forms of life" communicates the inconceivable nature of that reality. On another level, the incongruence between the admitted inadequacy of the diary as a chronicle and the emphasis on the importance of its message emphasizes its importance as a psychological record. On May 5, 1943, Wyleżyńska realized, "More and more, this diary is turning into a psychological investigation rather than a chronicle of events, as it was at the beginning." A few weeks later, on May 27, referring explicitly to the Jews she was trying to rescue, she records a revealing insight: "Beside the compulsion to record the facts, there is in me at all times a restless psychologist who wishes to untangle the puzzles of others [i.e., the Jewish fugitives] as well as [to understand] my approach to their peculiarities."

Wyleżyńska not only wanted to understand the Jews, but also her own response to their situation. This need evinces the self-critical aspect of her diaristic writing; it indicates both her willingness and her capability for self-analysis, the absence of which was very clear in Dąbrowska. Dąbrowska's consistent evasion of the Jewish tragedy and her inability to reconsider her competitive resentment of the Jews, even when the Jews had already "disappeared," strongly contrasts with Wyleżyńska's courage to observe, as objectively and as critically as she possibly could, the effect of the genocidal reality on the victims of the Holocaust and on her own psychological/moral constitution.

This shift from chronicling events to a moral and psychological probing of the self helps explain Wyleżyńska's unequivocal desire to publish the diary in its original, intact form. As a chronicler, she may have wished to have her acts of altruism on record (though many of them were encoded or merely alluded to in view of the German prohibitions). As a self-declared insightful student of psychology, she may also have been convinced that the intelligibility of the diary for the future reader was predicated upon the unsparing and uncompromising integrity of the diarist. In this sense, the diary represents what Charles Taylor defines as "a radical evaluation [which] is a deep reflection about the self"; it is a reflection which represents "this kind of responsibility for oneself . . . which is essential to our notion as a person."[7] The Jewish extermination presented Wyleżyńska with a challenge of radical self-evaluation, which she gradually came to perceive as the ultimate test of her moral personhood. As we shall see, she submitted herself to a rigorous reflective process which allowed her to study her moral self with remarkable integrity, while shaping her diary as an edifying life narrative.

Writing the Self as Moral Discipline

Even during the increasingly horrific persecutions of the Jews which culminated in the burning of the Ghetto, Wyleżyńska tried to maintain her faith in *Bildung*, the Enlightenment legacy of self-education toward moral and aesthetic self-improvement. She claimed that ethical vigilance needed to take the form of conscious self-assessment in an act of writing. "I suppose that not only a writer, but also every thinking person needs to write today," she mused, "in order to understand the situation and oneself. One's attitude toward present-day events is the touchstone of every person. Writing is the best evaluation of conscience."

Then she turned her attention from the fantastic landscape of the burning Ghetto to the inner landscape of the individuals who witnessed it, turning to listen to the reactions of passersby about "this atmosphere of horror." She observed that people were talking about "ordinary things," and that "very few even noticed the changed surroundings." Two days later, on April 30, she mentioned the Easter carousel in Krasinskich Square in front of the walls of the burning Ghetto, and wondered about this demonstration of "heartlessness" or perhaps of "lack of imagination." She ended up taking the blame as well: "We are all heartless. During Easter we worry more about the stew than about the fallen [i.e., the Ghetto Jews]. And so many of them die every moment." Like Iwaszkiewicz, who noted, with horrified amazement, the Warsaw Poles enjoying themselves in view of the burning Ghetto where his friends were perishing, Wyleżyńska also wondered at the general indifference toward the burning Ghetto.

As Martin Hoffman points out, "If the victim belongs to an outcast group, his or her misery may be attributed to false causes or responded to with indifference."[8] Stanley Cohen points to the mechanism of normalization, which makes it possible that "facts and images once seen as unusual, unpleasant, or even intolerable eventually become accepted as normal. . . . Normalization becomes neutralization, and then indifference."[9] Wyleżyńska was aware of the numbness, or "heartlessness," produced by an excess of horror.

At the same time, Wyleżyńska was also acutely conscious of persisting xenophobic attitudes toward Jews which made many of her fellow Poles approve of the German resolution of Poland's "Jewish problem." The diary is replete with evidence of growing Polish satisfaction with Jewish destruction. Of particular interest is Wyleżyńska's report from May 23, 1943, sarcastically entitled "From the anti-Jewish front of intellectually superior people," which talks about the prevalence of anti-Semitism at social gatherings of artists, writers, and intellectuals. She notes the revival of the derogatory epithet *Żydek* (Jewboy), which, she remembers, was unmentionable in intellectual circles during the prewar era. Now that the Jews have disappeared, Polish intellectuals refer contemptuously to their Jewish colleagues as Jewboys, and mockingly denigrate their work. She comments on their moral dishonesty and self-deception:

> One would have expected that the disaster caused by the common
> enemy [the Germans] would have reduced antipathy [toward the
> Jews], but this is not the case at all! Evidently, the cult of the
> mighty exists among those of our writers who have managed to

stay alive. Though their own existence has been precarious, they enjoy making fun of those who have been killed.

She also marvels at her colleagues' literary silence in view of the colossal events they were witnessing. "Epochal storms have been raging overhead, but these people are still bogged down in the past, treading water, sifting garbage, and writing about unworthy, forgettable matters."

Wyleżyńska's interpretation of the writers' anti-Semitic reaction as an indication of their will to power, even if it meant identification with the occupier, may well have been influenced by the fact that only five days earlier, on May 15, 1943, she was reading her beloved Julien Benda's 1935 *Délices d'Éleuthère*, in which the French intellectual expounds his perceptions of happiness and power. Benda saw power which brings greatness, rather than desire for social happiness, as the predominant force that moves humanity. In view of the rise of German fascism, he presciently warned about the victory of the will to power over the ideal of happiness, which he saw in the legacy of the Enlightenment. Wyleżyńska approvingly quoted Benda, "*Quand Saint Just disait que le bonheur est une idée nouvelle, c'était tout juste vrai pour la France. Pour le reste du monde, le bonheur est une idée folle.*" ("When Saint Just said that happiness is a new idea, it was true only for France. For the rest of the world, happiness is an insane idea.")[10] Benda claimed that the "Déclaration des Droits de l'Homme" ("Declaration of the Rights of Man") represented a mystical quality of happiness, which was unique to France.[11] While all other nations preferred the power of greatness, France alone saw the principle of equality and dignity of all human beings as the epitome of happiness.

Benda's position illuminates Wyleżyńska's explanation of the behavior of the Polish writers as a desire, even if illusory and only momentary, for power. Their dismissive attitude toward the murdered Jews, which denied the victims their dignity and equality, amounted to a repudiation of the universality of human rights. In this sense, their identification with the oppressor, rather than with the oppressed, deprived the writers of the happiness of insisting on the dignity of the Jewish victims. But whether her interpretation of the writers' behavior was influenced by Benda or not, Wyleżyńska's admiration of the French philosopher revealed the persistent struggle that she waged on the pages of her diary to remind herself of the liberal-humanistic ideals which seemed to have been disavowed even by the remaining, decimated intellectual elite of Warsaw.

The juxtaposition of Benda's postulation and "From the anti-Jewish front of intellectually superior people" reinforces Wyleżyńska's claim for the redeeming process of self-writing. Her reference to social happiness, à la Benda, evinced the vestiges of her hard-dying faith in the concepts of the Enlightenment. The proclamation of human rights was based on faith in the solidarity and fellowship of human beings, an ideal which communicated inclusion and which counteracted numbness, insensitivity, and "heartlessness" toward others. At the same time, the contrast between the genocidal reality and the happiness represented by human rights highlighted the irreversible loss of the civilized past. In her encounters with her fellow writers, Wyleżyńska was becoming aware that the ethical principles of the Enlightenment were incompatible with the present-day reality. But her estrangement from her Polish fellow writers did not mean that Wyleżyńska could seek comfort with her Jewish friends. As she was learning, the social reality of genocide estranged her from the Jews as well.

Autonomy, Altruism, and the Pursuit of Personal Happiness

On March 29, 1941, Wyleżyńska observed, "My 'moral corset' is my diary and my work for others." The metaphor of the "moral corset" communicated her staunch belief in self-imposed rigor and discipline as a key to ethical self; it also communicated her powerful sense of ethical accountability. The two characteristics of her "moral corset" — the diary and the work for others — are indicative of the components that she considered essential to her moral personhood. The placement of "my diary" before "my work for others" indicates that altruistic deeds were necessary but not sufficient to preserve her moral self; indispensable to moral integrity was the diaristic probing of the ethical and psychological self.

Wyleżyńska admitted that the need to assert her autonomy during a time of the negation of all freedom played a considerable role in her altruistic undertaking. Five times, from May 1941 to February 1942, she reiterated the maxim *tel est mon bon plaisir*, loosely translated as "[I do it] because I will,"[12] to emphasize her autonomous choice of the generally unpopular cause to help fugitive Jews. The imperious tone of the French maxim originally attributed to King Francis I emphasizes Wyleżyńska's freedom, nonconformity, and ethical disengagement from the consensus. She also emphasized the disinterestedness of her independently undertaken altruistic mission. Thus she declared that she never intended to act as a "professional activist"; her altruistic acts were meant to satisfy her need to do something for others. On February 13, 1942, she wrote, "I approached people who made me feel the need to give something of myself." On another occasion, she claimed that her will to act for the welfare of others had no ulterior motive: "When I do something good, the only reason is an absence of reason" (November 3, 1941). Another time she declared that her will was not associated with "self-sacrifice or duty" (Janurary 30, 1942), but rather by her wish to open up altruistically to persecuted Jews. Thus, she consistently perceived her "work for others" as the expression of her personal view and desires.

In a sense, Wyleżyńska's determination to act against mainstream anti-Semitic prejudice reflects her continuing adherence to progressive liberal causes. During her Paris years, she espoused the ideologies of pacifism, communism, and anti-fascism; she also opposed the Abyssinian war and Franco's regime in Spain, and she joined the Popular Front, the alliance of political parties in prewar France which aimed to oppose fascism. With the progression of the German conquest of Europe, she expressed her disappointment in the ideologies she had trusted: "Perhaps our hopes for the best possible world were just an illusion. This must be the case, despite Huxley's [pacifist and humanist] prophecies, despite Russell's [pacifist] advice on how one should act, despite all the things I wanted so much to believe" (1941). And on November 19, 1942, she remembered, "In the trusting atmosphere of the 1930s, when the specter of Hitler was still pale . . . democracy foundered. We were fooled by the hope of peace and then we failed to act against the most terrible murders in human history."

Wyleżyńska's alarm at the public collapse of progressive ideologies motivated her to practice these ideologies in her private sphere. But her decision to preserve her humanistic outlook by helping Jews also evinced her need to achieve personal happiness. She believed that attending unconditionally to others would actualize her moral potential, which would make her happy. Her conviction was inspired by Bertrand

Russell's 1930 philosophical treatise *The Conquest of Happiness*. Russell claimed that the happiness of modern man was hampered because "our traditional morality has been unduly self-centered." He argued that opening oneself altruistically to the world would result in happiness because alleviating the misery of others would make the benefactor feel powerful and at the same time would assure his "general liking" by the beneficiaries of his kindness.[13]

Sometime in the fall of 1939 or the beginning of 1941, Wyleżyńska accepted *à la lettre* the philosopher's prescription for happiness. She wrote: "Russell claims that one can liberate oneself from envy through an expansive and noble attitude toward others, an attitude which is an inexhaustible source of happiness because it assures general liking." She concurred with Russell: "This is my ethical principle — to see life through my friendly interest in others." She also quoted Russell's credo that to attain happiness, "one need distance oneself as much as possible from the self and turn toward the world." Scrutinizing her past, she asserted that even though she used to be self-centered, "I nonetheless have always been interested in others and, being privileged, I used to give the excess of my good fortune to others."

Wyleżyńska's determination to cultivate her altruistic potential brought forth considerable inner changes. In the early part of the diary, probably still in 1939, she wrote, "An accident or perhaps fate caused that I, a pacifist, might offer a little bit of help . . . even in my limited capacity." A few days later, she assessed her altruistic behavior:

> I have never imagined that an individualist, such as I am, could become so obedient. In the "idyllic" times of my not-so-sentimental education in the Paris of '35 and '36, I submitted to general discipline only in theory. Now, I am ready and willing to surrender. . . . Whatever belongs to the sphere of civil duties I fulfill like a soldier. . . . My attitude used to be rebellious. I have changed.

It is important to note that Wyleżyńska's "surrender" to the demands of altruistic life indicated her rebellious choice to practice Russell's prescription in a reality of the total collapse of moral reasoning and an unprecedented crisis of Western civilization, which certainly did not fit the reality that the philosopher addressed. In fact, Russell explicitly declared that his concept of happiness was confined to "day-to-day unhappiness which most of the people in civilised countries suffer," but not to "great catastrophes," or "any extreme cause of outward misery."[14] In one sense, Wyleżyńska's transposition of Russell's view of happiness to a time of genocide can be seen as an exercise of her autonomy to act because *tel est mon plaisir*. In another sense, her adherence to Russell's notion of giving to the needy indicates her expectation of continuing her relationships with her prewar Jewish friends.

While Wyleżyńska could not hope to be liked by her fellow Poles for helping Jews, it was reasonable to expect the "general liking" of the Jews she was rescuing. After all, as she noted in 1941, "All my life I have been attracted to Jews. Most of my female and male [friends have been Jews]. [I have always had] good relationships with them . . . have always found them like-minded . . . and have [identified] with their perspectives, cultural interests, and freethinking." And she might also have expected that while the decision to help Jews entailed great danger and required considerable risk-taking, it would endow her with a sense of autonomy and control which would deflect despair and depression. As Wyleżyńska envisaged it, her altruistic dedication to her Jewish friends, which she eventually also extended to Jewish strangers and children, would help her to achieve a state of happy selflessness. These goals did not materialize; instead, she was confronted with a situation the horror of which transformed her understanding of the self and others, as well as the nature and function of her diaristic writing.

Altruism Redefined

In her 1945 postwar recollections, Wyleżyńska's friend Zuzanna Rabska, a well-known writer and one of the Jews that Wyleżyńska helped to hide, wrote,

> Aurelia Wyleżyńska, a writer . . . a democrat in the broadest and most noble meaning of the word . . . was hiding Jews in her apartment on Lipowa. . . . She always hastened where unfortunate people needed moral support and encouragement [and] was not afraid of the traps of the Gestapo. . . . A few times, she

managed to get into the Ghetto, when she heard that a friend was having a breakdown. . . . Her warm and wise words healed wounds and eased suffering. She was fearless.[15]

Since Rabska wrote about Wyleżyńska after the war, the perspective and the point in time of her testimony raise the issue of the unreliability of recollections. Nonetheless it would have been possible to conjecture that this testimony of Wyleżyńska's freedom, courage, and generosity signals the "general liking" of Jewish fugitives, and therefore Wyleżyńska's successful actualization of Russell's theory of happiness in a time of terror. Yet Wyleżyńska's diaristic accounts of her direct interaction with the Jews she was helping, or her "charges," as she called them, disprove this assumption. In contrast with Russell's vision of altruism as a precondition for happiness, her altruistic activities brought forth deep disappointment in the Jewish fugitives and in herself.

Wyleżyńska's report of an incident on July 29, 1942, illustrates the complexities of the rescue situation. While visiting with Rabska in her Zalesie countryside hideout, which she had organized, Wyleżyńska fell into a cellar and broke her tail bone. Wyleżyńska reported that Zuza (Rabska), fearing that her identity might be revealed, opposed calling in the doctor, and then objected to transporting Wyleżyńska back to Warsaw by ambulance for fear of drawing attention to her presence, leading to eventual denunciation. Wyleżyńska noted Rabska's lack of concern not only about the pain of her injury, but also about her safety, pointing out that it never occurred to Rabska that Wyleżyńska was also at risk had she been found with hidden Jews. She harshly criticized Rabska's behavior and its detrimental effects:

> Zuza's psychotic, constant anxiety and her incessant sniffing out of danger create an atmosphere of turmoil which is bad for the nerves and paranoid with regard to the outside world. She [Zuza] argues that . . . every new person who knows the hideout may reveal the secret [and that] other Jews seeking refuge compromise those who have been hiding here.

Wyleżyńska followed this observation with a general value judgment of the fugitive Jews: "The surroundings around Warsaw are full of unfortunate fugitives, who flee from place to place hoping for a safe hideout. But there is no safety anywhere, and their situation can improve only if they find strength in themselves." At the same time, her sense of guilt and anxiety about Rabska's safety emerges in the rationalization "I can say with a clear conscience that neither my accident nor I myself was a cause for panic; Zuza's fear that [the accident] may harm [her] caused all this turmoil and anxiety." Finally, she tried to retract her criticism altogether: "I am noting these reflections with no intention of diminishing my friendship with Z. and out of my great compassion for her. My goal is to note this as a *signum temporis* [sign of the time]. Anyway, my observation also relates to others in a similar situation."

The Rabska episode is an example of Wyleżyńska's increasing dissatisfaction with others and with herself. She constantly vacillated between disparagement of the fugitives and a sense of guilt. Even as she was indicting the Jews' anxiety, selfishness, passivity, and inability to reason, she almost simultaneously faulted herself for her acerbic and unjustified judgment. Her critical view of the fugitives invariably confronted her with her own deficiencies, which, as she realized, defeated her goal of achieving the happiness of selflessness.

Consider, for instance, the temperamental shifts of mood and argument in the entry of November 8, 1942:

> I will surely go crazy from the ceaseless [demands of the fugitives] not to tell this, not to say that. All the time other people's affairs gravitate to me, as if I had in me some antidote to the lurking evil, which, in any event, lurks for all of us. Then somebody will say, with sincere sympathy, "You could have lived quietly, had it not been for me, for us . . . "

She follows with a justification which indicates her sense of guilt: "Certainly I am often too abrupt, but I console myself with my goodness and with my manner of helping . . . as if I were feeding not the closest, but rather the hungriest." Then she becomes irritated and angry:

> I am helpless when "somebody" confides in me her emotional or material worries. I am supposed to guarantee that our house will not be bombed, that the Gestapo will not come, that no-

body will take the things that have been deposited with me. . . . Some of the demands are comical, but the majority of them are dangerous and impossible to execute.

She concludes with a complete shift: "It would be unfair if I mentioned only their anxieties. There are many examples of courage, calm, and heroism. But we have the inclination to speak of the bad rather than of the good."

Altruistic dedication to the shelter-seeking Jews brought Wyleżyńska neither happiness nor self-contentment. A fantasy that she recorded on March 15, 1943, attests to her growing sense of having failed to become a better and therefore happy person: "At some point, after this never-ending war, all my charges [*podopieczni*] will meet in my flat for a reception. They . . . will show a certain degree of coldness toward the lady of the house because what she did for them was either too little or not good enough." The fantasy expresses Wyleżyńska's sense of failure. The desire to improve herself through altruistic action, which would give her a sense of empowerment and evoke "general liking," has failed. Ironically, she felt helpless vis-à-vis her "charges" whose expectations and needs she was unable to satisfy. On June 30, 1943, Wyleżyńska complained about one of them, Maria Mirska: "In response to all the good done for her sake, she bears grudges for things that have not been done for her, complains about every plan that did not work, and considers everything I do insufficient. I need to remind her of my efforts and show her the positive 'balance sheet' of the care she has received."

Wyleżyńska concludes, "I am afraid I will end up hating them." The helper has become the hostage of the hunted victims whose favorable opinion she has been unable to secure.

It is important to note that despite the worsening conditions of the Occupation that made the rescuing efforts increasingly difficult and risky, Wyleżyńska's altruistic efforts for the fugitives never faltered. In this sense, her work exemplified Lawrence A. Blum's postulation that "altruistic emotions are intentional and take as their objects other persons in light of their 'weal' and, especially their 'woe,'" as well as R. M. Hare's claim that "altruism . . . [means] giving "*more* weight to the preferences of others" than to our own.[16] Wyleżyńska's consistent and unhesitating dedication to the mission of rescuing Jews attests to her remarkable altruistic capacity. Her recordings communicate that she was in constant, personal contact with Jews who sought refuge on the "Aryan side"; she often gave them shelter in her own flat, which entailed the risk of denunciations by the neighbors; she tirelessly sought and negotiated safe hideouts with other rescuers; she planned moves from one place to another, and was indefatigable in obtaining false documents, or replacing the "burnt," stolen, or lost ones. On several occasions she ventured into the Ghetto to bring provisions and give comfort to acquaintances and friends.

However, the progression from her 1941 declaration of her affinity with the Jews, grounded in their common interests and similar ways of thinking, to her 1943 declaration of her resentment of the Jews is indicative of the transformation of Wyleżyńska's feelings of friendship for the Jews. The relationships she expected to maintain through her autonomous and altruistic decision to help her Jewish friends disintegrated in the reality of the Final Solution.

The Breakdown of the Empathic Horizon

The Germans' ideologically determined biological division of humanity into categories of the living and of the doomed invalidated the fundamental concept of empathy, namely the premise that "you" are another "I." The sentence of death which excluded the Jews from human society shattered the common horizon of shared values and mentalities. The Final Solution split the prewar horizon of intersubjectivity when the Polish rescuer assumed the role of caretaker of Jewish individuals. Even though the conditions of the Polish population under the Occupation were atrocious, the rescuers had incomparably more freedom of action and possibility of movement than the Jews they were hiding. Jews who decided to avoid or escape the Ghetto and hide on the "Aryan side" of Warsaw relied on their rescuers for every aspect of their physical existence. In many cases, they needed to pass as Christians, a situation that incurred not only the fear of being discovered by the Germans or blackmailed by the Poles, but also the emotional trauma of identity transformation. Wyleżyńska's use of the epithet "charges" in relation to the Jews she was helping attests to her perhaps unconscious recognition of the disjunction of the empathic horizon she used to share with her Jewish friends; no longer could they be considered the same as their Christian rescuers.

Most of Wyleżyńska's "charges," such as Rabska and Maria, as well as Julia Dickstein, a writer and translator, Ela, a painter, Robert, a doctor, and others who were not mentioned by name in the diary for security reasons, were deeply acculturated Jews who belonged to the prewar intellectual elite of Warsaw. They were scholars, artists, and writers with whom, in the prewar years, Wyleżyńska had shared the Enlightenment legacy of equality, rationality, freedom, tolerance, and, most significantly, human dignity. Now, as she was risking her safety, her freedom, and probably her life for the fugitive Jews, she watched with dismay, disbelief, and increasing disrespect how the individuals with whom she used to share ideas and feelings were transforming into self-absorbed, fearful, and degraded creatures. Their obsession with physical survival at any cost reinforced her contempt for them.

In the private sphere of her diary, Wyleżyńska was explicit about the fugitives' behavior, which she clearly did not like or respect. All she saw was desperation, self-pity, and incessant requests and demands, which she judged as extremely selfish:

> It is very unpleasant to write it, but here we need to say the truth. Not complaining about one's suffering is the only guarantee not only of survival, but also of securing the [positive] attitude of others. If a person endlessly claims that no one is as unhappy as she is, she will not make even the most Christian soul believe it.

She also cautioned against excessive complaining: "In theory, we are familiar with today's worst misery, but we lack the patience to hear about it all the time" (July 26, 1943). In essence, Wyleżyńska's idea of proper behavior of the victims of the Final Solution reflected prewar codes of discretion, bon ton, and, in general, good manners. To gain the rescuer's sympathy, the victims should maintain their dignity, preserve their composure, and keep mostly silent about their disorientation, fear, losses, and suffering. Her recommendations reflect her continuing thinking in terms of dignity, self-respect, and *Bildung*, qualities that marked her prewar enlightened milieu.

To preserve the good will of the helpers, tactful behavior was necessary, but not sufficient. Wyleżyńska's principal criticism pertained to the passivity of the hiding Jews. Resistance and militant action constituted the essence of Polish romantic patriotic heroism, but Wyleżyńska could not detect any signs of heroism in her "charges." For instance, she commented on the behavior of Robert, who, immobilized by fear, stagnated in his hideout:

> I have been reflecting on what a person in Robert's situation and others like him should do, but I am probably wrong, because I think in terms of normal existential reactions: to be or not to be. Either kill yourself or save yourself. There is a third alternative — a lack of will or indecisiveness — but apparently German psychotherapy intimidates weaker individuals.

Even though Wyleżyńska mentioned being "probably wrong," she perceived her reaction as "normal." Action would have evinced inner strength; instead, the Jews chose to be "weaker individuals" who submitted to "German psychotherapy." As Wyleżyńska saw it, the passivity of fugitive Jews amounted to an abject compliance with the occupier. In effect, the way she interpreted Hamlet's famous dilemma averred the humanistic existentialist concept of freedom in the face of overwhelming odds. Either deliberately choosing to die or embarking on a risky initiative to escape would have denoted the freedom to act.

Wyleżyńska's derogatory view of Jewish passivity does not indicate anti-Semitic sentiments. Rather, she saw the passivity of the Jews as a betrayal of the values of humanism in which she continued to believe; their inaction signified an abrogation of human autonomy and dignity. The transformation of Jews into contemptible creatures paralyzed by fear seemed to reaffirm the destruction of the Enlightenment legacy of the universality of equality, individual freedom, and the sanctity of human life. Dignified and autonomous conduct would have reaffirmed the validity of moral values. Wyleżyńska's view of Jewish weakness as reinforcing the barbarism of their persecutors challenged her persistent faith that the values of moral fortitude, rational thinking, and physical courage could potentially counteract the inherent dehumanization of genocide.

It was not only the humanistic weakness of the fugitives that proved difficult to accept. Wyleżyńska's helplessness when faced with their fears signaled her own anxiety about the unpredictability and incomprehensibility of the interminable rule of terror. Wyleżyńska's irritation with the fugitives' irrational behavior reflected her growing sense of impotence in a reality which defied all rational expectations. The moral disintegration of Polish society horrified her. After the destruction of the Ghetto, when the number of Jews in hiding increased, she observed the increasing cases of blackmail and denunciations of Jews to the Gestapo. Furthermore, for many Poles, the destruction of the Ghetto provided the cynical reassurance that "they will not have those [i.e., Jewish] rivals in a future Poland." Looking at the growing demoralization of the Polish population, she noted, "The moral epidemic is spreading despite everything, and the air is full of pollutants that weaker individuals absorb" (June 27, 1943). The metaphor of an epidemic reflects Wyleżyńska's desperation at the unrestrained moral disintegration of fellow Poles.

Caught between her despondency over the character weakness of the Jews and the moral corruption of the Poles, Wyleżyńska was finally impelled to admit the failure of the Enlightenment legacy in the reality of the Holocaust. She turned to André Gide, her "favorite author," whose diaries she called "a fifteen-hundred-page bible" (July 18, 1943), and whose "traces of wisdom" she used to "fish for" in the prewar times "in his diary and in his book, *Les nouvelles nourritures*" (Fall 1941). As in her readings of Benda and Russell, she searched Gide for the definition of happiness. Now in the horrific reality of Warsaw, still calling the French writer/diarist her "spiritual alter ego," she reread *Les nouvelles nourritures*, Gide's 1935 treatise about happiness and the future of humanity that he wrote when he was flirting with communism. On July 24 and 25, 1943, she noted that while Gide claimed his obligation was to be happy, he postulated that the fulfillment of this obligation was conditioned on the happiness of humanity at large. She quoted Gide, "*Mon bonheur est d'augmenter celui des autres. J'ai besoin du bonheur des tous pour être heureux*" ("My happiness is to augment the happiness of others. I need the happiness of all to be happy"), and noted that happiness according to Gide consists in goods which, as he explained, were, "*biens naturels, communs à tous*" ("natural goods, shared by all").[17] As Wyleżyńska saw it, Gide was an avowed proponent of human fellowship and the solidarity of all humankind.

The dissonance between Gide's utopian projection of humanity's happy destiny and the reality of humanity's barbarism shattered Wyleżyńska's trust in Gide: "I can no longer feed on confidence, faith in the future, and good advice for humanity. Today, these are inaccessible medications. What is André Gide thinking now, as he watches the fall of humanity? . . . I believed in his wisdom as I did in my own experience." The pain of Wyleżyńska's disappointment in the thinker she considered her soul mate and intellectual mentor is evident. She has arrived at the painful realization that Gide lacked the acuity to assess the human capacity for evil, and that the evil she was witnessing effectively voided all visions of the happiness of human solidarity and moral self-improvement of any meaning. Like Russell and Benda, who had failed to foresee the enormity of the moral crisis, Gide too failed to provide guidance and support in the battle for the values of humanism in a time of barbarism. It was a battle that Wyleżyńska seemed to be losing, and the pain of the defeat impelled a revision of her ethical Weltanschauung in the horrifying reality of genocide.

The Diary as Novel

The difficulties of reevaluating prewar conceptions of humanism were not lost on Wyleżyńska. With uncommon self-insight, she was trying to overcome her resistance to revise the values that guided her in her prewar life. As her diary shows, she was gradually realizing that her early aspirations to counteract terror by insisting on acting in the spirit of the Enlightenment turned out to be ineffective. She was coming to the conclusion that the Final Solution transformed all social attitudes and patterns of interaction. Perhaps most significantly, she was becoming conscious of her inner evolution, which transformed the diary from a factual chronicling of events into a psychological-ethical narrative.

On May 5, 1943, she realized that the diary has become an "An Unintended Novel" ("Powieść mimo woli"). The thematic focus of this novel centered on the protagonist-diarist's psychological and ethical problems as an actively engaged witness of the Jewish extermination. More specifically, it was following her evolving experience of the rescuer-victim relationship. On June 28, 1943, she formulated her subject: "The Jewish problem has emerged as the main theme of my diary. It was not chosen on purpose, but rather imposed by contact with people."

Though she did not name the "people" who shaped the diary's Jewish orientation, it is likely that they were the Jews, and more specifically, the Jews whom she was helping to hide and whose fate became the predominant aspect of her recordings. It is also possible to conjecture that the "people" were the Poles whose generally hostile attitude toward the Jews made the protection of Jews her diary's predominant theme. Whoever "the people" may be, Wyleżyńska's acknowledgment of the emerging importance of the Jews in her diary attests to her preoccupation with the impact of the genocide on "contacts with people," that is, on social interaction.

Unlike conventional fiction, the "unintended novel" was not conjured up in the author's imagination. Rather, its story line emerged out of her immediate responses to the increasingly tragic events that she was witnessing and felt compelled to record. In this sense, her diary was becoming a novel-like narrative of the protagonist-narrator's progression from her determination to reconfirm the precepts of liberal humanism in a time of terror to her realization of the breakdown of the Enlightenment tradition in the reality of genocide. Wyleżyńska's diary-novel is a testimonial of the author's psychological-ethical evolution. The unintended transformation of the diary into a novel answers Wyleżyńska's call for a literary "renewal." It signals that to remain meaningful when humanism is in crisis, literature can no longer represent an imaginative fictional reconstruction or interpretation of reality. As Wyleżyńska came to see, imagination falls short in the reality of genocide, and the impotence of imagination imposes a new order of values which rewrites the humanistic ethical code.

The Transforming Chapter: The Trauma of the Liquidation of the Ghetto

In April 1943 Wyleżyńska was marveling at the heroism of the Ghetto fighters.

> Reportedly, [the Jews] sent a short-wave message [to the Germans] with a threat, 'We are not afraid of you, [we] can persevere for two weeks.' And then? Glorious death! Under the circumstances, the virtue of personal gallantry in its military sense must be recognized as a most beautiful thing even by the pacifists. They have already broken a record! The defenders of Alcazar and Westerplatte have met their rivals.

In Wyleżyńska's exultant view, the Ghetto Uprising was comparable to the most glorious operations of resistance against oppression in history. The intrepid Ghetto fighters proved that a defense of human dignity at the price of honorable death was possible even during an unprecedented historical event of genocide. They seemed to reenact the heroic tradition which shaped Polish history. A similar perspective characterizes the report by Maria Kann, a member of the underground (Armia Krajowa), who compared the Ghetto Uprising to the Bar-Kochba revolt against the Romans.[18]

The Ghetto fighters not only proved the moral value of heroic action, they also illuminated the deplorable absence of such action among the Jewish fugitives on the "Aryan side." Learning about the Uprising, Wyleżyńska could hardly conceal her contempt for the fugitives. On June 28, 1943, she juxtaposed the contrasting aspects of Jewish behavior:

> Like a woman who holds on to the last, false glare of youth with transfiguring makeup, the persecuted [Jewish woman] supposes that [cosmetic changes] will cover up the past and assure the future. In addition to sympathy, these desperate attempts awaken a certain shade of — I don't know what to call it. . . . Whereas, in general, the stance of the Jews in the Ghetto represented their [i.e., the Jews'] rehabilitation. Some bunkers still go on fighting!

As Wyleżyńska saw it, the Ghetto heroes compensated for the dishonorable behavior of the fugitive Jews who strove to survive even at the price of self-degradation. Against their abject submission to the oppressor, the Ghetto fighters proved the ineffectiveness of "German psychotherapy" and affirmed their freedom to act. In this sense, the Ghetto Uprising seemed to reaffirm Wyleżyńska's faith in humanistic values; it also seemed to justify her disparaging attitude toward the fugitives. It looked as if the heroism of the Ghetto fighters proved the continuing validity of human dignity and autonomy.

Wyleżyńska's elation, however, was short-lived. The subsequent horror of the liquidation of the Ghetto defied any comparison to other historical cases of glorious insurrection. Against "glorious death," which in Tzvetan Todorov's terms represents the "heroic virtue" of death for some absolute goal or value, the Ghetto Uprising represented an "ordinary virtue," which signified the Uprising as a choice of the way to die.[19] The choice of the Ghetto inhabitants to die one way rather than another exacted the price of unimaginable inhuman suffering, which rendered meaningless any considerations of heroism or glory. On April 28, 1943, Wyleżyńska watched the suffocating billows of smoke arising from the burning Ghetto. In the midst of the Ghetto Uprising, the sunset was "terrorized by the earth's glow," she wrote, and "Warsaw resembled scenes from a futuristic film, which no memory could have sustained, no film director could have reproduced credibly, and which any written description would have misrepresented to an even larger degree."

The heroism of the Ghetto Uprising could not eclipse the horror of the liquidation of the Ghetto. Wyleżyńska's emphasis on the hellish, infernal sights which seemed to distort the cosmic order posits the liquidation as an ahistorical, otherworldly phenomenon. While on the conscious level the Uprising continued to evoke in Wyleżyńska a sense of triumph, enormous respect, and enthusiastic praise, the horror of the liquidation produced a traumatic response which decisively challenged her assessment of the event as a victory of humanistic ethics.

Wyleżyńska reported in her diary that on the first night of the Uprising, she heard the detonations in the Ghetto so close by that she felt "as if a train were passing through my room." She described this auditory "sensation" as being so terrible that "it could never be repeated," adding that it caused her "indescribable physical torment." As she was wondering whether the sensory experiences "symbolized an unsuccessful evasion" of something else, she had a fearful vision. She saw how "phantoms of people who are still alive settle at my bedhead. [They were] those who stayed outside the battlefield, but who belonged there." She identified them as fugitive Jews, realizing that "they will torment me as the emissaries of those who are perishing" (April 19, 1943). Nor did the acute physical reactions to the horror of the Liquidation cease when it was over. On July 28, while going by tramway through "a piece of the ex-Ghetto," she "looked at the walls, at the broken candelabra in the ruins of the synagogue. Blood congealed in my head and I felt how my skull was becoming shackled. This is how a river must feel when it suddenly freezes."

These detailed descriptions of her reactions to the images of destruction probe the overwhelming physical and mental impact of the liquidation of the Ghetto. Wyleżyńska's body responded instinctively with multiple somatic phenomena, such as the deafening train-like sounds, physical pain, the freezing of her blood, and the shackling of her skull. Her mind conjured up a fantastic image of phantoms which effaced the distinction between the fighters and the fugitives. Her vision of the indelible connection between those fugitives who were living on borrowed time and the Ghetto dead superseded Wyleżyńska's glorification of the Uprising, exposing it as an unsuccessful attempt to evade the trauma of the liquidation.

Having inscribed itself on her body and mind, the trauma confronted Wyleżyńska with the inescapable meaning of a reality circumscribed by the Final Solution. The intuitive reactions of her body and mind communicated the impossibility of entering the world of death of the Jews. On May 17, 1943, Wyleżyńska recorded a scene the horror of which signaled the inaccessibility of the Jewish world of death:

> Again my ears are full of human moans. . . . A mother has to toss a child off the balcony. The six-year-old knows what awaits him and instinctively fights with his small hands . . . he wants to live. . . . Those who are supposed to love and protect each other are struggling. The mother prevails and the child, falling down, catches on to another balcony. He hangs in the air. The flame envelops his dress. A German in the street shoots and kills him. . . . But he did not aim at his heart. In the meantime, his mother crushed her head on the pavement.

Images which redefined infanticide as an act of love refuted the romantic glorification of the "heroic" Ghetto fallen. More importantly, they challenged the "cowardly" passivity of the Jews who sought refuge. The liquidation of the Ghetto made Wyleżyńska realize that the sentence of death, which informed the existence of the Jews who were still alive, had severed them from the rest of humanity. Their classification as subhuman creatures doomed to extermination took away their identity as living subjects. This meant that Jews could no longer share a common horizon with non-Jewish human beings. It also meant that non-Jewish human beings were barred from entrance into the Jewish horizon of dehumanization and extermination. The impossibility to enter the situation of another whose right to life had been transformed into a death sentence separated Wyleżyńska from her Jewish friends with an unfathomable gulf which marked the end of empathy.

The Ethics of the End of Empathy

Variations on the hypothetical question "What would I have done?" frequently come up in Wyleżyńska's notations, especially in 1943, when the extermination of the Jews was beyond any doubt. For instance, on January 28, 1943, Wyleżyńska wrote,

> Death lurks for you [i.e., the hiding Jews] with double force, but what can I do? At the same time, the question arises, 'How would I have behaved in this situation?' I study the question diligently, wishing to give an impartial answer, in order to justify those who are concerned only with themselves.

Referring to Maria, Wyleżyńska wrote on April 27, 1943,

> To live alone, but to live, this is, at the moment, more important than the death of her sister . . . and the absence of news from her husband. Would he have reacted in the same way? Would I have? I get lost in these ruminations and cannot find any other solution except a call for indulgence. This is the only emotion we must have for everybody.

On May 2, 1943, she queried, "Who knows whether [if I had been in the same situation], I would have also been attached to this kind of an existence, that of an animal hunted in the jungle of the city?" Then, on June 28, she claimed,

> I have the courage to say that death is the only dignified solution. . . . I strongly believe that instead of becoming a burden for others, I would have found a solution. I examine myself all the time as to what I would have done. My answer to the question is positive and therefore negates life, but then again I treat the problem of clinging tenaciously to life in a theoretical manner.

The recurring question, "What would I have done?" signals Wyleżyńska's persistent attempts at empathic comprehension of the victims, while the consistent qualifications of the replies—the constant reminder that she does not speak from experience—communicate the impossibility of an empathic connection. Wyleżyńska progresses toward the realization that the situation of the persons for whom she was risking her life remained incomprehensible to outsiders, including her. Wyleżyńska's critical view of the fugitives as passive and undignified reflected her psychological unwillingness, and perhaps her inability, to acknowledge the ethically transformative meaning of the Final Solution. Eventually, the trauma of the liquidation of the Ghetto compelled her to work through her resistance. She was finally ready to acknowledge the unbridgeable distance between her reality and the reality of the victims.

On May 27, 1943, when the fires of the Ghetto were still raging, Wyleżyńska wrote,

> What would people not endure for the sake of survival! Their suffering attests to the desire for life that I would have not been able to imagine in the past and that I would not share today. Perhaps this is because the dangers that I have experienced are insignificant in comparison with their certainty [of death] and therefore do not engender internal resistance which takes the form of a desire to live.

Here Wyleżyńska displays a radical change of perspective. Her criticism of the fugitives had focused initially on their weakness, which implied either an inherent character flaw or lack of moral discipline. After witnessing the liquidation of the Ghetto she realized that the fugitives' desire to survive, which she had considered passive, even contemptible, was a form of internal resistance which she, as a non-Jew, could not comprehend. The fate that spared her from the Final Solution created a fundamental psychological and ethical disjunction between her and the victims. The decree of the Final Solution transformed the victim's psyche, creating an alternate ethical value system which privileged survival over freedom and dignity. And because it emerged from a situation which not only defied but indubitably defeated the humanistic legacy of the Enlightenment, this new ethics commanded respect.

Wyleżyńska's new understanding of the transformation of the victims led to an epiphany which redefined her understanding of her role vis-à-vis the victim. On the same day, May 27, Wyleżyńska wrote,

> Again I reach the conclusion, obviously more theoretically than practically, because it is easier, that my attitude toward my chosen or imposed "charges" — today I don't like this term, whose novelty used to amuse me — cannot depend on their unfavorable transformations. The only criterion of my modest operations needs to be an inner imperative, a feeling that I am obligated to be faithful to myself. They, succumbing to depression, anxieties, and all kinds of torments, can hardly remain the same as they used to be; but I, who was until now protected by fate, am accountable for every transgression of my obligations which I voluntarily undertook.

This insight reformulates ethics in a world of genocide. While acknowledging that empathic mutual understanding on a common emotional and mental horizon was no longer possible, Wyleżyńska accepted the otherness of the victims. Her awareness that she could not enter the world of the Final Solution made Wyleżyńska realize the weakness of her humanistic orientation; the genocidal edict invalidated the idea of all-encompassing human fellowship. Interestingly, the admission of the limitations of her humanistic Weltanschauung ensued in an attitude of tolerance for the incomprehensible Weltanschauung of the victims. Her realization of the unknowable terror of the world of the victims made her see the otherness of their subjectivity. Wyleżyńska's comment on her sense of dissatisfaction with the epithet "charges" signals a transformed view of the fugitives; now she is able to recognize the maturity of their endurance and stamina in the world defined by the Holocaust. She could no longer disparage the victims' incomprehensible horizon of fears, anxieties, and of the invincible desire to live.

Ironically, the unimaginable reality of the Final Solution revoked the notion of autonomy, because it imposed an obligation which nullified the capacity of her "royal" catchphrase *tel est mon bon plaisir.* Echoing the Kantian maxim of "moral imperative," Wyleżyńska declared that her altruistic action for the Jews was not her choice but her duty. Altruistic action has become an unconditional moral obligation. Happiness does not lie in the gratitude of the needy contrary to Russell, nor does it depend on human rights contrary to Benda, nor does it reflect Gide's vision of fellowship and sharing of common goods. Rather, happiness in a genocidal world consists in relentless attempts at postponing the end. The ethics of a time of atrocity redefined the position of the altruistic benefactor as subordinate to the needy, whose ultimate happiness now consisted in protecting their physical existence as long as she could.

Wyleżyńska's diary is a story of a struggle to remain human in a world which had lost its humanity. As a writer and a humanist, the diarist faced an aesthetic and ethical crisis, and the diary became the battlefield of her struggle against history. The aesthetic axis focused on the "end of language" in the reality of indescribable destruction, inexpressible horrors, and unutterable suffering and losses. The ethical axis emphasized the "moral ending" of a reality which transcended the powers of imagination. While the aesthetic axis entails a generic transformation from chronicle into a psychological-ethical exploration of the self and the world, the ethical axis shows Wyleżyńska's intense process of self-education in the new reality which invalidated all ethical values. Wyleżyńska's diary illustrates that the reality of genocide transformed the meaning of the ethics of empathy. It was no longer possible for all parties in human interactions to share equal expectatations. To preserve meaningful interactions in this reality, the genocidal categorization of human beings needed to be subverted and the humanity of those declared subhuman reaffirmed. For Wyleżyńska, the obligation to reaffirm the victims' humanity came to take precedence over all else.

CHAPTER 5

Zofia Nałkowska: The Silence and Speech of the Humanist Witness of the Holocaust

The drowning [Jews], who are pulling me into the abyss, still linger close by. The suffering of others has become more acute, more intense than one's own . . . and this mortal dismay. . . . Why am I tormenting myself? Why am I ashamed to live? Why am I unable to bear it?

Thus wrote Zofia Nałkowska (1884–1954), a prominent Polish writer, in her diary, on May 14, 1943, when the Warsaw Ghetto was burning.[1] Nałkowska's intense identification with the Jewish plight and her pain over the world's moral collapse reflected the humanistic, progressive Weltanschauung she absorbed in her parental home. She was born to Wacław Nałkowski, a distinguished geographer and idealistic lifelong advocate of social justice, and his wife, Anna, née Safranek, who shared her husband's ideals, collaborated with him on his scientific projects, and was the author of many geography texts. The Nałkowski home was a gathering place for the foremost progressive personalities, and this rarified atmosphere had an enormous influence on Nałkowska's intellectual growth. Nałkowski belonged to the sphere of radical Polish intelligentsia at the turn of the twentieth century which combined the positivist tradition with an ineluctable cult of knowledge. He believed in democratic freedoms, women's rights, and science, was vehemently opposed to clericalism and the old Polish aristocratic traditions, and was deeply invested in shaping a vision of the Polish nation in the future state. Extrapolating from the Darwinian evolution of species, he believed in a psychic evolution of humankind which delineated the history of social development. Having absorbed the intellectual atmosphere of her parental home, Nałkowska showed precocious interest in philosophy and psychoanalysis and read Nietzsche, Schopenhauer, Bergson, and Freud. She traveled widely in Europe and mastered four languages.[2]

Nałkowska started publishing fiction as well as press articles and essays in the beginning of the century. Her prolific writing career encompassed the prewar period, World War I, the interwar period of Polish independence, World War II and the German Occupation, and the first decade of the postwar communist regime. Her oeuvre includes fiction, drama, collections of novellas, stories, and literary sketches.[3] The *Diaries* (*Dzienniki*), which she started writing in 1896 (the extant manuscript begins in 1899) and continued until her death, extensively document her personal life, her life as a writer and a member of the intellectual milieu, and the historical era at large. In her youth, Nałkowska was active in the emerging feminist movement, and her early fiction focused on women's issues. At the time of World War I, Nałkowska became conscious of the brutality of war and adopted a pacifist perspective. Her fiction after the war explored the theme of the sociopolitical responsibilities of the individual. At that time, her writing interests shifted to the psychology of human behavior, as demonstrated by a series of short typological narratives, published as *Characters* (*Charaktery*; 1922).

In the interwar years, Nałkowska was increasingly skeptical about the ideological direction of the newly established Polish state. She watched the growing influence of the political right and its extreme anti-Semitic platform with apprehension. During this time, she reached the apex of her career; her fiction was translated into many languages and her plays were staged abroad. She became a public figure, a prominent member of the Professional Union of Polish Writers (ZZLP) and PEN club, as well as a social activist, focusing on causes related to prison conditions and the treatment of prisoners.

When the war broke out, Nałkowska fled Warsaw, but soon returned to the occupied city where she supported herself and her family by managing a tobacco store. During the war her beloved mother died and her Jewish brother-in-law committed suicide in Paris when trying to escape the Nazis, a fact Nałkowska kept secret from her sister. Her wartime writing focused on her diary, in which she recorded the hardships of the Occupation and the evolving Jewish genocide. After the war, she was appointed vice-president of the Main Commission for Investigating German War Crimes in Poland. Her work for the committee resulted in Nałkowska's masterpiece, *Medallions* (*Medaliony*; 1946), a groundbreaking literary documentation of war atrocities. In 1948 she wrote a few more "characters," concentrating on the mental and emotional consequences of the war experience. They were published together with the 1922 vignettes as *Former and Recent Characters* (*Charactery dawne i ostatnie*). Toward the end of her life, Nałkowska compiled a selection of her essays which was posthumously published in the volume *Vision Close and Distant* (*Widzenie bliskie i dalekie*; 1957). The volume opens with essays on Nałkowska's *ars poetica*. Her views of the social responsibility of the writer and the ethics of literary writing constitute an illuminating addendum to her diary, which demonstrates her conviction about the inextricability of the writer/diarist and the world.

Like the other Warsaw writers discussed in this book, Nałkowska responded to the Holocaust in the spirit of her formative ideological convictions. While watching the increasing atrocities committed against the Jews, she continued to abide by the universalism of the Enlightenment and by the socialist-humanist Weltanschauung of her parental home. Consequently, Nałkowska's attitude toward the destruction of the Jews differed remarkably from Dąbrowska's and Rembek's ambivalent, often hostile and dismissive responses. Those diarists drew upon the patriotic tradition of the exclusive destiny of the Polish nation, shaped by the romantic-heroic responses to Polish history of partitions and insurrections. In contrast, Nałkowska, a pacifist and cosmopolite, shared the universalist-humanistic responses to the genocide of the other diarists, Iwaszkiewicz and Wyleżyńska. At the same time, like each of the diarists, Nałkowska coped with the reality of the genocide in her own particular way.

Like Iwaszkiewicz and Wyleżyńska, Nałkowska was engaged in altruistic rescue operations, as demonstrated by her elaborately planned but ill-fated attempt to rescue Bruno Schulz. As later reports show, Nałkowska was in charge of planning and coordinating an elaborate operation to smuggle Schulz, a Jewish writer, her protégé and friend, from Drohobycz to Warsaw. Schulz was shot on the day of the operation.[4] In contrast with Iwaszkiewicz and Wyleżyńska, however, she did not predicate the redemption of humanism upon altruism extended to the victims of the Final Solution, but rather upon a courageous confrontation of the human proclivity for evil. She encapsulated her position in the famous aphorism, "People inflicted this fate upon people," which she used as the epigraph of *Medallions*.[5] An enlightened humanist-rationalist, Nałkowska did not attribute the Final Solution to an eruption of some metaphysical or supernatural powers; rather, she placed the responsibility on human beings who consciously and deliberately chose to destroy other people. Nałkowska's unambiguous acknowledgment of human evil illuminated her formative rational mindset, grounded in the tradition of the Enlightenment. The atrocities needed to be documented to assure the vitality of humanistic ethics. But the silence to which she was reduced by the horror as it was happening, a silence she was eventually able to break in *Medallions*, evinced the enormous emotional and mental difficulty of facing and bearing witness to the evil that people inflicted upon people.

Nałkowska was by no means detached from the Jewish tragedy. The opening quotation shows that the signs of distress emerging from behind the Ghetto wall evoked in her a visceral identification with the victims, an experience which she compared to drowning. The dramatic metaphor indicates a state of emotional disarray which made the composition of a comprehensible and meaningful testimony of the event problematic, if not impossible. The image of being helplessly engulfed reflects the impossibility of a rational, coherent response to the catastrophe. Iwaszkiewicz and Wyleżyńska also experienced difficulty in fully confronting the meaning of the reality of the Final Solution, especially when viewing the burning Ghetto, but while they managed to avoid the emotionally crippling effect of the horror, Nałkowska could not. For her the experiences of both victimizer and victimized not only transcended the comprehension of the witness, but also affected her physical and emotional well-being.

The *Diary*: Seeking to Imagine the Unimaginable

On February 4, 1944, Nałkowska wrote in her diary:

> I have brought here [i.e., to Adamowizna] a book, which I borrowed from [a downtown] reading room. . . . The pages are marked

with notations by people who read and studied it before me. . . . In the book, there is the stamp of another reading room, "Wirgina," 32 Elektoralna, from which most of these books were purchased, a former reading room in the annihilated Ghetto. And suddenly I see what this fact means and what the heaps of ruins which have replaced the whole quarter signify. I realize that there was not only family life there, not only little shops and cafés. There were reading rooms, a lot of them because they liked to read, girls from warehouses, boys from stores—they were all readers. There were old people's homes and kindergartens. There were organizations. This is a thing which is impossible to sufficiently comprehend or come to terms with. — I am still tormenting myself about the notebook of my Diaries which I burned that bad night. And thus was lost the time of those four months (in which there was also my visit to Wołomin and a lonely stroll to Górki on a glittering, sunny, frosty day after the snow). . . . This unrecoverable time seems to me doubly unrecoverable, because there is no record of it. I am inconsolable because [in the notebook] there was a lot about Mother and everything about the people behind the [Ghetto] wall, about their thing [i.e., the Jews' extermination], indeed, the most horrific thing in this horrible world.

As the date of this entry indicates, Nałkowska continued to imagine and reimagine the Ghetto long after it ceased to exist. The two discrete, yet associatively related parts of the narrative invoke the two main stages of the destruction. The first part tells of an encounter with a library book which brought back memories of the liquidation of the Ghetto in April and May of 1943. The second part refers to a diary notebook which Nałkowska had felt compelled to destroy; it had covered the period from September 1942 to January 1943, which included the deportations to Treblinka, during which 300,000 Jews perished.[6] Nałkowska's recollection of these past events in 1944, despite the intensifying German oppression of the Gentile population of Warsaw, indicates her persistent need to deal with them in some meaningful way. Dwelling on the destruction of the Jews in the pages of her private diary attests to the lingering trauma it caused. Nałkowska's focus on the past signals her continuing inability to reimagine not only the Ghetto events, but also other events recorded in the papers that she needed to destroy.

The Jewish provenance of the book that Nałkowska took with her to Adamowizna, the estate of her closest friend in the vicinity of Warsaw where she frequently stayed during the war, conjured up for Nałkowska a picture of Ghetto life. The notations of the Jewish readers in the book transferred her associatively back in time, where she imagined for a while that she had found herself on a shared empathic horizon with the Ghetto inhabitants. Like Wyleżyńska, who declared her prewar intellectual and emotional affinity with Jews, Nałkowska was reliving, for a moment, the prewar social climate. The notations in the book made her feel an intellectual affinity with the Ghetto readers, while the stamp of the Ghetto reading room in the book brought forth the familiar concept of communal organization. A metonymic representation of the Ghetto, the book constructed a momentary illusion, eliminating the unimaginable horrors behind it and allowing the diarist to perceive life there as an ordinary and familiar urban existence.

But the indelible reality of the Ghetto's annihilation defied Nałkowska's imagined reality of the Ghetto. The ruins of the Ghetto denied any attribution of normalcy to Ghetto life. The palimpsest of the Ghetto reading room in the salvaged book invoked the fate of the readers who, Nałkowska well knew, had been immolated in the fires of the Ghetto. While the book with its marked pages seemed to attest to the commonplace aspects of life in the Ghetto, the book's survival in an "Aryan" reading room exposed the deceptive nature of this imagined normalcy. The fact that such books, loved so much by their Jewish readers, had been sold to Polish reading rooms signified not only the increasing destitution of the Ghetto and the inexorable spiritual and intellectual deprivation of its inhabitants, but also the inhabitants' growing consciousness of the imminence of the Ghetto's final destruction. The starvation, disease, and abandoned corpses in the streets of the Ghetto, of which she was aware, exposed life in the Ghetto as a horrible charade, a travesty of normal life. In this sense, Nałkowska's association of life in the Ghetto with normal intellectual activities and social interactions reveals the futility of the diarist's imagining a horizon of empathic experience, which turns into an attempt to evade the genocidal reality of the Ghetto. Indeed, she herself acknowledges the illusory aspect of such a picture of Ghetto life. Like Iwaszkiewicz, who proclaimed his helpless incomprehension of the Ghetto burning, Nałkowska declared her inability to "sufficiently comprehend" the Ghetto's destruction.

The surviving Ghetto reading room book, which did not witness the death of its Jewish readers, invoked for Nałkowska another book, one of her diary notebooks, which apparently witnessed "everything," but did not survive to testify. Nałkowska burned the notebook for fear of its discovery by the Gestapo while they were inspecting a neighbor's apartment. The loss of the notebook caused her lasting remorse and self-reproach. Nonetheless, she did not make any attempt to reconstruct the events she remembered having recorded in the notebook, neither what befell the "people behind the wall" of the Ghetto, nor her visit to Wołomin, nor her stroll in Górki, nor even reminiscences of her recently deceased mother. As she saw it, the authenticity of the content was irretrievable because the real time in which the events had been recorded could never be recaptured.

This emphasis on recording occurrences in real time reflected Nałkowska's lifelong philosophy of the relationship between life and time. In her view, her diary was the battlefield of her war against time, the implacable enemy of life. The events — happenings, thoughts, feelings, and most importantly, the experiences of encounters with others — had to be solidified in an instantaneous recording in order to rescue them from dissipating and disappearing in the formlessness of time and the fluidity of memory. In this sense, the recorded events were integral to Nałkowska's authentic self: each of them, as filtered through her consciousness, reflected her original perspective. Thus on January 15, 1943, the day she resumed her diaristic writing, even as she was lamenting the burned diary, Nałkowska declared, "The only reason for my writing is my constant desire to halt life and keep it from loss and destruction." She maintained that such a narrative kept the events intact because the diary allowed her to "go back into my earlier life and rediscover the time which has elapsed since then by means other than memory" (April 28, 1941). The authenticity of events cannot be retrieved in our memories because the accumulation of subsequent events clouds our initial perception of the event at the moment it happened. A diary entry is authentic not because it is historically accurate, but because it has captured the diarist's perspective in real time. The diary seizes "the present, which, caught in flight and nailed to the dates, flutters to this day with life like a pinned-down butterfly" (April 28, 1941). Once documented, the event does not age, nor does the perspective of the diarist. Thus the diarist's unadulterated view of the world can be rediscovered in the diary's account of events, and its records of encounters with the world document the process of the diarist's inner growth and evolving identity.

The immense scope of Nałkowska's diaries attests to the seriousness of her diaristic *ars poetica*, which insisted on constant and copious recording. And the remarkable, half-century-long time span of the diaries reflects Nałkowska's obsessive battle against time. The pages of her diary marked victories over the ravages of time, an idea which explains her grief over the loss of the diary notebook. In view of Nałkowska's perception of the diary as her raison d'être, the burning of the notebook signified the loss of her authentic self in all the events she recorded in it. Nałkowska, however, puts special emphasis on the recordings of "everything" about the "people behind the wall" and their "most horrific thing" in this "horrific world," indicating her particularly deep sorrow over the loss of her accounts of the plight of the Jews, which must have included the 1942 deportations. The fact that a fear of the Gestapo caused her to destroy these recordings would suggest that Nałkowska's extreme anguish was caused by a sense of poetic and moral self-betrayal.

While we shall never know how detailed and accurate the recording of the deportations were, it is clear that, whether unable or unwilling, Nałkowska did not share her recollections. The extent to which she evaded the horrors of the deportations emerges in her response to Janusz Korczak's death. On January 26, 1943, Nałkowska was still deploring the "black stain of silence" of the missing notebook. She claimed that the loss severed her connection with reality and especially with the people who died in the time that she captured in the lost diary. She wrote, "K[orczak?] is different now than he was in the moment when I learned about his death. With his death a huge block of the past broke away from my life." Nałkowska indeed had known Korczak all her life; the famous pedagogue and pediatrician was a close friend of her family and especially of Nałkowska's father, with whom he collaborated on social projects. Undoubtedly the consciousness of his death must have signaled the end of a large chapter of Nałkowska's life. We also know that she supplied Korczak with cigarettes that the doctor was sending for from the Ghetto as long as it was possible.[7] At the time of the deportations, Korczak, who was the director of the main orphanage of the Ghetto, refused the opportunity to save himself that the Germans offered. On September 5, 1942, he led the children and the staff in a dignified and orderly fashion out of the Ghetto to Umschlagplatz. All were gassed in Treblinka.[8] Nałkowska's silence about the manner of Korczak's death speaks loudly about her resistance, perhaps reluctance to record the Jewish plight.

Nałkowska's reaction to the liquidation of the Ghetto offers a further indication about her inability to speak in concrete details about what was happening to the Jews. Like Iwaszkiewicz, who despaired over his helplessness while witnessing the burning Ghetto and recognized his failure to understand the horror, Nałkowska recognized her helpless watching of the event as moral compromise. On April 29, 1943, when the Ghetto had already been fighting and burning for over ten days, she exclaimed,

> I am next to it, and I can still live! Something, after all, is wrong with me. . . . I am being transformed into somebody else. How could I have been forced into this, when just to be next to it, just to live means to acquiesce with it? This is infamy, not only torment. This is horrendous shame, not just compassion. All the efforts to bear it, not to go insane, to somehow sustain one's self in the midst of this horror fill one with guilt.

Dismayed as she was at the tragedy of the Ghetto, Nałkowska experienced a painful sense of metaphysical guilt. As she saw it, her helpless witnessing of what people were inflicting on other people implicated her in the crime. She felt as if her passive presence at the scene communicated her agreement with the situation. The sense of complicity engendered guilt for being alive. It was perhaps a somewhat ironic reaction given that her burning of the diary notebook was motivated by a desire to escape physical danger. At the same time, her exclamations of self-reproach, which equated witnessing with acquiescence, reveal a consciousness of the vitiating effect of genocidal terror. Her unsparing self-judgment brought forth her self-accusation of cowardly collusion with the perpetrator.

In fact, the implicit way in which Nałkowska referred to the destruction of the Ghetto in her diary seems to explain the harshness of her self-judgment. Her cryptonym for Ghetto Jews as "the people behind the wall," and euphemisms such as "everything" for deportations and Jewish suffering, "the thing" for destruction, and "it" or "this" for the liquidation of the Ghetto, are but a few examples of the diarist's consistently vague language when discussing the Jews. Her consistent avoidance of precise references to people and events appears as yet another attempt to escape repercussions should the diary be seized by the occupier.

At a time when personal writing, and particularly writing about the Jews, was strictly prohibited and severely punished by the German authorities, no explicit references could be made to the atrocities perpetrated against the Jews. However, the guilelessness of her coded language — after all, it would have been not too difficult to gather the identity of "the people behind the wall" — reinforces the argument that her vagueness not only signified her fear of the oppressor, but also her inability to face the destruction of the Ghetto in writing. This supposition is supported by the conspicuous absence of any precise, concrete descriptions of the plight of the Jews anywhere in Nałkowska's wartime diary. While it is true that the wall concealed the horror taking place inside the Ghetto, the "Aryan side" of Warsaw constantly witnessed incidents concerning Jews. Nowhere does Nałkowska mention the Polish extortionists (*szmalcowniki*) who were blackmailing Jews in hiding, nor does she ever talk about the fugitive Jews seeking shelter or the teams of emaciated Ghetto inmates working on the "Aryan side." Only once, in her entry for January 14, 1942, does Nałkowska record anything to do with the Ghetto, and even then the reference is only indirect: "a small boy with beautiful dark eyes, serious, taciturn, rings the bell. Without any words, it is clear what is going on, everything is known. He eats bread with lard, I give him some money . . . while I hold back my tears."

Most conspicuously, perhaps, she kept silent about the infamous carousel in Krasinskich Square. Nałkowska must have known about it. The construction of the entertainment park in front of the wall of the burning Ghetto could hardly have been missed, and even if she had missed it, Nałkowska was present at Mrs. Morawska's apartment, one of the clandestine reading salons during the Occupation, the evening

Andrzejewski read his story "Holy Week," which included a description of the Easter carousel.[9]

Nałkowska seems not to have been able to bring herself "to pin down" on paper the horrific concreteness of the events that she was witnessing. Such reticence, however, did not characterize Nałkowska's diaristic approach to the oppression of the Poles. On May 10, 1944, a year after the liquidation of the Ghetto and a couple of months before the Warsaw Uprising, when the Occupation was increasingly brutal and the world seemed to be on the verge of an apocalypse, Nałkowska wrote,

> I am writing only to arrest, to stop life as it fleets away. Especially here, in the diary. But for whom? I used to think, rather vaguely, about some library or archives, where somebody might come to read it. Now I see that there will be neither libraries nor readers. It is clear that "Europe will become a desert," that it will be "leveled with the ground". . . . Air raids are destroying cities and people die in every way and under every circumstance. Nothing will remain. For me, it means that I will write and this will be the end. This is all. But nonetheless, it is. By writing, I save what is. The rest is beyond my reach. Indeed, the rest is silence.

This entry reflects a remarkable mood shift from despair to determination. Nałkowska seems almost energized by what she perceived as her mission: to continue recording a reality which foreboded the end of civilization. The allusion to Hamlet's last words, "the rest is silence," spotlights her heroic stance as a diarist "to save what is" by telling the story. Like Hamlet, who asks Horatio to tell his tragic history to Fortinbras, who will bring a new future to Denmark, Nałkowska wished to document the tragedy she was witnessing for the sake of the future. However, the apocalyptic context of Nałkowska's diaristic legacy differed from Hamlet's future-oriented injunction to tell his story. The story of *Hamlet*, as it has been told by Shakespeare and will be told, within that play's dramatic world, by Horatio, progresses from tragedy into the cathartic promise of a better, purer world. In Nałkowska's world of indiscriminate murder and the systematic elimination of archives, libraries, and all landmarks of civilization, her documentation of the destruction appeared to be the last vestige of humanism.

Indeed, there was no cathartic denouement in the following entry on May 12, 1944. Walking along Aleje (a Warsaw thoroughfare) on a spring day, beautiful, cloudless, and pleasantly warm, she exclaimed that despite all "life is wonderful." Right then, she suddenly observed,

> a car sneaks along the wide alley, and then one "Grim Reaper" [a German vehicle popularly associated with death], then two, then three. There are guns in the hands of those sitting on the benches. Our hearts sink and we think that they are heading for a roundup. But that's not it. Because right after them goes a truck completely covered in black cloth. Oh, this is what it is! With plastered mouths and tied hands, they [i.e., the prisoners] pass by, crowded, silent, probably drugged with something, blood pumped out, each with this knowledge, this torment, this panic.

A close reading of this episode, which I will title "A view from the street," reveals a meticulous literary construction which cannot be found in any of Nałkowska's references to the Jewish plight. Her depiction of Polish prisoners on their way to execution progresses in three consecutive stages. First is the description of the visible, moving vehicles. The diarist carefully sketches the convoy, counts the cars, and depicts the immobile, identical-looking armed military seated in the trucks. The description "guns in the hands" implies the mindless brutality of the executioners. The episode continues with the narrator-witness's imaginative penetration of the space behind the black cloth in order to describe the sight that the authorities wished to hide from the passersby, namely, the physically abused, half-conscious convicts. The final stage shows the diarist's compassionate identification with the mental torment of the prisoners. Thus the narrative moves from the uniform, physically threatening appearance of the oppressors to the concealed mass of tortured bodies, and finally to a sense of encompassing terror.

In contrast to Nałkowska's codified accounts of the Jews, the use of plural pronouns in phrases such as "our hearts sink" and "we think" in this succinct entry suggest a communally familiar situation which needs no further elaboration. The victims and the witnesses share the same horizon, and the bystanders have the empathic capacity to identify with the prisoners. Furthermore, the literary properties of the account—the con-

trasts of the beauty of the sunny spring day and the blackness of the prisoners' truck, of the author's initial happiness and her subsequent distress,
of the portrait of the powerful soldiers and the helpless victims, as well
as the present tense of the narrative — not only highlight the authenticity and the immediacy of the scene, but also foreground the authorial
voice of the diarist as she was skillfully "pinning down" the incident in
a carefully arranged series of images. Nałkowska's authorial command
over this account of victimized Poles is absent in her diaristic encounter
with the extermination of the Jews, which she claimed to have considered "the most horrific thing in this horrible world." While her grief still
allowed her to empathize with the experience of the prisoners and thus
to be able to witness to the brutal oppression of her fellow Poles, she
could not find the empathic presence of mind which would allow her to
understand and coherently describe the liquidation of the Ghetto.

A year before the incident "A view from the street," on Easter Sunday,
April 25, 1943, when visiting her parents' graves at the Powązki cemetery
adjacent to the Ghetto, Nałkowska's recording of her experience disintegrates:

> Above the cemetery wall, above the trees with their fresh glimpse
> of green, black clouds arise, like billows of smoke. Sometimes
> it is possible to see the flames, a swift shimmering sash in the
> wind. And to hear it over there, above the dark pansies on the
> grave. And to think of it. And to live.

Too overwhelmed to write any further, and yet unable to leave off in medias res, Nałkowska was nonetheless compelled to return to the ceme-
tery/Ghetto experience in the next entry. Thus three days later, on April
28, 1943, she acknowledged her inability to confront the situation of the
Jews behind the wall:

> Reality can be endured, because it is not given completely by
> experience, nor is it completely visible. It reaches us only in frac-
> tions of events, in shreds of accounts, in echoes of shootings —
> horrible and intangible — in billows of smoke, in fires which, as
> history claims, have "leveled [the world] to the ground," though
> nobody understands what these words mean. This reality, dis-

tant and at the same time right behind the wall, can be endured. But thoughts are unbearable. . . . The fate of people far away, the fate of people nearby, the dead [and] the dead. The big processions of the resigned. The leaps into the flames. The leaps into the abyss. A woman in this little garden, hearing the drops. A little boy in the window. Children in arms. I cannot bear the thoughts; they transform me.

While Nałkowska was able to cope with the painful reality of the convoy scene in "A view from the street" and to write empathically about the tormented bodies and minds of the convicts behind the black cover of the truck, the torment of "the people behind the wall" disabled her writing capacities. The artfully constructed representation of "A view from the street" contrasted dramatically with the increasingly unhinged, disoriented narrative of the second episode, which I will title "A view from the cemetery." It is true that both entries concern the infliction of suffering on innocent people under the German Occupation, and both draw a contrast between the beauty and joy of awakening nature and the despair and torment of the death-bound victims. Nonetheless, the differences between the texts are striking. In the former, the clarity of the narrative attests to a comprehensive, penetrating, and therefore controlling authorial perspective. In contrast, the author in the latter episode seems too aggrieved, bewildered, and terrified to maintain a centered perspective. In fact, when trying to penetrate the Ghetto wall imaginatively, the narrative voice disintegrates and the story falls apart.

Nałkowska's increasingly disjointed phrases, shifts of subject, and omissions obscure the description of "A view from the cemetery" and obfuscate its meaning. The confusion calls into question the plausibility of the testimony. It also makes the editorial endnotes that follow the entry in Hanna Kirchner's edition of the *Diaries* particularly pertinent. These endnotes clarify that the diary entry relates to the Ghetto Uprising and that its fragments reappear in the story "The Cemetery Woman" ("Kobieta cmentarna") in *Medallions*. Nałkowska's transformation of this entry into fictional form signals her later realization of the inadequacy of her diaristic representation of the Jewish genocide. The growing incoherence of her entry recalling the liquidation of the Ghetto reflected Nałkowska's failure to produce a meaningful record of the event in real time. The paralyzing dismay and horror not only disabled her communicative skills, but also precluded empathic connection with the horizon of the victims which would have made a certain degree of cognitive understanding of the Ghetto inhabitants possible.

Nałkowska had a lifelong literary and personal preoccupation with human relationships, and humanistic faith in human solidarity and fellowship. Her 1936 essay "On Writing" ("O pisaniu") emphasized the organic connection between the writer and humanity, which, she declared, should supersede "the egocentric tendency to break the world into the 'I' and the 'non-I.'" In fact, she claimed, the writer is inseparable from the world she explores in her writing: "The imperfection of the writer as a truthful witness derives from the fact that as an exploring subject he is made of the same existential matter as the object of his consideration."[10] In a poetic and passionate postwar declaration, Nałkowska reaffirmed her inveterate emotional and mental connection with people. Recording "a moment of silence and solitude" on January 1, 1950, she wrote, "I experience this moment more ardently than ever. . . . I experience it through my affinity with the world of people, to whom I feel stitched with the threads of their fate, while listening to the echoes of their words." Anna Foltyniak observed in her study of Nałkowska's *Diaries* that the writer's diaristic narrative was informed by her sense of an indelible connection with human beings. While aware of her particular perception of the world, Nałkowska forged her own identity by affirming her connections with the life histories and biographies of others.[11]

As "A view from the street" demonstrated, Nałkowska's empathic rapport with her fellow Poles persisted throughout the Occupation. Her testimony of the physical and mental torment of the convicts reflected a visceral identification with all Poles, who were victims of the rule of "collective responsibility" imposed by the Germans as retaliation for the actions of the Polish Underground.[12] In contrast, the fragmented narrative of "A view from the cemetery" displayed the limits of any empathic connection with the victims of the Final Solution. While watching, with dread and panic, the "most terrible of all" suffering of the Jews, Nałkowska was aware of her inability to comprehend, let alone express, the experience of people who were perishing behind the wall. The walled-in place was "another planet," governed by a concept of death, which separated Jews from other human beings. Unlike the terribly brutal, revenge-driven roundups, torture, and executions of the Poles motivated by the perception of the Poles as enemies of the regime, the burning of the people in the Ghetto was motivated by ideological indoctrination which defined the Jews as a non-human group condemned to systematic extermination. The treatment of the Jews defied any human explanation or rationalization.

Indeed, Władysław Szlengel, the Jewish poet behind the Ghetto wall, wrote before his death in April 1943:

> Your death and our death
> are two different deaths. . . .
>
> Your death will be marked by a cross
> mentioned in the press
> our death is a wholesale death covered up and forgotten.[13]

On the other side of the wall, walking in the cemetery among the graves covered with fresh grass and spring flowers, Nałkowska was aware of the unprecedented split of "the dead and the dead," that is, of the buried Christians and the burning Jews. The deliberate mass murder of human beings by other human beings signified a breakdown of the fundamental humanistic values of equality and dignity of all human beings. The categorization of Jewish and non-Jewish death showed that humanism had failed to provide effective defenses against the enemies of its most fundamental values. Eventually, on October 8, 1944, Nałkowska was capable of assessing and articulating coherently the impotence of humanism vis-à-vis human brutality: "The future reveals its horror in layers. Once we have transformed ourselves to bear one version of it . . . it turns out to be too easy, too banal . . . and we are exposed to a completely different formation of horror, against which we have no weapons whatsoever." But when watching the burning Ghetto in April 1943, she could only speak of the horror as "unbearable thoughts" which she was unable to articulate. The diarist who prided herself on "pinning down" her interactions with the world in real time had to acknowledge her incapacity as a recording witness of the "most horrible fate" of the "people behind the wall."

Medallions: Toward Humanistic Restoration

Medallions, Nałkowska's collection of short stories written in 1945 while she was serving on the War Crimes Committee and published in 1946, emphasizes Nałkowska's sense of moral obligation to let the world know about the Jewish extermination which she had failed to record at the time. The prompt completion of *Medallions* reflects Nałkowska's sense of urgency to record, in fictional form, the earliest testimonies of the genocide as they were given. The title of the work — which refers to tombstones bearing a relief of the deceased accompanied by a biographical inscription — symbolizes the restoration of the sanctity of life and dignity of death. As a metaphor, the medallion designates the process of testifying as an act of redrawing the effaced human image of the victims of the Final Solution. The stories restore the individuality of the victims and reintegrate them into the community of human beings. However, the subject matter of the stories, namely, the experience of the Holocaust, questions the strength of humanist ideals. In this sense, *Medallions* does not propose a return to the prewar humanistic Weltanschauung, nor does it promise to heal the trauma of the humanistic crisis created by the war. Instead, it raises consciousness of the impact of the Jewish genocide on humanistic ethics. Nałkowska's investigation of humanism within the context of a reality which denied Jews dignity and the right to live sounds a strong note of caution about the ultimate power of humanistic ethics in a time of mass murder.

On January 14, 1946, following an evening of literary readings, Dąbrowska wrote a disparaging criticism about *Medallions*, "Very weak — horror from the time of the Occupation. . . . Presented with the icy elegance of inner emptiness — it is boring and bothersome."[14] In contrast, on the occasion of Nałkowska's jubilee in 1952, Jarosław Iwaszkiewic deemed *Medallions* of preeminent ethical and artistic importance:

> I would like to dwell for a moment on a work of art, small in its dimensions, but great in its achievement, which you gave us and literature, after the war and the black night of the criminal occupation. Like a pearl diver, you brought out of the depths of this night a genuine jewel of restraint, intelligence, understanding, and analysis — and transformed it into a most serious

indictment of fascism and genocide. Only out of deep wisdom and great emotions can such art be born — seemingly restrained and remote, but in reality scorching and riveting. This is your great *J'accuse*, worthy of your great writing, your culture and your heritage. . . . No doubt everybody knows that I am speaking about *Medallions*. . . . This is your greatest achievement and, at the same time, the greatest achievement of every artist. You have found true beauty . . . in love for a human being, understanding his fate and joining with him, while giving up your proud, but no longer necessary rebellions . . . [and thus] you have discovered the highest and most authentic beauty that you have dreamed of. It is accessible to everybody, enraptures everybody, teaches everybody, and calls everybody to battle.[15]

While Dąbrowska's negative view of the theme of *Medallions* reflects her dismissive treatment of the Jewish genocide in her wartime diary, her inability to break away from the stereotypical vision of the realist genre of her own fiction seems to have prevented her from an objective evaluation of Nałkowska's innovative literary mode in her representation of the Holocaust.[16] In contrast, Iwaszkiewicz's appreciation of both the ethical and aesthetic aspects of *Medallions* reflects his own struggle with the barbarism of the Occupation and the Holocaust and his persistent faith in humanism. Well aware of Nałkowska's inclination to dominate,[17] Iwaszkiewicz praised her capability to forego her "proud rebellions," and to foreground the authentic stories of other human beings. Insightfully, he assessed Nałkowska's repudiation of fascism and genocide not as a vengeful search for justice, but rather as a reaffirmation of love and respect for other human beings. Iwaszkiewicz saw *Medallions* as Nałkowska's *J'accuse*. The reference to Zola and the Dreyfus trial is an allusion to the Holocaust which he could not mention openly in the communist cultural and political climate of the time. *Medallions*, for Iwaszkiewicz, is an idealistic struggle to restore a human image to the world by exposing the human capacity for the evil of genocide. In this sense, Iwaszkiewicz, who was deeply concerned about the humanistic potency of literature in the aftermath of the war, paid tribute to the morally edifying message of *Medallions*. As he saw it, the beauty of the accessible form, style, and content of the book demonstrated Nałkowska's "deep wisdom and great emotions" because it reached her readers on intellectual and aesthetic levels and at the same time impressed upon them the need to engage in a struggle for a more humane world. Iwaszkiewicz's comparison of the undertaking of *Medallions* to pearl diving invokes Nałkowska's wartime sensation of "drowning" or being sucked into "abyss." The metaphor of sinking into unfathomable horror communicated the loss of rational capacities and of the capability of coherent expression. In contrast, the image of pearl diving suggests a daring search which required "restraint, intelligence, understanding, and analysis" and which produced the unusual beauty of a luminous text.

Was Iwaszkiewicz aware that the cerebral, artistic construction of *Medallions* constituted a reaction to the emotions of horror and despair that silenced Nałkowska at the time of the Ghetto's destruction? Though unlikely, he might have heard about it from Nałkowska. Shortly before her death, in the 1954 article "About Myself" ("O sobie"), Nałkowska was still considering the silencing horror of the Holocaust:

> When I was writing *Medallions* I was not aware that I was using a different technique, or using a literary method different from that which I had used in my earlier books. The subject matter alone — so difficult to grasp mentally, and emotionally so unbearable — made me use a realistic medium. It was not a preconceived intention nor was it a conscious decision.[18]

Nałkowska's contention that her subject matter of the genocide determined the realistic form of *Medallions* complicates the accepted notion of literary realism. Literary realism, such as Dąbrowska's fiction, is an expression of the familiar which allows readers to see the text as a simile of their reality, because "what is written is *like* what I know."[19] The realistic design strives for a "truthful representation of real life, a depiction of commonplace events, characters, settings and typical circumstances."[20] The realistic genre highlights situations which can be easily associated with the quotidian, the customary, and the recognizable. It is the "art of creating an illusion of reality."[21]

In terms of its form, *Medallions* indeed adheres to the conventions of literary realism. The book imitates the circumstances of legal proceedings, presenting a compilation of testimonies by victims and bystanders, men and women of various ages, apparently chosen at random and recorded in real time by a member of the War Crimes Commission. This effect is heightened by the stories' authentic provenance from the genuine investigations of the War Crimes Commission, on which Nałkowska served. In addition, the linguistic register of the testimonies in *Medallions* conforms to the realistic genre by providing an indicator of the social class and level of education of the testifying characters. Finally, the succinct and factual narration of events reinforces the realism of the stories' plots because it affiliates them with the genres of documentary and reportage, which typically are grounded in historical facts or daily events.

However, the subject matter of *Medallions* defies the realistic mode. Genocide, an unprecedented and therefore unknowable and unfamiliar situation of unspeakable horrors, countervails the reality of everyday life. Nałkowska nonetheless asserted that the realistic medium was imposed upon her text by the subject matter. This assertion leads back to the diaristic inception of one of the *Medallions* stories, "The Cemetery Woman," which drew upon Nałkowska's failed attempt to record the liquidation of the Ghetto. Nałkowska's postwar transposition of the event, which she attempted unsuccessfully to depict realistically in her diary (as she depicted the incident in "A view from the street"), into a fictional context enabled her to produce a realistic representation of the "unreal" event that had eluded her in the real time of diaristic recording. Not only the time distance but also voices other than that of the diarist informed the presentation of the Jewish genocide in *Medallions* as a component of inconceivable, but nonetheless everyday reality.

In her study of *Medallions*, Helena Zaworska discusses the narrative configuration in "The Cemetery Woman" by pointing to the distribution of the roles of the tellers: whereas Nałkowska, the narrator, assigns to herself the description of the cemetery, the description of the liquidation of the Ghetto Jews in the second part of the story is entrusted to the simple, down-to-earth cemetery woman.[22] Nałkowska developed this character from the brief reference in her diary to "a woman in this little garden, hearing the bodies [of the Jews] dropping." In the second part of story, Nałkowska assumes the role of mere recorder of this woman's account. This self-conscious literary transmutation from active diarist to "passive" narrator that characterizes the stories finally allows Nałkowska to represent an atrocity which plunged her into an abyss of speechless despair through the voice of another.

While the construct of the cemetery woman mediates between the narrator and the event, it exposes Nałkowska directly to the woman's response to the event. The woman begins with a complaint: "We all live near the wall, and we hear everything that is happening over there. . . . People are shot in the street. They burn them in their apartments. At night such cries and weeping. Nobody can sleep or eat. Nobody can stand it." She follows with a rationalization: "They are also people, so one has pity for them. But it would be better for us if the Germans destroyed them. They hate us more than the Germans. If the Germans lose the war, the Jews will kill us all. Even the Germans say it. And it was on the radio . . . " Even as she strives to justify the destruction of the Jews, her anti-Semitic rationalizations break up as she is compelled to describe events that she not only heard but could discern from the distance:

> The worst is that there is no rescue. . . . They set the houses on fire and don't let them escape. So the mothers wrap the children in anything soft they have and throw them out to the pavement. And then they jump too . . . some with the smallest child in their arms. From one place we could see how a father was jumping with a small boy. . . . And even if we cannot see it, we can hear it. . . . All the time they jump like that. They prefer to jump than to burn alive.

The narrator reports that having finished her story, the cemetery woman "was listening for something. In the soft cooing of the cemetery birds, she recognized the distant sounds of bodies falling to the pavement. She picked up her watering can and walked to the yellow and navy-blue pansies on the graves."[23]

The story of the cemetery woman elucidates Nałkowska's claim that the subject matter of the genocide demanded realism. As the woman's story shows, even though she could only occasionally see them, the events of the destruction ineluctably penetrated her life, becoming an integral part of her reality. While she protests against the disruptiveness of the nearby genocide, the woman continues her work, planting and watering spring flowers in the cemetery. Her ability to distinguish the sounds of falling bodies from the sounds of the cemetery birds indicates that the tragedy behind the wall has become a mundane reality for the neighboring population.

In the story "By the Railway Tracks," the tragedy is no longer concealed behind a wall. A Jewish woman who was shot while escaping from a transport to an extermination camp is found by the inhabitants of a small Polish village lying by the tracks in an open space "like a hunted, wounded animal that the hunters forgot to kill."[24] The circumstances of the Jewish genocide have turned this woman into a hunted animal and transformed the villagers into "hunters" who must complete the task of killing her for their own protection. Providing any medical assistance or attempting to hide the fugitive would bring German retaliation on the village, and the woman "needed to die, one way or another."[25] When the Polish policemen show considerable reluctance to do it, one of the villagers volunteers and shoots her "like a dog."[26] The volunteer was a young man who had stayed with the woman all along, bringing her vodka and cigarettes, and who had seemed affected by the woman's situation. The story is told by an anonymous bystander, a witness who, as the authorial narrator records, "saw it and who could not understand the event which lived only in his memory."[27] At the end of the story, the anonymous witness's question suggests why the memory of the event persisted: "But why did he shoot her? It is unclear. . . . I cannot understand it. He seemed to take pity on her."[28]

The event changed the routine of the villagers for only one day, but it permanently undermined the anonymous witness's understanding of moral behavior. The fact that the scene would not recede in his memory emphasizes its traumatic impact, and his detailed account shows the extent to which the event became an inseparable part of his reality. The question of the killer's motives preoccupies him, but a clear answer eludes him. Did the killing of the helpless fugitive turn the villager into an implacable "hunter," or did it transform him into a mercy killer? Either possibility posits a moral problem. The first communicates the frailty of humanistic values; the reality of the genocide, which legitimized the killing of Jews, released the brutal instincts not just of the perpetrators but of the witnessing bystanders as well. Mercy killing, on the other hand, transforms the conception of violent death. In the reality of the Final Solution, the shooting of a helpless Jewess became an act of grace because it saved her from a worse death in the extermination camp. Whether committed out of cruelty or compassion, the killing of the Jewish woman by a Polish bystander signified an ethical reality which blurred the distinctions between good and evil.

The "medallions" produced by the cemetery woman and the anonymous villager depict their emotional and moral difficulties in coping with the genocidal reality which has ineluctably invaded their everyday lives. No qualms, however, seem to perturb the young soap-making assistant in the story "Professor Spanner," which opens the collection. His testimony, delivered to the commission, is devoid of any emotion; it is detailed, eager, and scrupulously factual. His description of guillotine executions of the prisoners, of boiling, cutting, and skinning their beheaded bodies, as well as of preparations of human fat for soap production, shows his complete immersion in the "scientific" reality of the Anatomy Institute.[29] As Zaworska observed, "Completely unconscious of his cruelty, the boy speaks of the reality of the fascist atrocities as if it were a normal, comprehensible reality in which he performed his daily duties."[30]

The conclusion of the assistant's testimony confirms his willingness not only to participate in recycling of human bodies into soap, but also to use the product. "In the beginning . . . I had shivers when I thought about washing myself with it. At home, Mother was disgusted too. But it lathered well, so she used it for laundry. And I also got used to it, because it was good." He concludes approvingly, "In Germany, people sure know how to make something out of nothing."[31] The "medallion" produced by the boy inscribes a shocking reality in which soap made of human fat is "something" and the human body is "nothing." Even more shocking is the boy's unperturbed, exclusively utilitarian, mental and physical integration into a reality which obliterated all respect for human life and the human body.

Nałkowska's witnesses/bystanders reveal degrees of adaptation to a reality governed by violent death and murder. The images of mothers with babies leaping from burning houses, of a helpless fugitive shot "like a dog," and of recycling of the human body into a commercial commodity reflect moral erosion which ends in a complete erasure of the sanctity of life and death. The influence of these events on the ethical constitution of the witnesses also raises the question of the extent to which the genocidal reality affected the moral world of the victims. Whereas the bystanders' stories illustrate the moral transformation of their everyday reality, the stories of the victims force the issue of moral norms in the reality of mass extermination.

The "medallions" of the victims portray disfigured faces and maimed bodies. The tellers are bereft of their families, relatives, and often their whole communities. They are somber, emotionally and physically exhausted people, who feel estranged and disoriented in the post-Holocaust world. Each of their testimonies is a record of hell on earth, unspeakable losses, suffering, and torment. Michał P., the protagonist in "The Man Is Strong" ("Człowiek jest mocny"), was assigned to digging burial trenches for the corpses of the Jews gassed in the trucks in Chełmno. When he discovered the bodies of his gassed wife and children, he asked to be shot. He was forced to continue working because, as his German tormentor assessed him, "The man is strong, he can work some more,"[32] whereupon he devised a successful escape into the forest. The woman in the story "Visa" ("Wisa") converted to Catholicism because "she was tormented by watching so much injustice and brutality. Thinking about Jesus helped her to endure it better."[33] Since she was documented as a Pole, she was not kept with the Jewish women in the camp. This probably saved her, even though she and her group of women were also brought to the Visa, "a meadow by the forest, under the trees" where the women inmates were left in the cold for hours on end before their eventual extermination.[34] The ordeal of the eponymous protagonist of "Dwojra Zielona" began when she hid in the ghetto of Międzyrzece. When she came down from the attic where she was starving, she was shot by the Germans and lost her eye. Feeling completely alone in the world, she went with other Jews to Majdanek, where she was tormented, starved, and beaten, but escaped the gas chamber. She volunteered to work in an ammunition plant, where she extracted her gold teeth to buy food. The storyteller in "The Bottom" ("Dno") underwent medical experiments in Ravensbrück. Beforehand she was incarcerated for two months in the Pawiak prison in Warsaw, where she was horribly tortured. She also worked in an ammunition factory, where people were driven by starvation to eat corpses, and where the inmates, treated sadistically by the guards, "were dying at the roll calls." The SS women kicked the corpses "to check if they were faking death."[35]

By no means does this brief summary do justice to the experiences told in these first-person narratives. Rather, it attempts to present a composite picture of the victims' reality of relentless torture, sickness, and starvation, of gassing and killing, and of a denial of dignity to the living and the dead. The sentence of mass murder did not transform the world of the victims; rather it replaced it with another. Unlike the bystanders who, in various ways and with differing levels of difficulty, incorporated the reality of the genocide into their everyday life, the ideology and tactics of the Final Solution devised a new reality for the victims deliberately constructed to eradicate, both physically and psychologically, the image of Jews as human beings before their extermination.

The four testimonies raise the question of the tenacity and tenuousness of human dignity in a reality of genocidal terror. The victims' desperate struggle for a measure of control over their deaths has already emerged in the bystanders' accounts in "The Cemetery Woman" and "By the Railway Tracks." Those accounts tell of the victims' affirmation of existential freedom by actively choosing the manner of their death rather than submitting to burning or gassing. In the testimonies of the survivors, autobiographical subjectivity complicates the investigation of the moral aspects of genocidal existence. The frequent silences that punctuate these accounts and the lacunae or reticence that disrupt the flow of the stories indicate that some aspects of the genocidal reality must remain inaccessible to the outside world. However, the stories that the victims were willing or capable of sharing reveal a growing complexity of the meaning of ethics in the reality of the Final Solution.

Significantly, the survivors do not tell their stories for the sake of revenge, nor do they intend to claim survival as a proof that justice prevailed. As Dwojra Zielona remembered the moment when the Soviets liberated Częstochowa (where, she mentioned, the entire Jewish population had perished) she says, "We welcomed them, but we did not shout for joy, nothing at all. . . . We had no strength left."[36] She informs her interlocutor/recorder that despite her loneliness, sickness, and exhaustion, she feels obligated to tell her story out of a sense of duty. "I wanted to live. Why? . . . To tell everything as I am telling you now. Let the world know what they did. I thought that I would be the only one alive. I thought that no Jew would remain."[37] Her sense of being the last Jew did not allow her to sink into resignation; on the contrary, it evoked in her the duty to tell about the extermination of the Jews. But as the last Jew, she lived not only to commemorate her people, but also to fulfill her obligation to inform the world of the atrocity committed against them. Thus, the tale that she is telling fulfills this obligation, because the testimony will instill the story of the Jews in the consciousness of the world. Her story reaffirms the humanity of which the teller and the victims in her tale had been divested. Despite the subject matter of unspeakable denigration and abuse, the act of telling reinforces the victim's sustained sense of self-dignity. The recording of the story by Nałkowska, the representative of the War Crimes Commission, reflects the penetration of Dwojra Zielona's story into the world that has the obligation to learn from the survivors not only the horrors but also the persistent humanity of the victims.

Dwojra Zielona's powerful sense of moral obligation toward her people and toward humanity at large motivated her wish to survive. In contrast, Michał P. survived thanks to other individuals' sense of responsibility to maintain the shared horizons of Jewish tradition and human fellowship. The people who helped him did it in the name of ideals that the Final Solution aspired to devalue and eradicate. Michał P. explains that on the day he found the bodies of his wife and children, "Two Jews hanged themselves in the cellar. I wanted to hang myself too, but a religious man talked me out of it."[38] Despite the horror of imminent death by gassing, there were Jews who not only continued to observe the prohibition of suicide, but also urged those who despaired to obey it. While some Jews transgressed and took their lives, Michał P.'s submission to the Law despite his terrible despair attests to his continuing faith in the sanctity of human life. Michał P.'s faith in humanity was reinforced in the course of his escape. A Polish peasant took an enormous risk by opening his house to the Jewish fugitive. Despite the danger of being found by his fellow villagers, who were looking for the fugitive, the peasant, as Michał P. remembers well, "Fed me, gave me a cap, and shaved me so I'd look like a human being."[39] The lifeline of Jewish ethics that the religious man extended to Michał P. corresponds to the peasant's extension of human fellowship. While the former saved Michał P.'s life, the latter restored to him the dignity of human physical appearance. The survivor's testimonial of these anonymous moral individuals proves the continuing relevance of humanistic values in the reality of genocide.

The survivors in the two other stories represent more complicated expressions of humanism. In "Visa," the convert protagonist scarcely hides her antipathy for the Jewish people. She opens her story with a declaration, "I don't dislike the Jews just as I don't dislike ants or mice."[40] The association of Jews with animals and insects implies the protagonist's acquiescence with the German perception of the Jews. In fact, her admission to having felt "curiosity like the Gestapo," while wondering how a cat would eat mice displays the extent of her identification with German sadistic propaganda.[41] Furthermore, her dissociation from her Jewish roots and her declaration of devotion to the Christian tradition implies her desire to disavow her Jewish roots completely. When she describes the Jewish women on the "Visa," she reveals no compassion for the "dirty, ulcerated, scabbed, sick, even dying" women of various nationalities, noting that "the Greek women were in the worst condition" because they were the weakest.[42] But all the women looked like inhuman creatures. Frozen, they moved together, "not like people, but like animals. Like a single mass . . ."

Yet, despite the contempt for the women reflected in their image as a mass of animals, the protagonist cannot refrain from telling how on a day when the sun came out, the "Greek women sang a national hymn. Not in Greek. They sang in Hebrew, the Jewish national hymn. . . . They sang beautifully, very loud and strong, as if they were healthy." And she offers an interpretation: "It was not physical strength, because they were the weakest. It was the strength of yearning and desire."[43]

In contrast to Dwojra Zielona and Michał P., whose self-identification as Jews was instrumental in restoring their ties with humanity, in "Visa" the protagonist's perception of Jews as animals indicates her deliberate denial of their humanity. However, the conclusion of her testimony with the story of the Greek women hints at a return of her repressed identity. Her acknowledgment of the Greek women's spontaneous affirmation of their identity as Jews, Zionists, and human beings shows her deep ambivalence about her identity. The explanation of the women's singing as an expression of "yearning and desire" for freedom is reinforced by the name of the anthem "Hatikva," which means "hope" and therefore attests to their rebellion against the abyss of despair and bestiality which preceded inescapable death. The protagonist's unwanted or unwilling, but nonetheless undeniable, recognition of the dignified humanity of the

Jewish Greeks reveals cracks in her anti-Semitic position. Inadvertently, perhaps, she found herself commemorating the women's assertion of humanism and dignity in the dehumanizing reality of the "Visa."

The story "The Bottom" presents a multilayered and complex humanistic response to human degradation. The protagonist describes the reaction of a German officer upon opening a sealed cattle car with a hundred women (including the protagonist herself) who traveled for seven days "with no water, no possibility to leave, relieving ourselves standing. We slept standing because there was no possibility to sit." The women, "drenched with sweat, faces blackened with dust, our clothes stinking, our legs covered with feces," were "howling like animals" for water.[44] The protagonist remembers that when the officer saw the women, "his eyes grew round and his fingers clawed in fear. He got so scared of us! He looked like a wild boar! Only after a while did he ask if anybody spoke German or French. Many did." The officer gives orders to bring them water and lets them out of the car to get cleaned up. Subsequently, he gives orders to open the men's transport, where the conditions were even worse. Then the women were sealed in again and nobody opened the car anymore. Some women went mad, and upon arrival in Ravensbrück, they were immediately shot. The teller cannot stop marveling, "You see, you see. Even the German got so frightened when he saw us."[45]

The German officer was traveling with a convoy of wounded soldiers and did not belong to the units of the SS and the Gestapo which dealt with the extermination of the Jews. Thus nothing in his war experience had prepared him for what he saw on the train. He was an outsider unexpectedly exposed to human beings who had been turned into filthy, howling animals. The horror of the women's dehumanization stripped him for a moment of his own humanity: he became speechless and assumed the look of a wild animal. In this sense, he intuitively imitated the women; their dehumanization dehumanized him. While the protagonist thinks that the German was afraid of the women, the vicarious nature of his reaction also communicates that the degradation of one group of people degrades the others as well. The officer's response to the situation shows his urgent desire to undo this state of degradation. His initial question about the languages the women speak claims them as people of culture, and the possibility that he gives them to clean up restores them to civilization. The German's intention to do the same for the men's transport further emphasizes that his response to the plight of the victims was motivated by his inherent humanism. For a short moment, the German officer transformed the genocidal reality of the women by redeeming their dignity as human beings. Immediately afterward, however, the dehumanizing treatment of the victims is reinstated and the reality of the Final Solution resumes.

The juxtaposition of humane and bestial treatment of the victims in "The Bottom" leads to the discussion of human nature in the concluding story, "Adults and Children in Auschwitz" ("Dorośli i dzieci w Oświęcimiu"). Here the testimonies confront the narrator Nałkowska with an understanding that human evil, which she encapsulated in the observation, "people inflicted this fate upon people," coexists with the realization that people are also capable of humanistic greatness in times of the greatest affliction. Thus she recounts stories of sadistic criminals who specialized in inventing methods of torture and murder at Auschwitz and clashing stories of courageous inmate-doctors who risked their lives to help the sick and needy in the camp. The penultimate episode, in which about 600 children selected for gassing escaped from their cells, "scattering around the camp," questions once more the nature of the human being. "The SS-men were chasing them back to their barrack. It was possible to hear from afar how they cried and begged to be saved, 'We don't want to go to the gas! We want to live!' "[46] But two of the children knocked at the window of one of the doctors.

> When he opened it, two boys, completely naked and numb with cold, entered. One was twelve and the other fourteen. They had succeeded in escaping the truck as it was approaching the gas chamber. The doctor hid the boys, fed them, and got clothes for them. . . . Risking his life every minute, he kept them until such time as they could show themselves in the camp without raising suspicion.[47]

The juxtaposition of the bestiality of the German children hunters and destroyers and the immeasurable generosity of spirit of the inmate doctors, who risked their lives for the children's sake, seems to indicate Nałkowska's faith in the power of humanism even under the most inhuman circumstances. From this perspective, the story confirmed Iwaszkiewicz's attestation of faith in humanism and in human beings as the most compelling quality of *Medallions*. However, Dr. Epstein's testimony, which concludes the final story, complicates Iwaszkiewicz's reading of *Medallions*. In the days of the liquidation of the children, Epstein noticed two fugitive children moving some sticks in the sand. When he asked what they were doing, they answered, "We are playing at burning the Jews."[48] The introjection of the reality of the extermination communicated the children's identification with the Germans. While obviously too young to grasp the annihilation that they faced, these children internalized the inhuman practices of perpetrators, making them part of their world. In this sense, the conclusion of the book revises the aphorism "people inflicted this fate on people." In the children's imagination, the Jews became sticks, inflammable, movable, and dispensable play objects, whereas the children assumed the roles of the powerful executioners of the burning. The pervasiveness of the genocidal mentality, capable of penetrating the consciousness of the child/victim, communicates the depth of Nałkowska's concern and uncertainty about the viability of humanism in a world imbued with Holocaust consciousness.

Nałkowska's response to the Holocaust demonstrates her own personal and professional transformation. Tying her self-image to her vocation of a writer, her diary and *Medallions* bear witness to her deepening understanding of the world and self. The reality of genocide pronounced a split between Nałkowska and the world of which she considered herself to be an integral part. Informed by the model of her parents, who believed in human progress and in one's obligation to devote one's lifetime to its promotion, she found herself facing a reality of genocide which emptied her fundamental beliefs of meaning. The horror of genocidal evil confronted her with her inability to bear witness, a realization which exposed the need for reexamination of the viability of the humanistic convictions. In this sense, Nałkowska's wartime experience represents a trajectory of self-reeducation, culminating with *Medallions*, which expressed not only her obligation as a humanist to present the story of the Jewish annihilation to the world, but also became an urgent act of self-rescue as a humanist and writer. The form of the testimonies attests to her readiness to learn the reality of genocide from others and her deference to the stories, as evidenced by her self-effacing role of authorial narrator, illuminates Nałkowska's deeper understanding of humanism. Unlike her formative prewar conviction in the eventual victory of the humanist idea, *Medallions* communicates that the strength of humanism lies in the absolute need to remain conscious of the human capacity for evil while maintaining faith in the human proclivity to goodness, whose victory is by no means assured.

CHAPTER 6

Stanisław Rembek: The Christian Witness of the Holocaust and the End of Polish Messianic Destiny

The altering perceptions of the Jews in the oeuvre of Stanisław Rembek (1901–1985) are puzzling. As Aleksander Kaczorowski has remarked,

> Is it inconceivable that the same man who wrote the profoundly moving descriptions of the Jews in his fiction was capable of such a degree of indifference in his *Diary of the Occupation* toward people that he saw as "only" Jews? How can we explain this contradiction?[1]

The references to the Jewish genocide in Rembek's wartime diary not only demonstrate obtuseness toward the victims, they also draw upon past anti-Semitic stereotypes in order to diminish the unfolding Jewish tragedy. Yet Rembek's literary work is populated with insightful and positive depictions of Jewish characters, all loyal and ardent Polish patriots. Rembek's changing views of the Jews in his diaries and literary works reflects the complex trajectory of his evolving nationalistic-religious Weltanschauung and a progression from the triumphalist assertion of the Polish people's Christian mission to a realization of the Poles' moral failure at the time of the Occupation and the Holocaust.

Rembek's formative self-identification as a patriotic Pole was shaped by the romantic tradition of the 1831 and the 1863 insurrections that conceptualized the suffering of the Polish nation in terms of Christ's Passion, and attributed a messianic destiny to the Polish people. The independence of Poland in 1918 and the victory of the new state in the 1920

Polish-Bolshevik war, in which Rembek fought as an officer, fortified his faith in Poland's military invincibility and moral superiority. In his autobiographical writing of the interwar period, Rembek displayed considerable anti-Semitic prejudices. In his fiction, however, he portrayed the Jews as patriotic officers fighting for Poland. Their selfless love for the motherland qualified them as comrades-in-arms. Such characterizations of the Jews highlighted Poland's democratic open-mindedness toward its Jewish citizens. Nonetheless, the Jewish faith of these soldiers prevented their full integration into Polish society, because as Jews they were excluded from the nation's Christian destiny. From a theological perspective, however, a Jewish presence was indispensable to Poland's redemptive destiny; the Jew sanctioned the Polish claim to a messianic calling as an affirming witness.

The 1939 defeat shattered the myth of Poland's invincibility. Rembek was deeply distressed over the incompetence of the military authorities, the indignities of the Occupation, and the loss of his identity as a proud reservist officer. Rembek's *Dziennik okupacyjny* (*Diary of the Occupation*) empathically recorded the physical and mental suffering of the Poles, while its observations of the evolving mass murder of the Jews showed deliberate indifference and indubitable anti-Semitic animosity. This reductive and insensitive treatment of the Jewish genocide reflected Rembek's need to reaffirm the Poles' honorable national character which would assure their special destiny among the Christian nations. Recognition of the unprecedented horror of the extermination of the Jews would have the contrary effect, diminishing the singularity of Polish heroism and martyrdom.

Rembek's treatment of the Polish attitude toward the Jews during the war in his postwar fiction, *The Sentence of Franciszek Kłos* (*Wyrok na Franciszka Kłosa*) and "A Letter to Churchill" ("List do Churchilla"), represents an astonishing ideological and theological turnabout of Rembek's diaristic perspective. Rembek's literary representation of the Occupation represents a far-reaching shift from his diary's silence about the moral dissolution of Polish society at that time. Rembek the writer reconstructed the Polish people's unethical wartime acquiescence in the extermination of the Jews which Rembek the diarist had evaded. This new perspective led Rembek to the realization that the immoral conduct of the Polish people violated Christian ethics and thus forfeited the Poles' singular destiny. The Polish contribution to the extermination of the Jewish witness of the Polish mission of redemption signified the loss of this mission and the victory of the forces of evil.

Rembek started his literary career in 1922–23 with *A Punitive Expedition* (*Expedycja karna*), a novel for adolescents,[2] but soon engaged in fiction for adults. In 1922, he published a novella, *Ripe Spikes* (*Dojrzałe kłosy*), which featured a Jewish Polish officer in the Polish army heroically waging a lost battle against the Bolsheviks in the 1920 war. He noted that seeing the story in print "has pleased me very much, because I have been very much attached to this novella."[3] In 1928 Rembek published his first full-length novel, *Revolver* (*Nagan*), about the Bolshevik war, in which three Jewish officers represent philosophical perspectives of the meaning of life in the reality of wartime, the main theme of the novel. In 1937 he published his second novel, *In the Field* (*W polu*), which also dealt with the 1920 war, for which he received the A. Asnyk Prize from the city of Kalisz and the Leventhal Prize awarded by Kasa Literacka. As Mirosław Lalak noted, because of the negative reactions of anti-Semitic critics to the conspicuous presence of Jewish soldiers in *Revolver*, Rembek refrained from featuring Jewish characters in his second novel.[4]

Rembek returned to Jewish subject matter in the wake of World War II with the 1947 publication of *The Sentence of Franciszek Kłos*. Rembek's last full-length work appeared in 1956. It was *A Ballad about a Disdainful Hanged Man and Two January Tales* (*Ballada o wzgardliwym wisielcu oraz dwie gawędy styczniowe*), which focuses on the 1863 failed Polish uprising against tsarist rule. In the first of the *Tales*, "A Delivered Relay" ("Przekazana sztafeta"), the Jewish characters, though stereotypically portrayed, turn out to be true Polish patriots and one of them is executed for his underground activities.

As his literary biography shows, Rembek was preoccupied with the theme of war, and his interwar novels gained him the reputation of the best battlefield novelist since Sienkiewicz and Żeromski. Maria Dąbrowska, who in 1938 nominated Rembek's *In the Field* for the Literary Prize of the literary publication *Wiadomości Literackie*, observed in her nomination letter that Rembek's novel "in many ways seems better than Remarque's *All Quiet on the Western Front*," and praised him for "having avoided the reportage 'style' and the pretense of formal simplicity."[5] Rembek attributed his predilection for military subjects to his family's long military tradition. He claimed a military lineage which, according to him, originated with his great-great-grandfather who took part in the French Revolution, continued with his great-grandfather who fought in the 1831 Polish insurrection, and was followed by his grandfather who fought in the insurrection of 1863.[6]

Attuned to the resurging hopes for Poland's independence during World War I, Rembek emulated the military model of his ancestors. In 1918 he quit high school, enlisted in the Polish army, and fought as an officer in the 1920 Polish-Bolshevik war. After his demobilization in the beginning of 1921, Rembek studied history and journalism at the University of Warsaw, where he took courses with the eminent Jewish historian Marceli Handelsman.[7] In 1928 Rembek traveled in Europe and stayed a few months in Algiers, where he worked as a draftsman in a local firm and served as a correspondent for the Polish press. Upon his return, he taught Polish literature and history in various high schools.

In 1935 Rembek married Maria Dehlen and, together with her two daughters from previous marriage, settled in Milanówek, a suburb of Grodzisko Mazowieckie in the vicinity of Warsaw. They stayed there throughout the war, enduring great deprivations. Rembek was constantly looking for work, holding temporary jobs as a teacher and a waiter, among others.

Under the communist regime, Rembek could not secure steady employment. For a time he worked in the Ministry of Culture, writing reviews for journals and magazines. From 1956 he lived in Warsaw, where he was employed in a public library. From 1956 to 1981 he was a member of PAX, an association for Catholics who cooperated with the communist regime, and wrote for its publications. In his final years, Rembek suffered from depression, which affected him throughout his life, and from lifelong alcoholism. He was hospitalized several times.

Rembek's literary work was practically forgotten under the communist regime. With the change of regime, he received considerable posthumous attention. In 1992, *A Ballad* was adapted into the film *Squadron* (*Szwadron*) directed by Juliusz Machulski. *The Sentence* was adapted into a radio program in 1997, and in 2000 Andrzej Wajda directed the novel's television production. Some of Rembek's manuscripts that were discovered in his papers were published in the 2004 collection *Churchill's*

Cigar (*Cygaro Churchilla*). Two of the stories in that volume feature Jewish characters. In "A Letter to Churchill" ("List do Churchilla"), a story which I will examine below, a hiding Jew undertakes the mission of a protector and defender of the Polish nation and its culture. In the other story, "In Trouble" ("W opałach"), a dashing young Jewish officer commands a successful underground rescue operation in occupied Warsaw. And in the story "Trees Blossom in Warsaw" ("W Warszawie kwitną drzewa"), Rembek remembers the heroism of the Jewish Ghetto fighters.[8]

Rembek's Diaries and Their Jewish Imprint

Rembek's personal writings consist of three diaristic texts: *Diaries: 1920 and Thereabouts* (*Dzienniki: Rok 1920 i okolice*), a record of the Polish-Bolshevik war and of the interwar period; "September" ("Wrzesień"), an account of his experience of the 1939 defeat; and the wartime chronicle *The Diary of the Occupation* (*Dziennik Okupacyjny*). These texts offer an insight into the historical turbulence of the writer's era as well as his evolving attitude toward the Jews. This attitude progresses from an ambivalent disposition toward Jews in the interwar years, to his determined dissociation from the Jews at the time of the German invasion, to his mental and emotional estrangement from the Jewish genocide at the time of the Occupation.

Diaries: 1920 and Thereabouts

Rembek's *Diaries: 1920 and Thereabouts*, published in 1997, covers the period of Rembek's military service as an officer in the 1920 campaign, his Warsaw studies, his constant search for work, and his efforts to write and publish. Following his demobilization, the entries become increasingly sporadic, frequently registering bouts of depression, illnesses, and various medical treatments. The diary concludes with the publication of *Revolver* in 1928, followed by a brief description of his stay in Algiers and a few entries from 1937.

 The first comment about Jews in *Diaries: 1920* sheds light on Rembek's formative ambivalence toward Jews. On November 29, 1918, Rembek notes, "Kozielewski [his teacher of Polish] spent the whole period talking about the Jews. He hates them very much and considers them the worst enemies of Poland. He convinced me to some extent, but not completely. I believe that no person, let alone a whole nation, can be entirely bad." Significantly, Kozielewski's anti-Jewish indoctrination took place only a few weeks after the declaration of the statehood of Poland on November 11. In view of the past 123 years of Poland's subjugation to the empires, which tore the country apart by inflicting endless suffering and disastrous devastation, Kozielewski's instigation of hatred for the Jewish minority as Poland's worst enemy was irrational. Perhaps even more disturbing was the impact of the teacher's anti-Semitic propaganda on his student. Even though Rembek knew that the aspersions the teacher cast on the Jews were motivated by hatred and that his slanderous generalizations about Jews would not have withstood any rational examination, he admitted to have found Kozielewski's view of the Jews plausible.

During his military service, however, Rembek forged a relationship with a Jew who was by no means an enemy. Bombardier Sztejnbach, a comrade-in-arms, came from his town, Piotrków, and had the same teachers in the school they both attended. When Sztejnbach died unexpectedly of typhoid fever, Rembek remembered him with sorrow, recalling their interesting conversations with affection and describing his funeral in detail. Later on, he commemorated Sztejnbach in *Revolver* by naming one of his Jewish characters after him. Nevertheless, the friendship with Sztejnbach did not change Rembek's mind about other Jews. Thus he had no qualms about bullying another Jewish soldier, Wasserman, for being shy and fearful, or derogatively describing an officer as "a Jew from Galicia, an exceptional coward, and a bluffer, who had no idea about artillery." His prejudice about Jews as cowardly soldiers emerges in his certainty that when this Jewish officer was released from the battery, he "gladly accepted" his dismissal.

Later on in civilian life, Rembek seemed more friendly toward Jews. In his diary entry of May 24, 1922, he mentioned that he did not like working for the newspaper *Kurier gnieznieński* because it sided too much with Endecja, then proudly noted having spoken twice in defense of a woman colleague who wrote an article which "presented a favorable view of the Jews."

Finally, in the single undated entry of 1923, Rembek presents a list of his friends in Warsaw, which included a Jew, Maksymilian Tejchner. Rembek's characterization of Tejchner highlights his divided mind about Jews:

> Tejchner, a Jew from Sosnowiec, has just passed his MD exams. He is a hard-working, highly cultured man, but so absorbed in gynecology that he sees everything through his professional perspective. His principles are completely materialistic, and therefore Bolshevik. He is a seducer of a demonic appearance. Apart from that, he possesses the flaws of his race: he is dirty, cowardly and greedy.

The incongruities of this portrait –Tejchner was a dirty doctor, a greedy Bolshevik, a cultured medical specialist, and a sex demon practicing gynecology — evince Rembek's thoughtless integration of the stereotypical view of the Jew. Yet his anti-Semitic prejudices notwithstanding, Rembek considered Tejchner a friend.

In the interwar *Diary:1920*, Rembek's ambivalent attitude to Jews shows that the negative stereotypes could be attenuated when social circumstances enabled friendly relationships. Such opportunities ceased with the German invasion, when the ruthlessness of the Germans' discriminatory policies against the Jews separated them from the Polish community.

"September"

"September"[9] is a detailed chronicle of the first month of the war and its multilayered traumatic experience. Responding to a misleading order from the retreating military leadership, Rembek, a reservist lieutenant, proudly led the men of Milanówek to take part in the defense of Warsaw. But rather than heroic exploits, "September" recounts Rembek's desperate attempts to join the fight, a search which ended in a distressing fiasco.

During the September campaign, Rembek wandered in Warsaw and its surroundings, often under heavy German bombardments, trying to enlist in a fighting unit. He was turned away at every step for lack of an official order of mobilization. His futile efforts made him see the absurdity of military bureaucracy at a time when the political and social institutions of the state had completely disintegrated. He gradually became aware of "the hopeless chaos dominating the highest echelons of our government."[10] At the same time, Rembek's happiness when he was allowed, by mistake, to join a military unit illuminates his unqualified self-identification as a Polish soldier ready to die for the motherland:

> Finally, I have joined the army. . . . All my troubles disappear . . . even the worries about my beloved family. I forget the exhaustion and the hunger. I am not afraid of anything. What are bombs and machine guns to me? Now I will not die helplessly; at worst, I will "fall". . . . I feel warm, safe, and happy. I am not alone.[11]

Army replaces family; in fact, it becomes his family, including him in a special, fearless comradeship of fighters, giving him a sense of dignity and imparting meaning to life and death. His subsequent dismissal from the unit made him feel lonely, abandoned, and disoriented like a child; it also afflicted him with an "unbearable sense of being useless."[12]

The traumatic realization of having lost his identity as a Polish officer was deepened by humiliating encounters with Jews. At one point, he was joined by some Jewish men who wanted to fight for Warsaw, but who quickly became scared of the bombardments. Feeling more secure with a veteran officer, they clung to him like helpless children. Rembek felt denigrated, and being in the company of cowardly Jews exacerbated his despair at having been excluded from the company of true fighters. When Rembek was later taken prisoner and forced to march with Jewish prisoners, he saw them as arrogant and unhelpful. Once in the prison camp, he recorded with contempt how the Jews were ingratiating themselves to the German enemies by offering them cigarettes, and how they were fighting unashamedly like wild animals for the bread the guards were throwing on the floor.[13]

At the same time, Rembek noticed that the Jewish prisoners were being singled out as the primary victims of the Polish soldiers in the group, who having joined forces with the German guards engaged in interrogating Jews, robbing them, and tormenting them sadistically. When one of the Polish soldiers spitefully declared Rembek a Jew, Rembek lost control: "'Damn it,' I screamed at him, 'Can you not distinguish between a Jew and a Pole!?'" He was not ashamed to observe that the vehemence of his response — which he presented in a direct quotation in order to stress the ferocity of his irritation — elicited startled glances from the people around.[14] Rembek evidently considered being associated with the persecuted and helpless Jews an unbearable insult. Ironically, the next morning, Rembek found himself equally helpless when pleading, in German, with a young German officer for permission to leave. Once the officer ascertained that he was not a Jew, Rembek was allowed to go home.

The demeaning and disturbing episode in the prison camp, which Rembek conflated with his humiliating experience with the Polish military, explains Rembek's unseemly outburst at the Polish soldier. In one sense, his denial of being a Jew reflected his fear of being included among people whose race made them helpless subjects of persecution. In another sense, the impetuousness of his shameless protest, which he showed no sign of regretting, expressed his shock at the transformation of his social position. It reflects his dismay at the swiftness with which the indignity of defeat erased his identity as an intrepid, valiant Polish soldier, rendering him indistinguishable from the passive, cowardly Jews. His subsequent pleading, in the enemy's language, with the all-powerful invader reinforced his shame and despair.

The debasement and self-debasement of Rembek's prison camp experience epitomized a long, humiliating sequence of events that made him feel ashamed, degraded, and defiled. Significantly, Rembek concludes his "September" travelogue with a symbolic act of self-cleansing. He reports that upon his return to Milanówek, "first of all, I bathed in the pond and then I washed and changed all my clothes, even the shoes, so that nothing would remind me of my three weeks of wandering."[15] But like Lady Macbeth, he could not remove with ablutions his disgraceful "spots" of shame, guilt, and regret.

Rembek's response to a prewar survey on the topic "Literature and the Soldier" ("Literatura a żołnierz") in November 1938 helps us understand his trauma during the September campaign. The survey, which was sent to a group of notable writers, was published in installments in the literary supplement of the daily *Armed Poland* (*Polska Zbrojna*) from October 1938 to January 1939. Thus, a few months before the war, Rembek claimed that

Polish society is military in the best sense of the word. Every Pole feels, first and foremost, that he is a soldier. . . . As represented by our Leader, our army plays a determining role in all aspects of our political, social, economic, and intellectual life. . . . Yet nobody can claim that the army has been politicized. Our officers are modest, well behaved, tactful, and knowledgeable. . . . Our soldiers are enthusiastic to serve and are ready for every sacrifice. Our reservists are dedicated to their units and would cheerfully answer every call. Should such a need arise, the whole nation will become a reliable, powerful, and forbidding instrument in the Leader's hands. Yet we are not aggressive toward our neighbors, and we do not cultivate any ideological, ethnic, or racist hatred. . . . In this sense, we can serve as an example to other nations, as we have many times in history.

Alluding to the great nineteenth-century romantic poets, he claimed, "We owe our exemplary character primarily to literature which instilled in us the virtue of chivalry and created a special type of a soldier—a fighter for a sacred matter—thus placing the military profession on a magnificent pedestal." He warned against "depriving the nation of its soldierly values. These values are personal and national honor, readiness for battle and sacrifices in the name of ideals, the ability to give up the individual self for the sake of collective action. . . . 'Duty' is the most beautiful term in our rich language." He went on to express his opposition to European pacifism which "was extinguished already in 1933 with the expulsion of Jews from Germany and their executions in the Soviet Union." "The pacifists," Rembek declared, "saved peace, but lost Czechoslovakia and influence in Central Europe, China, and the Mediterranean. At the same time, we [Poland] won security on the Lithuanian border, got Zaolzie, and doubled our [political] pertinence."

Rembek's ideological position was by no means unique; in fact, he was expressing the interwar Poland's triumphalist Weltanschauung. The national ethos of unconditional patriotism, uncommon chivalry, and superior moral standing that typified the ideological self-image of the country in the interwar period intensified even further with the increasing probability of a European war in the late 1930s. Exhilarated by the "miracles" of statehood in 1918 and the stunning victory over the Bolsheviks in 1920, the Poles were sure that their superior military force would easily fend off any potential attack.

Rembek's view of Poland as a nation of patriotic soldiers was confirmed in the 1939 siege of Warsaw, when "inspired by the Mayor . . . the citizens threw themselves into the defense, fighting the fires, supplying the defenders, tending the homeless, and burying the dead."[16] His belief in the country's invincibility, however, was destroyed by the ease and swiftness of the German invasion. This dismay was shared by all the diarists, who, stunned and dumbfounded, blamed themselves for their gullible trust in the baseless propaganda spawned by Poland's political and military authorities. Thus Zofia Nałkowska, having fled the capital in the first days of the war, described in her *Diary* the destruction of the countryside, the miserable throngs of refugees who were unprepared and deprived of everything, the columns of Polish soldiers taken prisoner, and the numerous German vehicles full of victorious German soldiers. She recorded her coachman's disbelief at the sight: "And they were telling us that those Germans had nothing to eat, yet how well they look. And they were saying that they had no gasoline, yet look how they travel." With boundless regret, outrage, and guilt, Nałkowska admitted thoughtlessness and self-deceit: "We let ourselves to be talked into keeping silent for the sake of the motherland; we allowed the cultivation of stupidity and catchwords, the cultivation of ignorance. . . . The reality was concealed from adults who were kept away from truth."[17]

At the time of the survey in 1938, however, Rembek's response represented the widespread conviction among the Poles of their exceptional moral and military virtues. Poland's superior moral standing in the Christian world was informed by the vision of romantic poets and thinkers, and predicated upon the chivalry and idealism of Polish military power. Whereas the European stance of appeasement proved detrimental to world politics, Poland had made many political gains in the international arena, while preventing any "cultivation of ideological, ethnic, and racist hatred" in Polish society. As Rembek saw it, European pacifist politics had already been proved wrong as early as 1933, with the persecutions of Jews in Germany and the Soviet Union. By referring to Jewish persecutions in other countries, Rembek alluded to Poland's tolerance toward its Jewish minority. To perpetuate the myth of Poland's moral superiority, Rembek chose to ignore Endecja's powerful fascist propaganda and its virulent anti-Semitic platform.

Such blatant misrepresentation of Poland's social, political, and moral reality on the eve of the war underscores Rembek's desire to hold on to the ethos of Poland as an exceptional nation-state of special, even sacred standing. Contrary to undeniable evidence, Rembek insisted that Poland's external politics of balancing power and peace went hand-in-hand with its internal politics of tolerance. Prophetic literature shaped the military and religious identity of the nation as a community of citizen-soldiers. Indeed, Rembek's vision of Poland echoed Mickiewicz's concept of the "democratic messianism of the nation," which imparted an obligation to shape Poland's political life "in accordance with the idea of Christian morality."[18] Rembek's studies of Polish history with Handelsman may have further reinforced this view. As Handelsman saw it, the Polish national narrative was modeled on Christ's story, whereby the country's long history of suffering and patriotic struggle, which culminated in the rebirth of the state, was seen as a reenactment of the Passion and Resurrection. Such a mythic perception of history determined the sacred obligation of the nation to spread the Christian message of moral redemption.[19] This self-perception as a nation bearing a sacred message pervaded the collective consciousness of the Poles.

The ideology of Poland's singular position among Christian nations collapsed in September 1939. Poland's unexpected defeat shattered the triumphalist self-image which had lulled the nation into delusions of military-religious superior uniqueness, and, as "September" shows, radically transformed patterns of behavior and social conventions among all segments of Polish society.

The Diary of the Occupation

Rembek's wartime diary starts in 1940, becomes less systematic in 1943, and ends abruptly with a single entry in January 1944.[20] It describes the hunger and cold, the unceasing terror of the Gestapo roundups, the deportations, attacks by the Polish underground on German positions and trains, and the Germans' retaliatory executions of civilians. The diary also records the constant menace of the gangs roaming in the forests surrounding Milanówek and Grodzisko, as well as the complex relationships of the Poles with the Volksdeutsche in the towns. Rembek observed the continuous flow of trains transporting the German and Italian soldiers eastward and westward during the German offensive against the Soviet Union, and scrupulously recorded even the most unreliable and unfounded rumors about military operations, defeats, and victories in Europe. He documented his trips to Warsaw where he taught in underground schools, met with other impoverished writers in the "Literary Kitchen" ("Kuchnia Literacka"), and occasionally tried to sell his family's remaining valuables to replenish their scarce supplies of food and coal. He also chronicled his attempts to alleviate the stress and monotony of the constant struggle for survival by visiting the local tavern to drink, share rumors, gossip, and speculate about the end of the war.

There are frequent references to Jews in the diary. Rembek conscientiously narrated everything he heard about the Jews as well as what he witnessed in Grodzisko and in the Warsaw Ghetto, through which he passed on the tram several times. He touches on the prohibitions imposed on the Jews in Grodzisko, their 1940 expulsion from Grodzisko and "resettlement" in the Warsaw Ghetto, the 1942 deportations followed by the liquidation of the Ghetto, the extermination of the Jews in Treblinka, and the executions of Jews who were found in hiding. Notably, however, even though Rembek continued recording intermittently in 1943, he did not mention the Ghetto Uprising.

The accounts of Poles and Jews interweave, presenting a composite picture of the unfolding Occupation and the evolving Jewish genocide from the perspective of a Polish observer. The editor of the *Diary of the Occupation* sees Rembek's text as a "chronicle" which is valuable "not only for historical reasons, but also because of its detailed depiction of the social reality in occupied Poland," which included the "horrific exodus of the Jews from Grodzisko and the strange silence in town that followed."[21] Indeed, the diligent documentation of events and situations, facts, rumors, and hearsay defines the diarist as a chronicler of the historical progression of the war in the context of a small town and, more specifically, of the socioeconomic experience of the Occupation. But Rembek's chronicling of the Polish experience of the Occupation was not limited to concrete, material hardships, such as roundups and food shortages; the diary also documented the exacerbating emotional toll of the situation. Not only did the diarist frequently complain of being depressed, but he also frequently observed the escalating depression of those around him. Horrifying events and ominous rumors intensified the pessimistic mood, and the anticipation of further disasters triggered anxieties, fears, and the general sense of hopelessness.

Thus on May 10, 1940, Rembek wrote, "All around a depressive mood dominates because of German roundups. Apparently, through the length and breadth of the territory of the *Generalgouvernement*, a hunt, unprecedented in history, for people of all positions, gender, and ages has been taking place." On June 11, 1940, he noted that upon reading in the newspaper about "Italy joining the war, I was so shaken that I become numb and went to see Saloni [a friend] who told me that he had got sick at the news." On June 20, 1940, he stated, "I feel terribly upset, as I am being constantly fed stories about arrests, tortures by the Gestapo, and mass executions in Radom, Firley, Starachowice, and in Tomaszów. . . . Because of my distress, I could not write." On September 18, 1940, he confessed, "I was tormented by gloomy thoughts, especially in connection with the war and with the poverty at home. . . . We hear close cannon and rifle fire. Most probably the military exercises of the armies which were moved to Milanówek and Grodzisko. . . . Nonetheless, my nerves were shot." On April 30, 1941, he observed, "General despondency about the nearing [German-Soviet] war and the expected resettlements of the Poles in the east." On June 16, 1941, he discussed the apocalypse with Julek, a friend who visited to help him overcome the depression. They reached the conclusion that the horrific events on earth corresponded to astrological/cosmic upheavals. On June 24, 1941, he noted, "Masses of rumors and hearsay. The saddest is that Warsaw is being bombed again by the Bolsheviks." On September 22, 1942, he documented, "Roundups take place even on the train. In Milanówek they took 28 people at night. A bleak mood dominates." And on November 4, 1942, he surrendered to hopelessness: "I feel so depressed that I can no longer cope with the diary. Anyway, everybody is depressed." Soon afterwards, the diary stopped in medias res. Despite his constant attempts to write, the circumstances of the Occupation paralyzed Rembek's capacity to chronicle; the prevailing hopelessness silenced the expression of mental and physical suffering.

The recurring observation of the collective mood of depression in Rembek's account indicates that mental affliction became a salient component of Rembek's perspective of the reality of the Occupation. It also highlights the importance that he attached to the social uniformity of this response. It might be that this emphasis on communal despondency reflected Rembek's need to rationalize or justify his own proclivity to depression. The constant reference to general depression might also have helped Rembek satisfy his compulsive need for a sense of belonging which was already evident in his desperate search for a military unit in "September."

While the inclusive motif of depression attests to Rembek's personal need to feel part of the collective, the association of the general mood of depression with atrocities beyond the confines of the small community of Milanówek-Grodzisko signals the tenacity of his ideological creed of Polish brotherly fellowship, illustrated by his postulation of one's absolute "duty" toward the collective over individual interests in the prewar survey. Reaffirmations of Polish patriotism emerge throughout the diary. Thus, upon visiting Warsaw on the first anniversary of the September campaign on August 31, 1940, Rembek noted that the "Tomb of the Unknown Soldier, with its extinguished torch, was drowning in white and red flowers. It was constantly surrounded by passersby. People were taking off their hats and a passing policeman saluted." A few weeks later, again in Warsaw, he observed "an optimistic mood despite the horrific persecutions. One is struck by the extraordinary solidarity of people from all walks of life." On November 11, 1941, he reported irritation ensuing from a meeting in Warsaw with his friend Jaś Waśniewski, "who has not changed his attitude of hatred toward the Polish people and of his pleasure in all its misfortunes." In the same entry he mentions "the great number of turtles drawn in chalk on fences and building walls"; the images were underground propaganda urging slow work in the service of the occupier. On April 1, 1942, he also observed that he saw anchors — the underground symbol of "Fighting Poland" — on walls throughout Warsaw.

In view of Rembek's continuing faith in the solidarity of the Polish nation, it is not surprising that he often attributed the depression he believed he shared with his townsfolk to news and rumors about the persecutions of Poles across the *Generalgouvernement*. The depressive mood that he detected in his community transcended local concerns, communicating a shared response to the Occupation among unrelated individuals who nonetheless cared about their fellow Poles. It is obvious that he wished to see himself on an empathic horizon which included all suffering fellow Poles. Rembek's emphasis on Polish solidarity under the Occupation applied exclusively to the Christian Poles. His compassionate response to the reported or rumored persecutions of Poles contrasted starkly with the hostile insensitivity he exhibited toward the persecutions of Jewish citizens. Neither the humiliating defeat followed by the terror of the Occupation nor the incomprehensible horror of the genocide seemed to have affected his formative views about the singularity of the Polish nation and the indelible otherness of the Jews. They represent the diarist's insistence on privileging the suffering of the ethnic Poles by diminishing, trivializing, and even doubting the severity of the Jews' suffering.

Recounting his meetings with Polish escapees from the Soviet Union, he constantly denounces Jewish collaboration with the Soviet victimization of the Poles. In this sense, Rembek echoes his teacher Kozielewski, who saw the Jews as Poland's worst enemies. On April 5, 1940, he records meeting a woman who escaped from the "horrific Bolshevik persecutions of the Poles." She informed him that "the Jews there beat up and torment the Poles for every uttered Polish word." On July 13, 1941, another woman who arrived from the Soviet Union recounted that "the Bolsheviks treated the Poles very badly. They were deporting the families who had relatives on our side to Siberia, and the Jews were assisting them enthusiastically." Clearly, the prewar slander of the Jews as *żydokomuna*, an anti-Semitic term for communist Jews which implied they were conspiring with the Bolsheviks against Poland, continued to be operative in wartime.

Some of Rembek's observations reiterate the negative prewar view of Jews as ubiquitous and intrusive. On March 18, 1940, he was pleasantly surprised by the scarcity of passengers on the tramway "perhaps because the Jews have been prohibited from using tramways and trains." And on April 18, 1940, he reported how he and his father availed themselves of "a decent sauna because the Jews were prohibited from using the public bath." The prewar propaganda about Jewish economic dominance reverberates in his observation of Grodzisko on February 27, 1941, after the deportation of the Jews: "The streets seem empty without Jews, but their absence has had a positive impact on the town's economic life. Anyway, a number of them have already returned on various pretexts."

Rembek's adverse wartime view of the Jews exceeds anti-Semitic pre-war stereotypes. His continual affirmation of the greater suffering of the Poles leaves no doubt about his bias. On April 15, 1940, he argued that the Jews were treated much better by the Germans than the Poles: "People talk about the terrible oppression of Poles in Piotrków and about the greatly improved lot of the Jews. They are not executed, nor are they sent to labor camps; they are free to move and trade. Apparently they were supplied with matza for the approaching holidays." On November 5–18, 1940, he claimed that the rumors about Jewish suffering were greatly exaggerated: "The Germans promised terrible repression of the Poles and the slaughter of all Jews. In the end, they just beat up a few Jews in the Ghetto." On March 28, 1941, he blamed the Jewish persecutions for aggravating the situation of the Poles: "Some gloomy rumors from Siedlce, where the army allegedly organized a Jewish pogrom, which involved burning houses. The gendarmes were called and of course they started persecuting the Polish population, arresting probably 160 people."

Even Rembek's reports of the 1942 deportations, the liquidation of the Ghetto, and the exterminations of the Jews in Treblinka demonstrate his consistent attempts to highlight Polish suffering and minimize the Jewish plight. "In Ursus, an escaping Pole shot two Germans. Massive executions are expected again," he writes on May 20, 1942, then offhandedly adds: "In the Ghetto, apparently eighty thousand Jews have died since February." A little later, he notes, "From about July 20, the Germans started the liquidation of the Ghetto. Apparently, 836 people were killed that day and among them all the Poles who happened to be there." He deplores the fact that nobody checked their identity cards (July 31, 1942). In the same entry, he attempts to diminish the totality of the Jewish destruction. "Presumably everyday they deport 600 Jews in sealed cars from the railway station. Nobody knows where they are taken. In the meantime, in Piotrków the ghetto has not yet been hermetically sealed, and in Częstochowa apparently they [the Jews] can move freely. At the same time, horrible terror against Poles rules there." On August 7, 1942, he recorded hearsay about the mass murder of the Jews, for which he obviously failed to find a comparative instance of Polish suffering: "It is rumored that in Treblinka, Warsaw Jews have supposedly been finished off. In cars strewn with burned lime and chlorine, they bring 150 at a time. The corpses are unloaded into enormous pits, dug out by excavators. Then everything is plowed over. In this way, supposedly, one hundred thousand have been already deported from Warsaw." Another rumored piece of information about the destruction of the Jews followed: "It is said that the small ghetto up to Chłodna [a street] has been completely cleansed" (August 14, 1942). Nonetheless, on September 16, 1942, he still questioned the totality of the Ghetto liquidation: "Presumably, Warsaw Ghetto has been finished off, though opinions differ. At any rate, I see Jewish labor units going to or coming back from work all the time." And on November 4, 1942, he was still trying to diminish the scope and the horror of the destruction: "There are supposedly thirty thousand Jews left in Warsaw. Apparently, a sealed train with Jews from Częstochowa went through Milanówek. They were offering 20 złoty for a glass of water but nobody responded for fear of the Germans. In Piotrków they somehow have not touched the Jews."

These references demonstrate Rembek's willful dissociation from the victims. I would argue that overlapping rhetorical strategies, such as juxtaposition, diversion, doubt, and detraction communicate Rembek's persistent efforts to belittle the plight of the Jews. His expression of anti-Semitic biases diverts attention from the present-day mass murder of the Jews to the biased prewar attitude toward Jews as enemies, intruders, and exploiters. Doubts about the scope of the extermination — some of the Jews return from the Warsaw Ghetto to Grodzisko, some of the ghettoes remain unsealed, some Jewish labor units are still seen in Warsaw even though the Ghetto was liquidated — diminish the totality of the liquidation. Finally, the insistence on the dubiousness of the information detracts from the authenticity of the Jewish destruction. Modifiers such as "allegedly, "presumably," and "it is said" qualified the destruction of the Jews as rumor, gossip, or hearsay. Such modifications question the factual accuracy of the report, thus diminishing its emotional impact.

The consistent depreciation of Jewish suffering aimed to highlight the generosity of spirit of the Polish people and their sense of fellowship and solidarity even as they were coping with terrible personal hardships. The frequency of the references to Jews, however, raises questions about the effectiveness of such a competitive strategy. As the discussion of Maria Dąbrowska has shown, the glorification of the Polish story of suffering was also possible by ignoring the Jewish story altogether.

The stunning reversal of Rembek's attitude to the Jews in his postwar fiction raises poignant questions about the generally indifferent and often hostile attitude toward the Jews in his wartime diary. It is possible that during wartime, Rembek's progressing depression, exacerbated by the unending war and its humiliations and deprivations, compelled him to maintain his idealized patriotic image of the Poles and their particular destiny. It seems, however, that once the war was over he could no longer suppress his consciousness of the moral disintegration of Polish society under the Occupation.

In order to appraise the radical shift in Rembek's views of the Jews and of the Poles in his postwar fiction, it is necessary to examine the prewar representations of Jews in his early novella, *Ripe Spikes*, and his first novel, *Revolver*. The juxtaposition of Rembek's pre- and postwar views of Polish Jews suggests that the reversal of his orientation evolved out of his wartime experience, and especially from his critical perception of the Polish experience at large, even though he refrained from — or was incapable of — admitting it on the pages of the *Diary of the Occupation*.

Interwar Fiction: The Polish Messianic Destiny and the Affirming Jewish Witness

The presence of Jews in Rembek's fiction is indispensable to the theological fundamentals of his nationalist ideology. A devout Catholic, Rembek adhered to the vision of Poland's Christ-like destiny propounded by the nineteenth-century romantic poets with its obligation to "spread the idea of Christian morality among the nations." As Rembek's prewar response to the survey "Literature and the Soldier" shows, in his ideological schema, the messianic promise of the Polish people was ineluctably intertwined with the national mission of chivalric military struggle for independence.

The Jews in Rembek's interwar literature are active participants in the military life of Poland while serving as witnesses who corroborate Poland's special religious destiny. As ardent patriots, these Jewish soldiers fight for the independence of Poland on a par with their Polish comrades; as Jews, however, they are unable to internalize the messianic destiny of the Christian Poles. The perennially frustrated yearnings of these Jews to integrate themselves into the Polish life of faith affirm the superior position of the Christian Poles.

In his interwar fiction, the novella *Ripe Spikes* and the novel *Revolver*, Polonized Jewish characters — both named Szwarc, both officer cadets — fight fearlessly in defense of independent Poland against the Bolshevik invader. Their patriotic valor demonstrates their indubitable love for the Polish motherland; it also signifies unfulfilled aspiration to find faith in Christian Providence. Having abandoned their Jewish origins — though, as the narrator makes clear, they still look and behave like (stereo)typical Jews — both Szwarcs are aware of their inability to embrace the Christian religion. Excluded from Christ's grace, they find themselves in an existential limbo. The theological no-man's-land of the Jewish soldiers is of fundamental importance to Rembek's national-religious Weltanschauung. Both the desire of these Jewish characters to access Christian faith and their consciousness of their exclusion testify to the messianic promise of the Poles, who in Rembek's view are all Christian soldiers.

The officer cadet Szwarc in *Ripe Spikes* was proud to serve in a fighting unit which "protected him from objections to his Jewish origins."[22] Wishing to prove his loyalty and courage, he undertakes to lead a dangerous military operation which he quickly realizes is doomed to failure. Indeed, the mission fails and Szwarc and his soldiers face inevitable death. What preoccupies Szwarc at this critical moment is his inability to find faith in divine providence: "Having rejected his native faith, he never stopped believing in God . . . and searched for the Truth to the point of exhaustion."[23] While he believes in the existence of God, he is unable to put trust in divine mercy and the grace of salvation. When the situation on the battlefield gets desperate, a mysterious figure wearing the badge of a paramedic appears. But the man does not attend to the maimed bodies; rather, in an awe-inspiring manner, he sets out to save souls by demanding that the dying soldiers confess their sins and affirm their faith in God. Finally, he engages in a theological exchange with Szwarc. In response to Szwarc's demand for evidence of a merciful God, the priest postulates that God has already showed his love and mercy when he revealed himself to humanity in the man Jesus. Eventually, just before his death, Szwarc relinquishes his doubts and experiences a redeeming epiphany: "Everything became clear and there was nothing more to discuss and he believed in everything this stranger was telling him." Having been granted the love of Jesus, he enters a state of grace and is baptized at the very moment of death: "Suddenly he saw the priest above him. He was moving his hand above him speaking something solemnly. The cadet officer felt drops of water on his face though the sky was brightening. . . . 'Are you Elijah?' he said with last breath."[24] Szwarc's acknowledgment of Elijah, to whom both Jesus and John the Baptist are compared in the New Testament, attests to his baptism. He remains on the battlefield, dead but with his eyes wide open to finally see the Truth.

Like his namesake in *Ripe Spikes*, Szwarc in *Revolver*, "even though from Jewish origins, had a hot and generous Polish heart."[25] Yet despite his loyalty and readiness for patriotic self-sacrifice, he was considered less chivalrous and more cowardly than a Polish-born soldier. Szwarc was quite aware of this biased opinion. "Had I been a Catholic Pole," he complains to his Polish friend, "I could have deserted from the army, instead of fighting so many years for Poland. I could have been the worst coward and crook and nobody would have blamed me for anything."[26] When his friend suggests conversion, Szwarc does not protest the unfairness of such a solution. Instead, he confesses a theological predicament:

> I would have liked to convert. Not in order to attain a higher social standing — it would have rather held me back socially — but only because I like your faith. I have studied it. But I cannot believe it. I lack something. Perhaps something your priests call sacrificial grace. . . . It is different to see the beauty of a faith from putting one's trust in it. In the meantime, I don't believe in anything. I am still searching.[27]

The Jew's perception of his origins as a fate which precludes grace affirms the Christian Pole's inherent state of grace, which enables faith in salvation that is unattainable to the Jews. In Rembek's theological view, the Jew may admire the beauty of Christian virtues and appreciate Christian dogma, but he cannot accept the Christian message, nor can he surrender to its attraction and make it internally his own. Szwarc's frustrated aspiration to espouse Catholicism serves to affirm the superiority of the Polish nation. From a theological perspective, the recognition of the Jew, the descendant of the first Chosen People, that he has no access to divine grace which now belongs to the Polish people is quintessential to the Polish messianic mission. Unlike the typical rationalization of anti-Semitism as a response to the Jewish refusal to receive Christ the Redeemer, in Rembek's fiction the Jew desires Christian redemption from which he is ineluctably excluded (at least in his lifetime, as is shown in the case of the first Szwarc). This is an important distinction, because it implies Rembek's consideration of the Jew, especially a Jewish soldier-patriot, as an indispensable witness validating the Poles' special Christian destiny.

Postwar Fiction: The Murder of the Witness and the Loss of the Mission

Rembek's postwar fiction treats Poland's special Christian destiny in a remarkably different way. Polish collaboration with the Germans in the extermination of the Jews revoked Poland's special destiny. The utter destruction of the affirming witnesses of Poland's messianic mission signified the collapse of the fundamental Christian ethics of love and mercy. Rembek's novel *The Sentence of Franciszek Kłos* and his short story "A Letter to Churchill" illustrate how the conduct of the Poles towards the Jews during the war reflected moral degeneration which unleashed indiscriminate violence of apocalyptic proportions. This regression to barbarism decreed the rule of satanic evil.

The epigraph and the closure of *The Sentence of Franciszek Kłos* construct a frame for the apocalyptic trajectory of the novel, which castigates the moral disintegration of Polish society under the Occupation. The epigraph quotes a famous hymn by the prominent Polish poet Jan Kasprowicz, "Holy God, Holy and Strong" ("Święty Boże, Święty Mocny"). The message of this hymn, diametrically opposed to the romantic poets' vision of Poland's messianic mission, attests to Rembek's ideological and theological transformation. The hymn depicts the ultimate human tragedy when, having descended into the abyss of despair, the human being renders homage to Satan, who has installed the sinister rule of death in the heavenly spheres. The horrifying climax of the hymn sets the mode of growing despair and hopelessness in Rembek's novel: "O Satan!? You grabbed the skeleton under its arm / and as high as its gleaming scythe / you grew up to the heavens / and there has been no thunder! / with inconsolable mourning / I kneel before you."[28] A heavenly "thunder" would have reaffirmed the presence of the divine justice. However, the reconfirmation of the implacable rule of satanic evil at the conclusion of Rembek's novel precludes redemption.

The story of Kłos's life and death in *The Sentence* is based on an authentic event that Rembek documented briefly in his diary on July 30, 1943: "In Grodzisko, policeman Kłos, who went especially after illegal traders, was shot." In his study of the case, however, Marek Nowakowski shows that the postwar memories of the Grodzisko residents were more foreboding. Decades later they testified that "Kłos, a Polish policeman (*granatowy policjant*), a collaborator and a serial murderer, was sentenced and executed by the Armia Krajowa."[29] The factual foundation of Rembek's novel highlights what his major critic, Mirosław Lalek, called the "originality of Rembek's text," namely, Rembek's thematic focus on the collaboration of the Poles with the occupier and on the general hostility of the Poles toward the Jews. As Lalek mentions, the question of collaboration was only raised openly "forty years after the publication of Rembek's work."[30] In this sense, Rembek's extreme criticism of the Poles as collaborators, persecutors of the Jews, or passive, acquiescing witnesses under the Occupation counteracts the trend of "heroic-martyrological tones focusing on Polish solidarity which typified postwar Polish literature."[31]

The novel's final episode shows the townpeople congregating in front of the coffin of the dead protagonist at a small chapel in the center of town. Rembek's nameless first-person narrator tells the story of Kłos, which takes place in the fictional town of Brodnia, of which the narrator is a resident. The narrator remembers the general mood of intense animosity for Kłos after his execution by members of the underground. "The hatred and the joy at the revenge were so powerful that they even overcame the dread of [German] reprisals."[32] The universally hateful attitude toward the dead man is clearly shown in the absence of any acknowledgment of Kłos's mother, who pushed her way through the crowd to the casket where she kept crying, "My son! My son! My son!" As the narrator remembers, the crowd let her pass, but remained unmoved by her grief. Nobody made an effort to comfort the bereaved mother; nobody extended sympathy. The novel's conclusion reiterates the apocalyptic message of the epigraph:

> We watched the scene [of the mother with the dead son] making neither sound nor movement. During all that time, none

of us uncovered our heads. All our faces were stiffened, all our hearts were locked: they were filled with the worst calamities that hubris and satanic malice managed to spread over our villainous and sad planet.[33]

To the narrator, the people in front of the casket were, metaphorically speaking, as rigid as the corpse lying before them. Their covered heads, blank faces, and hardened hearts communicated their emotional deadness.

However, the narrator is sincere enough to disclose that his identification of "hubris and satanic malice" in the community's response to Kłos's death emerged only at the time of the writing of the story. At the time of the event, he shared the other townspeople's perception of Kłos's violent death as the "victory of justice." He even saw Kłos's death as an omen of forthcoming redemption: "It finally appeared that our misery had reached its peak and that a tarrying God had resumed the rule of justice."[34] In retrospect, however, the unanimous approval of Kłos's death did not signal the restoration of God's just order; the malevolent sense of self-righteousness it engendered represented rather the victory of the satanic order of evil. The assessment of the execution of Kłos as a proof that justice has prevailed was necessary to displace a truth that nobody in the community, the narrator included, was ready to face: "Only today do I understand that reaction. In a situation of betrayal, the closer the relation between the traitor and the community, the greater the desire for revenge. Kłos was born, raised, and known in our town, thus we knew him too well not to hate him with deathly determination."[35]

Only years later did the narrator gain insight into the psychological mechanism that motivated such intense hatred of the dead man. Kłos's execution by the underground defined him as a traitor. The acknowledgment of the executed criminal as a native son and lifelong member of the community would have raised doubt about the town's solidarity with the underground, which might have brought forth further acts of revenge. At the same time, the recognition of having produced a traitor might have reflected badly on the town's self-image, confronting it with its accountability. Therefore the execution of Kłos incurred a compulsive need to erase all affinity with the dead man, whom everybody had known from infancy: "We looked at him with attentive curiosity the way one would look at a hunted predator, which was too dangerous to meet when it was alive."[36] The image of Kłos as an animal denied him his humanity, whereas his identification as a predator typified him as a menace which justified his execution.

The intense estrangement from Kłos after his death illuminated the extent of the townspeople's moral distortion. As long as Kłos was alive, his crimes were excused with a claim that "basically he was not a bad man. He killed [some people] because he was drunk and his other murders were provoked by Kranc, his evil spirit. Had it not been for vodka and bad company, he could have been an honest man and a loyal citizen."[37] Such exonerating rationalizations attest to the town's complicity with his heinous crimes. At a deeper level, the determined disavowal of Kłos signaled the residents' recognition of their culpability that they wished to erase. This view of the town's moral corruption foregrounds the narrator's concluding, sinister apocalyptic vision of a world dominated by forces of evil.

The construction of the final episode juxtaposes the narrator's real-time agreement with the collective with his postwar reassessment of this position. At the time, the narrator seemed to acquiesce willingly with the consensus. His postwar perspective, however, reveals another reason for his joining the collective, namely, the social pressure to conform. For instance, he realizes that at the funeral he refrained from taking off his hat in the chapel not only because at that time he was in agreement with the others that "respect for the sacredness of the place must give way to just contempt and rightful hatred," but also because "I was anxious not to be accused of any measure of solidarity with the dead renegade."[38] The narrator's postwar "I" realized that belonging to the wartime communal "we" required corroboration of the community's hypocrisy and willful self-deception.

This view of social consensus differs considerably from Rembek's diaristic view of Polish society. In the *Diary of the Occupation* Rembek stressed the unanimous public commemoration of the heroes of the September campaign, the spontaneous proliferation of the underground signs (anchors and turtles) urging sabotage and resistance, and even the widespread depression, which he attributed to the unbroken ties of empathic Polish fellowship. The discrepant views of Polish society in the diary and the novel beg the question of the relationship between

Rembek the diarist and his fictional first-person narrator in *The Sentence*. Does the novel represent an unsparingly self-critical reappraisal on Rembek's part of his attitudes and behavior during the war? More specifically, does the novel's twofold narrative, with its separate present and past trajectories, reflect a reassessment of Rembek's faith in Polish special destiny? I would argue that the significant discrepancy between Rembek the diarist's wartime opinion of the Poles and Jews and that of his postwar fictional first-person narrator enhances the plausibility of the supposition. In addition, while the multiple correspondences between the two texts support the argument of an autobiographical element in the novel, the diary's considerable omissions and evasions, especially in relation to the Jews, which subsequently emerge in the fiction, testify to the diarist's postwar self-revision. It seems to me that the enormous contrast between Rembek's ideological and theological position in his diary and in his postwar fiction tells a personal story which merits the trespassing of the generic boundaries of diary and fiction.

The closeness of the diary and the novel is stressed by the replication of a great number of geographic, sociological, and historical facts from the *Diary of the Occupation* in *The Sentence*. As mentioned, the novel was conceived out of the recording of Kłos's violent death in the diary. Like the authentic Milanówek-Grodzisko, the fictional Brodnia was located in the vicinity of Warsaw where, like Rembek the diarist, his fictional narrator visited frequently. Brodnia's tavern was a meeting place of notables who, like in the authentic Dąbkowski tavern in Grodzisko, gathered there to exchange rumors, trade gossip, and engage in heavy drinking. Furthermore, the professional identification of the narrator as a mason and a historian who lectured on history to the reservists' club resonates with Rembek's multiple occupations, such as draftsman, post office clerk, history teacher, and reservist officer.

The most relevant evidence, however, of Rembek's desire for a critical reassessment of Polish society, himself included, does not lie in the obvious situational or biographical correspondences between the two texts. Rather, it is the importance of the 1943 liquidation of the Ghetto in the novel, an event which is not even mentioned in the diary. Indeed, the plot of *The Sentence* starts in April with the observation that with the liquidation of the Ghetto, many Jewish fugitives escaped to the countryside where they hoped to find safe hiding places. The novel ends with the execution of Kłos by the underground. Kłos was condemned to death for cooperation with the German authorities, which included confiscation of food owned by the Poles, sending the Poles to labor camps, and extorting the Polish population. The crime that sealed his fate was killing a member of the underground military organization.[39] Significantly, Kłos's horrible murders of Jews, which the narrator describes in great detail as proofs of Kłos's growing bestiality, were not mentioned in Kłos's indictment by the underground. Clearly, the underground did not consider such murders to be crimes.

With respect to the Jews, therefore, the underground was separated by only one degree from the German position. While the murder of Jews was officially sanctioned by the Germans, it was not considered a punishable deed by the underground. As the narrator recalls, "In connection with the liquidation of the Ghetto . . . a new dictate was issued by the *Generalgouvernement*," which Alojzy Schwick, a Volksdeutscher and the commandant of the police station in Brodnia, delivered in a special speech. "Jews should be killed wherever found. It is forbidden to shoot Poles."[40] In fact, as the narrator shows repeatedly, the topic of hidden Jews dominated the conversations in the tavern. When Schwick said to Chomiński, the owner of the tavern, "We know that tens and hundreds of thousands of Jews are hiding among the Poles," the man hastened to assure him, "We do not hide Jews." Schweik, however, was not satisfied. "You should cooperate with us in finishing them off. It is for your own good," he told the tavern's Polish patrons.[41] Even among themselves, these men never expressed any objections to the order to kill Jews, but they were intrigued by the German prohibition on killing Poles who were hiding the fugitives. Mayor Korkowski sought reasons for such leniency in the German defeats on the eastern front.[42] In contrast, headmaster Rządek detected more complex reasons: "Since the Germans are busy liquidating the Jews, they want to pit them and the Poles against each other. Then it will be our turn." But he agreed with Schwick that "though the Ghetto was liquidated, tens and hundreds Jews are hiding with Poles," and remarked that "all the same, they murder so many of the Jews hiding in Brodnia and the vicinity."[43]

Indeed, while some Poles were trying to rescue Jews, others took full advantage of the German injunction to find and liquidate the fugitives. For Kłos and his fellow policeman, Volksdeutscher Kranc, searching for Jews became an exciting game and a favorite pastime. The narrator tells how "every morning they would drink, go to the station, and then embark on their hunting expeditions which consisted in catching and murdering Jews, many of whom, as the headmaster Rządek stated correctly, were hiding in Brodnia and its surroundings."[44] Kłos and Kranc were in competition for the number of Jews each of them managed to murder. When Kłos with manic zeal shot a Jewish family of five at point blank, Kranc half-jokingly complained that Kłos had deprived him from reaching his goal of fifty, proudly exposing the forty-nine marks on his gun representing the number of Jews he had shot.[45]

In contrast with Rembek the diarist, who evaded the issue of hiding Jews altogether, the narrator of *The Sentence* expressed concern about the safety of the fugitive Jews, noting their lack of caution: "Once they recovered from the horrors of the Ghetto, they were wandering everywhere attracting bands of spies, Volksdeutsche, and blackmailers." He was aware that the Jews faced danger not only from marginal groups, but also from "denunciations of the neighbors [of the rescuers], especially women, usually old women."[46] But as the narrative shows, the proclivity to blackmail and denounce hiding Jews was not the purview of old women; it was common and widely spread in Brodnia. This becomes clear in the episode of a church service conducted by Father Międlik who, as the narrator reports, was a priest of "great righteousness and even saintliness," but ironically "was not a handsome man, and his big, fleshy lips and a huge crooked nose made him look like a Jew. Because of that he had some unpleasant encounters with the Germans."[47] Despite his "bad looks" and the suspicion about his origins, Father Międlik, with brave disregard for spies, denunciators, and collaborators, publicly pleaded with his parishioners to consider the fate of the Jews with Christian mercy and compassion.

As is the custom, after the service on the first Friday of September, the priest said the litany of the Sacred Heart of Jesus, a prayer for the redemption of the sinners: "Many do not know You at all, many turned their backs on You, contemptuous of your commandments." He then begged for the deliverance of the prodigal sons from sin: "Make them return speedily to their parental home. Make all those who still wander in the darkness of paganism recognize Your light." Then, unexpectedly, the priest continued with a prayer for the Jews: "And look with a pitiful eye at the sons of the nation which used to be Your beloved people. May they also partake in Your merciful spring of redemption and of life."[48]

Implicitly, the prayer for the Jews exposes the parishioners' regression to dark paganism in their refusal to fulfill the Christian obligation of compassion for the Jews who, as the priest reminds his congregation, were God's chosen people. Father Międlik's prayer implies that the congregation has deteriorated to paganism, because it had abandoned the light of God's truth. Redemption lies in "knowing God," and the understanding that His "parental home," which is illuminated with the light of truth, can be reentered upon the recognition of the Jews as God's people. The priest's public intercession for the Jews in front of the church full of parishioners attests to his courage to defy the German injuction; it also attest to the prevalent anti-Jewish behavior of the town he knew and which he set out to mend.

Indeed, Kłos, who is present at the service, is dumbfounded. "How is it possible?" he asks himself. "The priest is praying for Jews? At this time? Is the Catholic Church in favor of Jews?"[49] His questions were answered when Kłos made his confession to the priest. Kłos defended his actions by repeating the German dictate: "I generally killed only Jews." Father Międlik tells Kłos that the Christian ethics of mercy and love evolved from the commandments given to the Jews. "God Almighty said, 'Do not kill.' Not even your enemy. And our Master, Jesus Christ added, 'Love your enemies. Do good deeds for those who hate you.'" He does not leave Kłos in any doubt about right and wrong. "Thus, even if you consider Jews your enemies, as a Christian you are forbidden to cause them any harm." He counters Kłos's animosity for Jews by reminding him that "Jesus himself was of this nation, as well as the Holy Mother and all the apostles. . . . Jesus loved his people as a human being. Haven't you heard how he wept over Jerusalem prophesying her fall?"[50]

Father Międlik makes heroic attempts to save Christian humanism by restoring the awareness of Christian affinity with the Jews. For the sake of its Christian identity, the congregation must extend compassion and protection to the Jews. His teaching that Jesus was a Jew and a human being who loved and was compassionate toward his fellow Jews was meant to reinstate a consciousness of the sanctity of human life. In this way, he attempted to rescue his flock from regression into the pre-

Revelation era of "dark paganism" which did not know the commandment not to kill. The survival of Christianity, as he saw it, depended on the attitude toward the Jews who were declared non-human targets of extermination. By advocating for humane treatment of the Jews, the priest waged a battle for the Christian soul of the Polish people.

The priest's battle for humanism was lost on the bloody battlefield of Brodnia's marketplace. The execution of eighty Poles in retaliation for an underground act of sabotage was interrupted by a retaliatory attack by the underground forces. In the fierce, indiscriminate killing that ensued, Kłos took the side of the Germans, and engaged, as if amok, in shooting the helpless, panicking Polish men, women, and children, as well as the underground fighters. The priest's failure to prevent humanity's regression to barbarism is symbolized by the statue of the Holy Mother and the ruins of the Goldman building, which face each other across the savagery in the marketplace. The tragic incongruity of the Holy Mother benevolently smiling on a massacre highlights humanity's abysmal moral fall. Meanwhile, the ruins of a building which once belonged to a murdered Jew have been turned into an execution place of Poles and Jews alike. The license to kill one group of people — the Jews — unleashed the murderous instincts of humanity at large. Christian mercy and compassion were replaced with unrestrained hatred and malicious pride, which pronounced the implacable rule of evil.

Ironically, the shade of redemption that may be detected in *The Sentence* lies in the novel's concluding and conclusive declaration of the absence of redemption. The narrator's announcement of the victory of satanic evil shows a rebirth of the moral capability to distinguish between good and evil. He submits to the satanic dominion with "inconsolable mourning." The narrator's capacity for both retrospection and introspection allows him to examine himself and the fallen world through the lens of defeated humanism.

While the narrator's moralist voice in *The Sentence* invokes the ethical norms of the lost world of humanistic civilization, the construction of the narrator in the short story "A Letter to Churchill" precludes such moral partiality. Władek, the first-person narrator, positions himself as an observer and a transcriber, and this claim to objectivity is reinforced by the subtitle "A True Story." In fact, the story consists of Władek's accounts of two seemingly unrelated episodes.

The first episode, which Władek narrates as an observer, takes place in occupied Warsaw, when the underground "started settling accounts with the German police and administration."[51] Władek describes the lawlessness, terror, and emotional obtuseness of Warsaw. Having arrived in the city to meet his cousin Zygmunt, he finds the streets empty for fear of violence, while random shots punctuate the silence, causing the few passersby to flee. During his short walk, Władek actually witnesses the shooting of a German officer in broad daylight by four people who have chased the officer in a car. The body was left in the street. Then, instead of the expected meeting with Zygmunt, Władek finds his cousin's body at a hospital morgue full of people searching for their relatives in the piles of murdered, massacred, desecrated corpses. Zygmunt's funeral is hastily performed, with perfunctory attendance of family and friends who pay little attention to the service while discussing business matters and other mundane affairs. Zygmunt's violent death remains unexplained.

The second part of "A Letter to Churchill" is Władek's transcription of a story he was told after the funeral. The storyteller, Artur Szmeller, most probably a Volksdeutscher, was Zygmunt's friend as well as Władek's former comrade-in-arms in the Polish-Bolshevik war and later his roommate in the academic dorm in Warsaw — all implicit references to Rembek's interwar biography. Szmeller became an SS officer, who came back from the eastern front. Fond of jokes, Szmeller eagerly tells Władek about a funny incident that happened to him and his two German comrades-in-arms, Kurt Walz and Wenzel Claus.

Claus's figure and demeanor bore an uncommon resemblance to Winston Churchill. While enjoying themselves in Stanisławów during the liquidation of the Ghetto, the officers happened to find a letter addressed to Churchill from one Ludwig Ajzen. Ajzen, a Jew, wrote to Churchill from his hiding place, begging the British prime minister to save his family. Having decided to play a trick on the obviously insane Jew, the group arrived at the hideout, where Claus impersonated Churchill. The officers sadistically terrorized Ajzen's horrified wife and daughters and their distraught Polish women-rescuers, while Ajzen, who believed that Churchill had indeed come to their rescue, was overcome with joy. So was Szmeller, who recalled feeling "simple human joy — *Schadenfreude* — especially since it involved the Jewish enemy and since the Polish women should have known better and could have made money doing some trading rather than taking money from Jews." Later he mentioned that the rescuers were even more stupid than he had imagined because they were hiding the Jews altruistically, out of friendship.[52]

Preparing for the departure for London, Ajzen goes to dig up a jewelry box in the garden. There Claus is attacked by Ukrainian policemen, who beat him up and want to kill him. Ajzen gives them the box and saves Claus's life. Subsequently, as Szmeller recalled, he addressed Claus:

> Mr. Churchill — he sobbed, stroking his hands — I saved you. I committed embezzlement because for your life I gave away the jewels and the gold that my clients deposited with me, but, so what, your life is worth more than my good reputation. Had you been killed, the whole Polish nation would have perished, Polish culture would have been lost, everything in the world that is forthright and noble would have been destroyed.[53]

When Ajzen follows the officers to their apartment, Claus shoots him on the staircase because, as he explains, he "deserves some satisfaction for the beating by the Ukrainians." The story ends with Szmeller's final recollection: "I said to Claus, 'Do you know the funniest thing about this hullaballoo? That you with your own hands killed the benefactor who actually saved your life.' 'Ha, ha, ha' — we all roared with laughter."[54]

In a sense, Władek's transcription of Szmeller's story is a representation of the world dominated by satanic hubris and malice that came into being in *The Sentence*. It is a world whose evil rulers are automatons programmed to destroy "with joy" all that is "forthright and noble." Modeled loosely on the passion of Christ, with the poignant absence of the resurrection, this story illustrates a state of irredeemable barbarism which proclaimed the negation of Christian ideals. The Jew, transformed from victim who begged for rescue into a Christ-like savior, sacrifices himself for the Polish nation and Polish culture, which he sees as the epitome of all that is good and honorable in the world. Ironically, Ajzen, a Jew condemned to extermination, enacts the messianic destiny of the Polish people, while the roaring laughter of his murderers, which echo the mockery of Jesus on the cross, declares the annihilation of the very idea of redemption. In this sense, the "funny" incident that Szmeller tells the narrator is also a story of the triumph of the German ideology of murder over the Christian dogma of life and love. In another, perhaps even more ominous sense, Szmeller's compulsive need to tell this horrific story to his former Polish comrade, with whom he fought for the redemption of the Polish nation, reflects a degree of mindless hubris and self-unconsciousness that results in the impossibility of redemption.

The narrator/transcriber's conspicuous silence seems to reinforce the hopelessness that Szmeller's story transmits. In this sense, the two parts of "A Letter to Churchill" complement each other. The objective mode of the narration communicates the terror that rules over occupied Warsaw and the last Jews of Stanisławów. Even though the former is dominated to a large degree by the underground and the latter by the German army, both worlds display a reality of unconscionable brutality and a lack of awareness of the moral fall of humanity. The story's two episodes are thus connected by the motif of the obliteration of respect for human life and death. The sanctity attributed to the human spirit and body has been devalued. Indeed, in a world where violence, indifference, and Schadenfreude have become the norms, madness takes on a new meaning. The Jew in the story, who, like his Polish rescuers, continues to operate according to the old world's norms of love, compassion, and care for another has become an anachronism, a relic ironically governed by the Christian ethics that the Polish nation was meant to emulate. From this perspective, Ajzen's "insanity" is the inability to comprehend the horrific parody of the "Churchillian" enlightened world, where the values of justice, love, and compassion have been replaced with a reality of murder and terror devoid of the consciousness of sin.

Rembek's witnessing of the Jewish genocide displays considerable complexity. The vacillations between sympathetic views of the Jews in his literary works and the anti-Semitic attitude of his personal recordings that peaks in the *Diary of the Occupation* are hard to reconcile. We can only conjecture that the Occupation presented the writer with ideological difficulties that he found impossible to face, let alone resolve. As his thinly disguised autobiographical fiction after the war demonstrates, his patriotic nationalistic conviction of Poland's military and moral superiority fell apart during the Occupation.

Dąbrowska, whose formative ideological positions about Polish superiority and stereotypical anti-Jewish views resembled those of Rembek, did not adjust her attitude towards the Jews as a result of the Holocaust. Her postwar resentment and envy toward the remnants of Polish Jews reflected to a large extent her prewar prejudices. In this sense, Dąbrowska's lack of compassion for the Jews at the time of their destruction represented her authentic response to the Holocaust.

Rembek's postwar fiction, however, sheds a different light on his wartime attitude. The tenor of these writings permits us to understand the contrasting themes in the diaries of identification with Polish suffering and of detachment from the plight of the Jews as a psychological stratagem to conceal a third, most problematic narrative that indelibly linked the Poles and the Jews, the hunter and the hunted. This narrative was the story of the Poles' attitude toward the extermination of the Jews, which, as Rembek's narrative discrepancies suggest, he could only face after the war, and even then tell only through the lens of fiction. It is perhaps possible to argue that the need for emotional and ideological defenses under the Occupation compelled Rembek to avoid facing the pernicious Polish attitude toward the Jews and to cling to the prewar ethos of Polish Christian singularity. This conjecture gains support from the drastic ideological transformations that emerge in Rembek's postwar fiction. While Polish society's descent to the darkness of paganism, powerfully deplored by Father Międlik in *The Sentence*, exacted the loss of its stature as a Christian moral beacon to the nations, the ideals of mercy and love that they betrayed did not disintegrate. As the story of Ajzen demonstrates, the persecutions of the Jews by Christians restored the safekeeping of the commandments and the human values of the Revelation to the Jewish people. In view of Rembek's fundamental belief in Poland and its messianic calling, the radical transformation of his theological-ethical Weltanschauung reveals an uncommon capacity for self-examination; it also illuminates the depth and the complexity of the ethical predicaments that the event of the Holocaust posited for humanity.

To Witness the Experience
of Witnessing

The preoccupation with the Holocaust has not abated. The publication of Saul Friedlander's seminal 1996 volume, *Probing the Limits of Representation*, which examined both scholarly and artistic interest in the Holocaust since the 1970s, did not by any means constitute a conclusive appraisal of the phenomenon.[1] Despite Lyotard's warning that "no one can — by writing, by painting, by anything — pretend to be witness and truthful reporter [of the Holocaust] without being rendered guilty of falsification and imposture through this very pretension,"[2] writers, essayists, artists, filmmakers, playwrights, video and television producers, and others have continued to create representations of the Holocaust. The ethicists among the growing numbers of Holocaust scholars have pondered the paradox of the proliferation of imaginative representations of the "incomprehensible" and therefore "indescribable" experience of Holocaust suffering.

For instance, James Hatley argues that the obsessive response to the victims' plight is rooted in the fact that the harm caused by the Holocaust has been "irreparable." Since the trauma of the Holocaust persists, it impels the post-Holocaust witness to pay constant attention to the story communicated by the victim-witness. The horrific and irremediable aberration of basic human ethics "does not allow life to return to normal," and thus "the witness is called to insomnia," which precludes healing and closure. Thus, Hatley's witness, who "inherited the Shoah only in its aftermath," remains alert to "the incessant call to righteousness."[3] From Hatley's perspective, our persistent attempts to reconstruct the Holocaust experience attest to a forever-unfulfilled desire to repair the irreparable ethical wound that the Holocaust inflicted on humanity at large.

Gary Weissman attributes the continuing interest in the Holocaust to its elusiveness. Because "we cannot experience or witness the reality of the Holocaust itself . . . we are still searching for ways to *feel closer* to that horror." The inaccessibility of the event creates a lacuna which produces the fantasy of the "nonwitnesses" who did not experience the Holocaust to "feel the horror" of the victim-witness. Weissman questions whether the artistic representations of the Holocaust which intend to confront the nonwitness with the horror of the event lead to understanding of the event. He also doubts the effectiveness of personalizing the horror, as practiced in the U.S. Holocaust Museum, whereby the nonwitness takes on the identity of the witness-victim. As he sees it, the obsession with representations of the Holocaust demonstrates an effort to reduce the experience of the Jewish genocide to "shapes and sizes we can cope with."[4]

These discourses show that consciousness of the Holocaust has produced a prolonged psychological and moral crisis, which has ineluctably affected the post-Holocaust generation. The desire to alleviate the inherited trauma has engendered a desire to relive vicariously the traumatic experience of the victim. The impossibility of entering the "planet of death" of the Holocaust victim is doomed to failure and, as Lyotard claims, has resulted in falsified reconstructions of the world of the Final Solution.

The enormity of the genocidal crime certainly explains the fixation of "nonwitnesses," the inheritors of such a horrific legacy, on the source of the trauma, namely, the world of the victim. *The Ethics of Witnessing* submits that a possibility for approaching the world of the Holocaust lies in the perspective of the non-victim witnesses. These individuals watched the Jewish destruction in its real "sizes and shapes" and were confronted then and there with its ethical ramifications, which they recorded in their wartime diaries. Presented in their private life stories, the diarists' direct, often spontaneous insights with regard to the Holocaust allow us to see not only the world of the Holocaust through the eyes of another, but also another's response to the horror. In other words, the diaries make it possible for the post-Holocaust nonwitness to approach the second degree of separation, namely, to engage vicariously in the experience of the non-victim witness. These unmediated testimonies also make it possible to follow the psychological-ethical impact of the traumatic event on the witnesses' mindset and worldview.

Here a caveat is in order. I am fully aware of the teleological structure of my subjective incursion into the diarists' minds. The narratives that I have constructed out of their diaristic notations and entries cannot possibly represent conclusive or definitive interpretations of the diarists' psyches and personalities; such a claim would be presumptuous and obviously untrue. The examinations of the diaries in this book represent merely my naturally limited perception of the texts. I would argue, however, that the advantages of my analytical attempts to understand the diarists' minds, Weltanschauungs, and motivations outweigh the limitations of my subjective readings of their personal texts.

To begin with, the diarists, with the exception of Rembek, planned the publication of their diaries; in fact, as I have shown in the book, they were determined to have them published, and some of them engaged in editing the diaries for publication even before the end of the war. As experienced writers, they must have been conscious of the fact that once their private life stories entered the public sphere, they would be open to their readers' appraisal, interpretation, and criticism. Their eagerness to publish their subjective perceptions of the war and their responses to the brutality of the German occupier, which culminated in the extermination of the Jews, attest to the importance that they attached to their experience and to the message for posterity that it contained.

Indeed, as this study has shown, the direct testimonies of the Holocaust horror in the diaries underline the trauma that motivates today's preoccupation with the elusiveness of the Holocaust experience, and its irreparable consequences. To paraphrase Czesław Miłosz, as "Christians who looked at the Ghetto," the diarists were separated from the burning Jewish people not only by the Ghetto walls; they also acknowledged their lack of imagination and even stamina to grasp the relentlessly evolving genocide that they were witnessing directly. In this sense, the real-time non-victim witnesses established a negative empathic horizon with today's nonwitnesses: both groups lack the imagination to comprehend the victim's experience; neither is capable of contending with the ethical crisis that the reality of the Jewish experience represented. This failure to establish an empathic horizon with the victim constitutes an empathic horizon which connects the experience of the Holocaust and post-Holocaust witnesses.

But, as this book shows, each of the diarists failed to connect with the victim in a different manner. The spectrum of the struggles with the reality of the Holocaust that the five diaries represent provides an invaluable lesson about the nature of witnessing. The variety of responses to Jewish suffering—from Dąbrowska's deliberate dismissal, to Rembek's willful belittling which he corrected in his postwar *Sentence,* to Iwaszkiewicz's altruistic dedication and humanistic despair, to Wyleżyńska's altruism as moral self-correction, and to Nałkowska's traumatic silence which she broke in her postwar *Medallions*—teach the complexity and the variability of responses to another's plight. The subjective truthfulness of each of these diaristic responses raises our consciousness of the tenuousness of the ethics of witnessing. In this sense, this study of the diaries suggests that an orientation shift is necessary for nonwitnessing seekers of the Holocaust experience of suffering. It also brings to the fore the injunction of moral self-examination on the present-day witness of present-day atrocities. An examination of the diaries impressed on us the witness's obligation of constant self-evaluation when confronted with the ongoing suffering and violence of today's world.

Chapter 1

1. Iwaszkiewicz, *Notatki*, 85. Unless otherwise stated, all the translations from the diaries and other Polish texts quoted throughout this book are mine.

Roman Kramsztyk was a painter and graphic artist; Aleksander Landau, a musician; Paweł Hetz, a poet, essayist, translator, and editor; Józef Rajnfeld, a painter and draftsman.

2. The liquidation of the Ghetto was also the subject of Jerzy Andrzejewski's long story "Holy Week" ("Wielki Tydzień"), originally written in 1943, then rewritten and published in 1945 (Andrzejewski, *Noc*, 65–211). Other contemporaneous descriptions of the Warsaw Ghetto destruction include Szymanowski, "Likwidacja getta"; Kann, "Na oczach świata"; and Sarnecki, "Z otchłani."

3. For the intersubjective aspect of empathy, see Zahavi, "Beyond Empathy."

4. "To be sure, Hitler's plans for Poland stipulated the complete destruction and dismemberment of the Polish state, the annihilation of the Polish intellectual and political elite, and, in turn, the colonization of Polish population" (Finder and Prusin, "Jewish Collaborators," 123). See also Grabowski, *Szantażowanie Żydów*, 97–123; and Biskupski, *The History of Poland*, 97–123.

5. Poles received the highest number of Righteous Among the Nations medals, a special recognition of the State of Israel of the Gentiles who rescued Jews. Baum, "Projekt 'Światła w ciemności," 36, quotes courageous Poles who explain their altruism by claiming "W nieszczęściu trzeba podać rękę. Ktokolwiek nie przyjdzie" ("In unhappiness one needs to extend one's hand. No matter who comes"). Another source of help and rescue was Żegota (Rada Pomocy Żydom; The Polish Council to Aid Jews), a branch of the underground organization Armia Krajowa [Home Army]. Żegota was co-founded by Zofia Kossak-Szczucka in 1942.

6. Jan Gross claims: "[The Holocaust] took place in full daylight and was witnessed by millions of Poles who . . . by and large did little to impede it, to slow it down, or to interfere with it." Quoted in Finder, "Introduction," 7.

7. Engelking-Boni, "Psychological Distance," 52.

8. Finder, "Introduction," 8.

9. Ringelblum, *Polish-Jewish Relations*, 6–7.

10. For the English translation of the poem, see Polonsky, *"My Brother's Keeper?"* 49–50. For a historical survey of the event, see Szarota, *Karuzela na placu Krasińskich*.

11. Karski, "An Early Account of Polish Jewry Under Nazi and Soviet Occupation," 265, 269.

12. An English translation appears in Polonsky, *"My Brother's Keeper?"* 34–53. The article was first published in *Tygodnik Powszechny* on January 11, 1987.

13. Miłosz's own English translation of "A Poor Christian Looks at the Ghetto" appears in Polonsky, *"My Brother's Keeper?"* 51.

14. I realize that the concept of nationalism exceeds the component of ethnicity, as defined by cultural features such as language and religion. The distinction between ethnicity and race also presents problems, as Thomas Hylland Eriksen claims: "Ethnicity can assume many forms, and since ethnic ideologies tend to stress common descent among their members, the distinction between race and ethnicity is a problematic one" (*Ethnicity and Nationalism*, 5). This is certainly true of the Polish Jews in the context of Polish nationalism, in which prejudicial perception blended the cultural and religious differentness of the Jews with the supposed distinctness of the hereditary characteristics of their "race." My use of the terms "nationalism" and "ethnicity," here and throughout, with relation to Polish-Gentile and Polish-Jewish interactions includes both the components of religion and racism.

15. See Polonsky, "The Fate of the European Jews, 1939–1945," 198.

16. See, among others, Engel, "On Reconciling the Histories of Two Chosen People"; Polonsky, "The Fate of the European Jews"; Głowacka and Żylinska, *Imaginary Neighbors*; Steinlauf, *Bondage to the Dead*; Zimmerman, *Contested Memories*; and Cherry and Orla-Bukowska, *Rethinking Poles and Jews*. See the responses to Błoński's article in Polonsky, "*My Brother's Keeper?*" and Steinlauf, *Bondage to the Dead*, especially 89–121 ("Memory Reconstructed"). See also Polak and Polak, *Porzucić etyczną arogancję*, especially 223–35.

17. Shallcross, *The Holocaust Object*, 84, claims that "since ashes preserve the individual incarnation and markings [circumcision], their undeadeness and in-betweenness are understated, to say the least. Ashes are not the substance in which life still lingers, but the agency from which individual life resurrects itself in an unorthodox way." In contrast, I would suggest that since the poem is told from the perspective of the "poor Christian," he understands the uncircumcised differentness of his "broken body," while, ironically, the ashes of the burned Jews can be distinguished by the differences in their "luminous vapor." For interpretations of the destruction and the "guardian-mole," and the speaker's guilt, see also Nathan and Quinn, *The Poet's Work*, 17–18, and Fiut, *Moment wieczny*, 71, 73–74.

18. He might be referring to Darwin's *The Origin of Species*, but it seems to me that the biblical references — patriarch, Jew of the New Testament, the Second Coming — point to the hierarchy of species in the story of Creation.

19. By referring to Jesus (of Nazareth) rather than Christ, Miłosz places the Christian Messiah in the Hebrew tradition. "Jesus" is the translation of Joshua, which means salvation, thus emphasizing the humanity of the Messiah.

20. Among many cases of Poles helping Jews despite their anti-Semitic biases, the most famous example represents Zofia Kossak-Szczucka, a prewar Polish writer, who did not hide her anti-Semitism. During the war, she was a cofounder of Żegota, an underground organization, which was helping Jews. In her wartime underground articles, and her pamphlet, *Protest*, she called on the Poles to extend help to Jews, yet never changed her anti-Semitic orientation. Nonetheless, in 1985, Kossak-Szczucka was posthumously awarded the title of Righteous Among the Nations by the State of Israel. See Cherry and Orla-Bukowska, *Rethinking Poles and Jews*, 5. For the subject of anti-Semitic rescuers of Jews, see also Tec, *When Light Pierced the Darkness*.

21. This problem is raised in Tych and Tych, "Świadkowie *Shoah*." I am indebted to Mrs. Lucyna Tych for her archival research of non-Jewish documents, which was greatly helpful to my research.

22. Grabowski, *Szantażowanie Żydów*; Engelking, *Donosy do władz niemieckich*; Oliner and Oliner, *The Altruistic Personality*.

23. See, for instance, Shapiro, *Holocaust Chronicles*; Leociak, *Text in the Face of Destruction*; Patterson, *Along the Edge of Annihilation*; Zapruder, *Salvaged Page*; Vice, *Children Writing the Holocaust*; Garbarini, *Numbered Day*; Kassov, *Who Will Write Our History?*; Kruk, *The Last Days*; and Lehnstaedt, "Who Will Write Their History?"

24. Leociak, *Text in the Face of Destruction*, especially the chapter "Why Did They Write?" 77–96.

25. Brenner, *Writing as Resistance*, and Brenner, "Voices from Destruction."

26. In Shapiro, *Holocaust Chronicles*, only two articles appear in the section "Polish Bystanders." Gross, "Two Memoirs from the Edge of the Destruction," discusses the diary of Maria Dąbrowska, whom he unequivocally considers an anti-Semite, and the diary of Dr. Zygmunt Klukowski, which he considers an unequivocal proof of the Polish population's awareness of the Holocaust. Opalski, "The Holocaust in the Diaries of Zofia Nałkowska, Maria Dąbrowska, and Jarosław Iwaszkiewicz," claims that these diaries present evidence of prevailing Polish aloofness and detachment from the fate of the Jewish people. Kirchner, "Holocaust in the Diaries of Zofia Nalkowska and Maria Dabrowska," 106, accuses Opalski of intentional misreading and claims that the diaries of Nałkowska and Dąbrowska evince identification with the Jews and the desire to help the victims.

27. Iwaszkiewicz, *Notatki*, 116.

28. Walicki, *Philosophy and Romantic Nationalism*, 239–91. See also Janion and Żmigrodzka, *Romantyzm i historia*.

29. Girard, *Le journal intime*, ix–x.

30. Boener, "The Significance of the Diary," 42.

31. Nussbaum, "Toward Conceptualizing Diary," 129.

32. For a historical overview of the concept of *Bildung*, see, for instance, Gadamer, *Truth and Method*, 8–17. Lejeune, "The Practice of the Private Journal," 195–96, discusses the requirement of young girls in the nineteenth century to write diaries "for moral and educational reasons."

33. André Gide (1869–1951); his diaries extend from 1889 to 1950. Samuel Pepys (1633–1703); his diaries extend over a decade, from 1660 to 1669. Maria Bashkirtseff (1858–1884) started her diary at the age of thirteen.

34. Nussbaum, "Toward Conceptualizing Diary," 131, 134; Boener, "The Significance of the Diary," 42.

35. See Jauss, *Toward an Aesthetic of Reception*, 22–25; Gadamer, *Truth and Method*, 300–305; Mandel, "Full of Life Now," 66–72.

36. For the restrictions on the intelligentsia, and especially on writers to write and publish, see, for instance, Lucas, *Forgotten Holocaust*, 8–13; and Gross, *Fear*, 3.

37. Taylor, *Sources of the Self*, 11–12.

38. Kant, "What Is Enlightenment?" 3, 4.

39. Smith, *The Theory of Moral Sentiments*, 1, 114, 115.

40. Sueber, *Rediscovering Empathy*, 1.

41. Stein, *Collected Works*, 11, 38. *The Problem of Empathy* was Stein's doctoral thesis, which she wrote under Husserl and completed in 1916. Stein converted to Catholicism in 1920 and took the vows of the Carmelite Order in 1933. She perished

in Auschwitz in 1942. For a detailed discussion of her philosophy of empathy, see Brenner, *Writing as Resistance*.

42. Hunt, *Inventing Human Rights*, 40–42, 29, 32.

43. Bateson, "These Things Called Empathy."

44. On these two perspectives, see Kögler and Stueber, *Empathy and Agency*.

45. See Hoffman, *Empathy and Moral Development*.

46. In paricular, my approach draws on Edith Stein's doctoral study, *On the Problem of Empathy*; on Thompson, "Empathy and Consciousness," who grounds his argument in Stein; on Tooms, "The Role of Empathy in Clinical Practice," an analysis of Stein and especially her theory of the living body; and on Zahavi, "Beyond Empathy," 151–67.

47. Iwaszkiewicz, *Ciemne ścieżki*, 114.

48. Gide, *The Journals*, 3:354 and 4:47.

49. Woolf, *A Writer's Diary*, 337.

50. Camus, *Notebooks*, 337.

51. Iwaszkiewicz, *Notatki*, 48.

52. Rembek, *Wyrok*, 105–6.

Chapter 2

1. The heroic acts of rescue of Anna and Jarosław Iwaszkiewicz are summarized in Gutman, *Encyclopedia of the Righteous*, 287. I also have copies of the file (marked by the number 956) that Maria Iwaszkiewicz-Wojdowska, the daughter of the Iwaszkiewiczs, submitted with the application for the medal of the Righteous Among the Nations for her parents. The file includes Maria's recollections of the Jewish individuals her parents helped, and the testimony of Joanna Kramsztyk-Prochaska, for whom the Iwaszkiewiczs arranged a hiding place together with her mother in the vicinity of their Stawisko estate. Some of the rescued individuals appear under coded names in Iwaszkiewicz's wartime diary. Maria concludes her recollections with the following statement: "My parents saw the help they extended to endangered people as a natural thing and never sought any distinctions or awards. Now, when their home has become the Museum of Anna and Jarosław Iwaszkiewicz, I, their daughter and the curator of the museum, wish to have a proof of their acts."

2. Iwaszkiewicz, "W Stawisku."

3. For the Jewish theme in Iwaszkiewicz's fiction, see Maciejewska, "Zagłada Żydów w twórczości Jarosława Iwaszkiewicza."

4. Iwaszkiewicz, *Wiersze Zebrane*, 249–53.

5. Drobniak, *Jedność i różnorodność*, 42, 50, 10.

6. These great national Polish poets are mentioned in Iwaszkiewicz's poem "Do Pawła Valéry" ("To Paul Valéry"), in *Wiersze Zebrane*, 285–87.

7. Iwaszkiewicz, *Dzienniki*, 107.

8. Ibid., 108.

9. Ibid., 112–16.

10. Iwaszkiewicz, *Książka*, 5.

11. Zawada, *Jarosław Iwaszkiewicz*, 203.

12. Ibid., 204.

13. Iwaszkiewicz, *Książka*, 6.

14. Ibid., 5.

15. Ibid., 382.

16. Ibid., 184, 185, 186.

17. Iwaszkiewiczowa, *Dzienniki i wspomnienia*, 70.

18. Iwaszkiewicz, *Notatki*, 9. All quotations from the wartime diary used in this book come from Zawada's edition.

19. Quoted in Michlic, *Poland's Threatening Other*, 146–47.

20. For instance, Mieczysław Grydzewski [originally Gryncendler], who was of Jewish origins, established and edited the literary journals *Pro Arte et Studio* and *Skamander*, and later *Wiadomości Literackie*. These publications were instrumental in shaping Polish modernist literature in the 1920s and 1930s.

21. See, for instance, his recollections of prewar and postwar Jewish friends, Tuwim, Słonimski, and Szyfman in *Aleja Przyjaciół* (*The Alley of Friends*). Iwaszkiewicz supported Julian Stryjkowski and played an instrumental role in the publication of his *Głosy w ciemności* (*Voices in Darkness*) in 1956. Iwaszkiewicz was also the father-in-law of Bogdan Wojdowski, a prominent postwar Polish-Jewish writer. I am indebted for the information about Stryjkowski and Wojdowski to Prof. Monika Adamczyk-Garbowska.

22. Radziwon, *Iwaszkiewicz*.

23. Iwaszkiewicz, *Książka*, 35–36.

24. Iwaszkiewiczowie, *Listy 1922–1926*, 195, 180, 205.

25. Iwaszkiewicz, *Książka*, 210.

26. Iwaszkiewiczowa, *Dzienniki i wspomnienia*, 56.

27. Fein, *Accounting for Genocide*, 33.

28. Iwaszkiewicz, *Notatki*, 102.

29. Ibid., 103.

30. Ibid., 10.

31. Ibid., 16.

32. Ibid., 111.

33. Ibid., 109.

34. Iwaszkiewicz, *Książka*, 8, 9.

35. For the romantic tradition, see, for instance, Janion and Żmigrocka, *Romantyzm i historia*. For an analysis of the Kraków and the Warsaw schools of Polish historiography, see Serejski, *Naród a Państwo*, especially, 177–307. See also Davies, *Heart of Europe*, especially 175–208. On the Kraków and the Warsaw schools and the "Jewish question," see Engel, "On Reconciling the Histories of Two Chosen Peoples," 922–26.

36. Iwaszkiewicz, *Książka*, 178, 179, 180.

37. Ibid., 189.

38. Iwaszkiewicz, *Notatki*, 48.

39. Ibid., 84.

40. Ibid., 82.

41. Ibid., 6.

42. Ibid., 104–9.

43. Ibid., 89.

44. Ibid., 89–90.

45. Ibid., 90.

46. Ibid., 85.

47. Drobniak, *Jedność i różnorodność*, 69.

48. Iwaszkiewicz, *Wiersze Zebrane*, 285–87.

49. Iwaszkiewicz, *Ciemne ścieżki*, 114.

50. Drobniak, *Jedność i różnorodność*, 19.

Chapter 3

1. Drewnowski, *Rzecz russowska*, 43.

2. "Doroczny wstyd" ("Annual Shame") appeared in *Dziennik Popularny* on November 24, 1936.

3. Drewnowski, *Wyprowadzka z czyśćca*, 6: "Słonimski kept declaring that nobody since Stefan Żeromski had such moral authority." Słonimski was of Jewish origin.

4. Próchnik, "Antysemitism," 25, 26.

5. Drewnowski, *Rzecz russowska*, 29.

6. Drewnowski, *Wyprowadzka z czyśćca*, 23.

7. I was unable to obtain a copy of the publication in the United States. My quotations are taken from the full text sent to me by Dr. Sławomir Buryła with Prof. Drewnowski's permission. I thank them both for their most kind cooperation. In the notes, BUW refers to the Biblioteka Uniwersytetu Warszawskiego (Library of Warsaw University); BN, to the Biblioteka Narodowa (National Library); and ML to the Muzeum Literatury (Museum of Literature).

8. BN/ML CD no. 8, vol. 14, 8.XII.1955–31.XII.1956.

9. Drewnowski, *Wyprowadzka z czyśćca*, 29.

10. Ibid., 184.

11. Ibid., 186–87.

12. Mencwel, "Dąbrowska wobec Stalinizmu," 82.

13. Borkowska, *Maria Dąbrowska i Stanisław Stempowski*, 114–15.

14. Drewnowski, *Wyprowadzka z czyśćca*, 184.

15. Gross, "Two Memoirs from the Edge of the Destruction," 224.

16. BN/ML CD no. 4, vol. 9, manuscript, notebook 13.VI.1940–18.XI.1940.

17. April 22, 1943: "We saw billows of smoke above the Ghetto where the fighting apparently still continues"; April 26, 1943: "In general it is beautiful weather; it is sunny and it is spring. But outside the window there are still huge clouds of smoke from the Ghetto. Half of Warsaw is burning"; April 27, 1943: "Through the window, the cloud of smoke is still visible. It is horrible and fearful thoughts overpower my mind" (BN/ML CD, no. 4, vol. 9, notebook 2.IV.1943–1.IX.1943).

18. Drewnowski, *Rzecz russowska*, 42–8.

19. Ibid., 47.

20. Ibid., 50.

21. Abramowski, *Filozofia społeczna*, 209. See also Drewnowski, *Rzecz russowska*, 53–57.

22. Dąbrowska, *Życie i dzieło Edwarda Abramowskiego*, 30.

23. Drewnowski, *Rzecz russowska*, 46.

24. Ibid., 46–47.

25. Janion and Żmigrodzka, *Romantyzm i historia*, 52. On the issue of "Universal Brotherhood" see also Walicki, *Philosophy and Romantic Nationalism*, 249.

26. Dąbrowska, *Pisma Rozproszone*, 186, 189–90, 191. The story, "Wspomnienia" ("Reminiscences"), was first published in 1927.

27. BN/ML CD, no. 8, vol. 2, 11.XI.1917–31.XII.1927

28. The Polish Minority Treaty, signed in 1919 at the Versailles peace conference, promised to protect the rights of all minorities in the Polish state. The Constitution of the Polish Republic of March 17, 1921, reconfirmed the spirit of the treaty, promising freedom of conscience and religious denomination to all Polish citizens as well as equal rights regardless of their religious denomination.

29. See, for instance, Paczkowski, *The Spring Will Be Ours*, 21–23.

30. See Steinlauf, *Bondage to the Dead*, 12–16.

31. For example, Pease, *Rome's Most Faithful Daughter*, 123, notes that "in 1937 the Polish Catholic Press Agency called for 'a statesmanlike solution for the Jewish problem in Poland.'"

32. Paczkowski, *The Spring Will Be Ours*, 17.

33. I am referring to Andrzej Walicki's distinction between "political" pluralistic nationalism, the product of Western Enlightenment, which promoted a humanitarian and progressive democratic sovereignty of the people, and the "cultural" linguistic nationalism which promoted "a closed and monolithic society with authoritarian government." See Walicki, *The Enlightenment and the Birth of Modern Nationhood*, 2, 5.

34. Steinlauf, *Bondage to the Dead*, 16–17.

35. For the discussion of Polish anti-Semitism in the interwar period see, for instance, Gutman, "Polish Antisemitism Between the Wars"; Melzer, "Antisemitism in the Last Years of the Second Republic"; and Szymon Rudnicki, *Równi, ale niezupełnie*.

36. Scheler, *Ressentiment*, 25, 29, 30 (emphasis in the text).

37. For an extensive historical survey of the campaign against Jewish students, see Rudnicki, *Równi, ale niezupełnie*, 135–56.

38. "Her words," claims Rudnicki, "[which] reflected the opinions and the position of the majority of the Polish intelligentsia, gave moral support to the beaten [Jewish students]" (Rudnicki, *Równi, ale niezupełnie*, 150). See also Libera, *Dąbrowska*, 76–77.

39. BN/ML CD, no. 8, vol. 4, 26.IX.1934–31.XII.1936.

40. BN/ML CD, no. 8, vol. 5, 1.I.1937–7.IX.1939.

41. BN/ML CD, no. 8, vol. 5, 1.I.1937–7.IX.1939 (emphasis in the text).

42. Stempowski apparently urged Dąbrowska to confront publicly the anti-Semitic incidents at the universities. See Borkowska, *Maria Dąbrowska i Stanisław Stempowski*, 17–19, 105–6.

43. BN/ML CD no. 8, vol. 5, 1.I.1937–7.IX.1939.

44. Rudnicki, *Żywe i martwe morze*, 58–89.

45. BN/ML CD, no. 8, vol. 5, 1.I.1937–7.IX.1939.

46. "The only four individuals that I loved — Marjan [Dąbrowski, her husband], Stach [Stanisław Stempowski, her partner], Jerzy [Stempowski, Stanisław's son], Stasia [Stanisława Blumenfeldowa] — emerge in front of my eyes. Three of them [Marjan, Jerzy, Stasia] are dead." BN/ML CD no. 4, vol. 10, 2.IX.1943.

47. BN/ML CD no. 4, vol. 9, 2.IV.1943–1.IX.1943.

48. Dąbrowska, *A teraz wypijmy*, 179.

49. Dąbrowska, *Przygody*, 394–413.

50. BN/ML, CD no. 4, vol. 10, 2.IX.1943–5.X.1945.

51. BN/ML, CD no. 4, vol. 10, 2.IX.1943–5.X.1945.

52. For Warsaw deprivations see, for instance, Lucas, *The Forgotten Holocaust*, 30.

53. Ibid., 10, 12.

54. Gross, *Fear*, 5.
55. BN/ML, CD no. 4, vol. 10, 2.IX.1943–5.X.1945)
56. See, for instance, Grabowski, *Szantażowanie Żydów*.
57. See Szapiro, *Wojna żydowsko-niemiecka*.
58. See, for instance, Polonsky, "The Fate of the European Jews."
59. BUW/BN/ML, CD no. 9, notebook 63, 17.XI.1959–2.III.1960.
60. Gross, *Fear*, 5, 6.
61. Snyder, *Sketches from Secret War*, 198.
62. BN/ML, CD no. 4, vol. 10, 31.I.1947–16.VI.1947.
63. Drewnowski, *Wyprowadzka z czyśćca*, 189.
64. July 20, 1960, Muzeum Literackie, Warsaw, Dział Rękopisów inw. 4608.
65. Tel-Aviv, November 20, 1960, Muzeum Literackie, Warsaw, Dział Rękopisów inw. 4608.
66. BUW/BN/ML, CD no. 9, notebook 74, 11.IV.1960–13.V.1960, s. 1320–1361 19.VIII.1960.
67. BN/ML, CD no. 8, vol. 11, 1.IV.1951–3.VII.1952.
68. BN/ML, CD no. 8, vol. 13, 2.I.1954–5.XII.1955.
69. BN/ML, CD no. 4, vol. 10, 16.VI.1947–13.VII.1947.
70. BN/ML, CD no. 8, vol. 8, 5.XII.1948–17.XI.1949.
71. BN/ML, CD no. 8, vol. 10, 7.VII.1950–1.IV.1951.
72. BN/ML, CD no. 8, vol. 14, 8.XII.1955–31.XII.1956.
73. BN/ML, CD no. 8, vol. 7, 26.XII.1947–5.XII.1948.
74. BN/ML, CD no. 8, vol. 7, 26.XII.1947–5.XII.1948.

Chapter 4

1. For academic references to Wyleżyńska's diaries in connection with religious rituals under the Occupation, see Leociak, "O obecności sacrum"; in connection with the phenomenon of prostitution, see Grabowski, "Prostytucja w okupowanej Warszawie"; in connection with Polish negative response to Jews in the Holocaust, see Urynowicz, "Stosunki Polsko-Żydowskie."

2. Her works include, among others, a 1913 study of Ryszard Berwiński, a 1919 biography of Narcyza Żmichowska, and the historical narrative *Maria Leszczyńska na dworze wersalskim* (*Maria Leszczyńska in the Court of Versailles*; 1923); the novels *Niespodzianki* (*Surprises*; 1924) and *Księga Udręki* (*A Book of Torment*; 1925); the study *L'emigration polonaise en France* (1928); a travelogue, *Z duszą twoją na ramieniu: Listy z Hiszpanii* (*With Your Soul on My Shoulder: Letters from Spain*; 1933); and a translation from the Russian of D. Mereżkowski, *Narodziny bogów: Tutankhamon na Krecie* (*The Birth of Gods: Tutankhamon on Crete*; 1926) and, from the French, of W. Mickiewicz, *Memoirs* (1926, 1927, 1933). She also wrote numerous articles and essays in Polish and French, many of them on women's issues.

3. To the best of my knowledge, Dr. Marcin Urynowicz from the Instytut Pamięci Narodowej (Institute of National Memory) is working on an annotated edition of the diary. Despite extensive inquiries, I was not able to find much information about the author and even less about the diary.

4. *Ad usum* refers to the expression "ad usum Delphini," which designated censored texts suitable for the Grand Dauphin, son of Louis XIV. Wyleżyńska wanted to preclude the possibility of censoring her text.

5. Wyleżyńska is alluding to Horace Ode 3.30, "Exegi monumentum," in which Horace declares that he has contructed a memorial to himself through his poetry which will give him immortality. She is also referring to Pushkin's 1836 poem "Exegi Monumentum," in which Pushkin, echoing Horace, also claims that his poetry will become a monument which will be known to all peoples of Russia and will outlive any other monumental constructions and memorable conquests.

6. With this phrase Wyleżyńska again alludes to Horace, Ode 3.30, now recalling the sixth line, "non omnis moriar" ("not all of me will die [because my poetry will live forever]"). Pushkin also used Horace's line in his poem. I want to thank my good friend Dr. Debra Hershkowitz for the reference to Horace.

7. Taylor, "Responsibility for Self," 299.

8. Hoffman, "Prosocial Motivation," 269.

9. Cohen, *States of Denial*, 188.

10. Benda, *Délices*, 36 (my translation).

11. Ibid., 37.

12. She repeats the phrase on May 14, 1941; June 20, 1941; November 3, 1941; January 30, 1942; and February 13, 1942.

13. Russell, *Conquest of Happiness*, 30, 31, 32, 39, 77.

14. Ibid., 2.

15. Zuzanna Rabska (1888–1960) was a writer and a poet, and owned a large collection of bookplates. She was the daughter of Aleksander Kraushar and wife of Władysław Rabski, a well-known critic and publicist. The source of her testimony: Polska Zjednoczona Partia Robotnicza, Komitet Centralny. Wydział Historii Partii— Archiwum. Syg. 231/3.

16. Blum, *Friendship*, 12; Hare, *Moral Thinking*, 129 (emphasis in the text).

17. Gide, *Les nouvelles nourritures*, 227, 226 (my translations).

18. Kann, "Na oczach świata," 75–76.

19. Todorov, Facing the Extreme, 15–16.

Chapter 5

1. The chapter epigraph is from Zofia Nałkowska's diaries, which are taken from the multivolume edition by Hanna Kirchner; the translations are mine. All entries will be cited by date.

2. See Pieńkowska, *Zofia Nałkowska*, 9–13.

3. Among her writings are the novels *Kobiety* (*Women*; 1906), *Węże i Róże* (*Snakes and Roses*; 1914), *Hrabia Emil* (*Count Emil*; 1920); the autobiographical *Dom nad łąkami* (*A House on the Meadows*; 1925), *Granica* (*Border*; 1935), and *Węzły Życia* (*Knots of Life*; 1948); the drama *Dom Kobiet* (*House of Women*; 1930); and story collections including *Koteczka czyli białe tulipany* (*A Kitten or White Tulips*; 1909) and *Między Zwierzętami* (*Among Animals*; 1915).

4. See Kirchner's note 3 on January 27, 1943.

5. Nałkowska repeated almost identical versions of this phrase on July 28, 1944, in *Medaliony*, 121, and in *Widzenie*, 461. The phrase "Ludzie ludziom zgotowali ten los" literally means "people boiled/cooked this fate to people."

6. Notebook no. 46 covered the period from September 5, 1942, to January 15, 1943. The deportations began in July 1942 and ended in January 1943. See Kirchner's remarks in *Dzienniki V*, 420 note 1, and 424, note 2.

7. Kirchner, *Nałkowska*, 519.

8. On Korczak see Kirchner's note 1 in *Dzienniki II*, on the entry of September 11, 1910, and note 2 in *Dzienniki V*, on the entry of January 26, 1943. The name Korczak was inserted by Kirchner, who claims that "from the context it is possible that she refers to Janusz Korczak, whom the writer knew from her earliest youth."

9. Iwaszkiewicz, *Notatki*, 89–90.

10. Nałkowska, *Widzenie*, 61.

11. Foltyniak, *Między "pisać Nałkowską" a Nałkowskiej "czytaniem siebie,"* 107–8.

12. For instance, on October 15, 1943, Nałkowska wrote, "They announce [though the megaphone] a whole list of names of those executed today. Later, the names of those who will be executed if the attacks don't stop. . . . The principle of pure chance underlies collective responsibility."

13. Szlengel, *Co czytałem umarłym*, 105.

14. Quoted in Kirchner, *Nałkowska*, 591.

15. Iwaszkiewicz, "Do Zofii Nałkowskiej" ("To Zofia Nałkowska") in *Cztery Szkice Literackie*, 89–90.

16. For critical reception of *Medallions*, see Kirchner, *Nałkowska*, 588–92.

17. See, for instance, Gombrowicz, *Proza (Fragmenty) Reportaże*, 203, on Nałkowska's writing in 1935: "Nałkowska is a cold egoist and a cultural egotist, who would not allow anybody to stupefy her, and would not surrender one iota of her standards."

18. Nałkowska, *Widzenie*, 24.

19. Frye, *Anatomy of Criticism*, 135–36 (emphasis in the text).

20. Wellek, *Concepts of Criticism*, 228, 231.

21. Lodge, *Modes of Modern Writing*, 25.

22. Zaworska, *"Medaliony" Zofii Nałkowskiej*, 35.

23. Nałkowska, *Medaliony*, 91–92. I am aware of the translation of *Medallions* by Diana Kuprel (Evanston, Ill.: Northwestern University Press, 2000), but have chosen to provide my own translations.

24. Nałkowska, *Medaliony*, 97.

25. Ibid., 98.

26. Ibid., 99.

27. Ibid., 94.

28. Ibid., 99.

29. For a detailed analysis of the investigation of soap production in the story, see Shallross, *The Holocaust Object*, 55–71.

30. Zaworska, *"Medaliony" Zofii Nałkowskiej*, 47.

31. Nałkowska, *Medaliony*, 79.

32. Ibid., 116.

33. Ibid., 108.

34. Ibid., 109.

35. Ibid., 85.

36. Ibid., 106.

37. Ibid., 104.

38. Ibid., 116.

39. Ibid.

40. Ibid., 107.

41. Ibid., 108.

42. Ibid., 109.

43. Ibid., 110.

44. Ibid., 85.

45. Ibid., 86.

46. Ibid., 123.

47. Ibid., 123–24.

48. Ibid., 124.

Chapter 6

1. Kaczorowski, "Balada o Grodzisku."

2. The novel was published in installments in a youth biweekly, *Ognisko*.

3. Rembek, *Dzienniki—Rok 1920 i okolice*, 171. The novella was first published in installments in *Kurier Gnieźieński* in 1922 and reprinted in *Cygaro*, 102–37.

4. Lalak, "Postać Żyda," 30–39.

5. Quoted in Siedlecka, *Wypominki*, 200.

6. Stanisław Rembek in interview with Zbigniew Irzyk, *Kierunki* (May 11, 1978).

7. Marceli Hendelsman (1882–1945) was actively engaged in public life, a patriot and a fighter for Polish independence. During World War I, he was connected with Piłsudski's legions, and he fought in the 1920 Bolshevik war. Rembek does not mention this fact, nor does he mention anywhere that during World War II Hedelsman went into hiding in Milanówek, from July 1942 to June 1944, where he collaborated with the Polish underground. He was denounced to the Gestapo and deported to the concentration camp Gross-Rosen and eventually to Dora-Nordhausen, where he died in March 1945. See Hendelsman, *Rozwój*, 9–10.

8. Rembek, *Cygaro Churchilla*, 285–301, 301–27, 369–70. As the editor notes, the stories were found in Rembek's unpublished papers. I have examined Rembek's papers in the National Library of Rare Manuscripts in Warsaw, but was unable to establish the dates of the stories. The editor of the collection groups the stories according to their historical themes, but does not specify any dates. I would like to thank Maruta Rembek-Stępniewska, Stanisław Rembek's stepdaughter, and her husband Karol Stępniewski for giving me the permission to access Stanisław Rembek's papers.

9. Rembek, *Cygaro Churchilla*, 141–254. The editor refers to the text as "extremely valuable September notations," so it is hard to determine whether it is a diary or a memoir. On my examination of the papers, I encountered the same difficulty. The narrative is divided into chronological segments marked by titles rather than dates. The meticulous recording of the episodes makes it plausible to conjecture that Rembek wrote the piece on the basis of the notes that he took on his journey.

10. Rembek, *Cygaro Churchilla*, 227.

11. Ibid., 182.

12. Ibid., 219.

13. Ibid., 201–2, 249, 251.

14. Ibid., 253.

15. Ibid., 255.

16. Davies, *Rising '44*, 84.

17. Nałkowska, *Dzienniki*, September 19, 1939; October 4, 1939.

18. See Janion and Żmigrodzka, *Romantyzm i historia*, 52.

19. Handelsman conceived nation as a family of individuals united by territory, the sense of shared destiny, the same language, common culture, and common ethnic origins. Handelsman detected in Polish nationalism the emphasis on the uniqueness of the Polish nation, whose struggle for independence was also a "redemptive revolution for the world" which marked its calling as "Christ-like redeemer of humanity" (Handelsman, *Rozwój*, 26, 37).

20. Rembek, *Dziennik Okupacyjny*. All citations to entries in this diary are by date.

21. Nowakowski, "Introduction," in Rembek, *Dziennik Okupacyjny*, 5, 6, 7.

22. Rembek, *Cygaro Churchilla*, 105.

23. Ibid., 110.

24. Ibid., 130.

25. Rembek, *Nagan*, 176.

26. Ibid., 178.

27. Ibid., 179.

28. Jan Kasprowicz (1860–1926), a prominent Polish poet, dramatist, and literary critic, compared to Adam Mickiewicz. Deeply religious, his later poetry draws upon the Holy Scripture and the Christian tradition. *Hymny*, his major poetic creation, focuses on the unceasing struggle between good and evil, in which the arena of the battle is the human soul. Human pleading for mercy meets with silence from the distanced God. See Hutnikewicz, *Młoda Polska*, 104–24.

29. Nowakowski, "O Wyroku na Franciszka Kłosa," 105.

30. Lalak, *Między historią a biografi*, 68, 93. Armia Krajowa was a major underground organization. "Granatowy policjant," literally, a "navy policeman," was so called because the Polish police in the German service wore navy uniforms.

31. Lalak, *Between History and Biography*, 71.

32. Rembek, *Wyrok*, 156.

33. Ibid., 157.

34. Ibid., 158.

35. Ibid., 156.

36. Ibid., 157.

37. Ibid., 156.

38. Ibid., 158.

39. Ibid., 18.

40. Ibid., 40.

41. Ibid., 64.

42. Ibid., 75.

43. Ibid., 74–75.

44. Ibid., 77.

45. Ibid., 46–47, 82.

46. Ibid., 77.

47. Ibid., 93.

48. Ibid., 94.

49. Ibid.

50. Ibid., 105–6.

51. Rembek, *Cygaro Churchilla*, 285.

52. Ibid., 294.

53. Ibid., 299.

54. Ibid., 300.

Epilogue

1. Friedlander, *Probing the Limits of Representation.*

2. Lyotard, *Heidegger,* 45. Of course, Elie Weisel and Theodor Adorno also claimed the incompatibility of the aesthetic and the Holocaust experience.

3. Hatley, *Suffering Witness,* 2–3, 103.

4. Weissman, *Fantasies of Witnessing,* 5, 209, 211, 23 (emphasis in the text).

BIBLIOGRAPHY

Abramowski, Edward. *Filozofia społeczna: Wybór pism* [*Social Philosophy: Selected Writings*]. Warsaw: Państwowe Wydawnictwo Naukowe, 1965.

Andrzejewski, Jerzy. *Noc* [*Night*]. Warsaw: Czytelnik, 1945.

Aronson, Alex. *Studies in Twentieth-Century Diaries: The Concealed Self.* Lewiston: Edwin Mellen, 1991.

Bartoszewski, Władysław, ed. *Triptyk polsko-żydowski* [*Polish-Jewish Triptych*]. Warsaw: Rada Ochrony Pamięci Walk Męczeństwa, 2003.

Bateson, C. Daniel. "These Things Called Empathy: Eight Related but Distinct Phenomena." In *The Social Neuroscience of Empathy*, edited by Jean Decety and William Ickes, 3–17. Cambridge, Mass.: MIT Press, 2009.

Baum, Marzena. "Projekt 'Światła w ciemności — Sprawiedliwi wśród Narodów Świata'" ["Project 'Lights in Darkness — Righteous Among the Nations'"]. *Midrasz* 9.

Benda, Julien. *Délices d'Éleuthère.* Paris: Gallimard, 1935.

Biskupski, M. B. *The History of Poland.* Westport, Conn.: Greenwood, 2000.

Blum, Lawrence A. *Friendship, Altruism and Morality.* London: Routledge and Kegan Paul, 1980.

Boener, Peter. "The Significance of the Diary in Modern Literature." *Yearbook of Comparative and General Literature* 21 (1972): 41–45.

Borkowska, Grażyna. *Maria Dąbrowska i Stanisław Stempowski.* Kraków: Wydawnictwo literackie, 1999.

Brenner, Rachel F. "Voices from Destruction: Two Eyewitness Testimonies from the Stanisławów Ghetto." *Journal of Holocaust and Genocide Studies* 22, no. 2 (2008): 320–40.

——— . *Writing as Resistance: Four Women Confronting the Holocaust — Edith Stein, Simone Weil, Ann Frank, and Etty Hillesum.* University Park: Penn State University Press, 1997.

Camus, Albert. *Notebooks 1942–1951.* Translated by Justin O'Brien. New York: Alfred A. Knopf, 1965.

Cherry, Robert, and Annamaria Orla-Bukowska, eds. *Rethinking Poles and Jews: Troubled Past, Brighter Future.* Lanham: Rowman and Littlefield, 2007.

Cohen, Stanley. *States of Denial: Knowing About Atrocities and Suffering.* Cambridge, Eng.: Polity, 2001.

Dąbrowska, Maria. *A teraz wypijmy . . . Opowiadania* [*And Now We Shall Drink: Stories*]. Warsaw: Czytelnik, 1981.

——— . *Pisma Rozproszone* [*Dispersed Writings*]. Edited by Ewa Korzeniewska. Kraków: Wydawnicto Literackie, 1964.

——— . *Przygody człowieka myślącego* [*Adventures of a Thinking Person*]. Warsaw: Czytelnik, 1972.

——. *Życie i dzieło Edwarda Abramowskiego* [*Life and Work of Edward Abramowski*]. Warsaw: Wydawnictwo Związku Polskich Stowarzyszeń Spożywców, 1925.

Davies, Norman. *Heart of Europe: The Past in Poland's Present*. Oxford: Oxford University Press, 2001.

——. *Rising '44: The Battle of Warsaw*. New York: Viking, 2004.

Drewnowski, Tadeusz. *Rzecz russowska: O pisarstwie Marii Dąbrowskiej* [*The Matter from Russow: About the Writing of Maria Dąbrowska*]. Kraków: Wydawnictwo Literackie, 1981.

——. *Wyprowadzka z czyśćca: Burzliwe życie pośmiertne Marii Dąbrowskiej* [*Moving out of Limbo: The Stormy Posthumous Life of Maria Dąbrowska*]. Warsaw: Państwowy Instytut Wydawniczy, 2006.

Dreifuss (Ben Sasson), Havi. "We Polish Jews? The Relations Between Jews and Poles During the Holocaust—The Jewish Perspective [Hebrew]. Jerusalem: Yad Vashem, 2009.

Drobniak, Piotr. *Jedność i różnorodność: Europa w twórczości Jarosława Iwaszkiewicza* [*Unity in Diversity: Europe in the Work of Jarosław Iwaszkiewicz*]. Wrocław: Wydawnictwo Uniwersytetu Wrocławskiego, 2000.

Engel, David. "ARH Forum: On Reconciling the Histories of Two Chosen People." *American Historical Review* (2009): 914–29.

Engelking-Boni, Barbara. *Donosy do władz niemieckich w Warszawie i okolicach w latach 1940–1941* [*Denunciations to German Authorities in Warsaw and Evirons in the Years 1940–1941*]. Warsaw: Wydawnictwo IFIS PAN, 2003.

——. "Psychological Distance Between Poles and Jews in Nazi-Occupied Warsaw." In Zimmerman, *Contested Memories*, 47–54.

Eriksen, Thomas Hylland. *Ethnicity and Nationalism: Anthropological Perspectives*. London: Pluto, 1993.

Fein, Helen. *Accounting for Genocide: National Responses and Jewish Victimization During the Holocaust*. Chicago: University of Chicago Press, 1979.

Finder, Gabriel N. "Introduction." *Polin* 20 (2008): 3–55.

Finder, Gabriel N., and Alexander V. Prusin. "Jewish Collaborators on Trial in Poland, 1944–1956." *Polin* 20 (2008): 122–49.

Fiut, Aleksander. *Moment wieczny: Poezja Czesława Miłosza* [*The Eternal Moment: The Poetry of Czesław Miłosz*]. Kraków: Wydawnictwo Literackie, 1998.

Foltyniak, Anna. *Między "pisać Nałkowską" a Nałkowskiej "czytaniem siebie:" Narracyjna tożsamość podmiotu w "Dziennikach"* [*Between "Writing Nałkowska and Nałkowska's Self-Reading": Narrative Identity of the Subject in the Diaries*]. Kraków: UNIVERSITAS, 2004.

Friedlander, Saul, ed. *Probing the Limits of Representation: Nazism and the "Final Solution."* Cambridge, Mass.: Harvard University Press, 1992.

Frye, Northrop. *Anatomy of Criticism: Four Essays* (Princeton, N.J.: Princeton University Press, 1957).

Gadamer, Hans-Georg. *Truth and Method*. London: Continuum, 2006.

Garbarini, Alexandra. *Numbered Days: Diaries and the Holocaust*. New Haven, Conn.: Yale University Press, 2006.

Gide, André. *The Journals of André Gide*. Translated by Justin O'Brien. New York: Alfred A. Knopf, 1947–51.

——. *Les nouvelles nourritures*. Paris: Gallimard, 1935.

Girard, Alain. *Le journal intime*. Paris: Presses Universitaires de France, 1963.

Głowacka, Dorota, and Joanna Żylinska. *Imaginary Neighbors: Mediating Polish-Jewish Relations After the Holocaust*. Lincoln: University of Nebraska Press, 2007.

Gombrowicz, Witold. *Proza (Fragmenty) Reportaże, Krytyka Literacka 1933–1939 [Prose (Fragments) Reportages, Literary Criticism 1933–1939]*. Kraków: Wydawnictwo Literackie, 1995.

Grabowski, Jan. "Prostytucja w okupowanej Warszawie i w Dystrykcie (1939–1945)" ["Prostitution in Occupied Warsaw and in the District (1939–1945)"]. In *Parlamentaryzm, konserwatysm, nationalism [Parlamentarism, Conservatism, Nationalism]*, edited by Jolanta Żyndul, 271–89. Warsaw: Wydawnictwo Sejmowe, 2010.

———. *Szantażowanie Żydów w Warszawie, 1939–1943 [Blackmailing Jews in Warsaw, 1939–1943]*. Warsaw: Wydawnictwo JFIS PAN, 2004.

Gross, Jan Tomasz. *Fear: Anti-Semitism in Poland After Auschwitz — An Essay in Historical Interpretation*. New York: Random House, 2006.

———. "Two Memoirs from the Edge of the Destruction." In Shapiro, *Holocaust Chronicles*, 219–31.

Gutman, Israel, ed. *The Encyclopedia of the Righteous Among the Nations: Rescuers of Jews During the Holocaust*. Jerusalem: Yad Vashem, 2004.

———. "Polish Antisemitism Between the Wars: An Overview." In Gutman, Mendelsohn, Reinharz, and Shmeruk, *The Jews of Poland*, 97–109.

Gutman, Israel, Ezra Mendelsohn, Jehuda Reinharz, and Chone Shmeruk, eds. *The Jews of Poland Between Two World Wars*. Hanover: University Press of New England, 1989.

Hare, R. M. *Moral Thinking: Its Levels, Method and Point*. Oxford: Clarendon, 1987.

Hatley, James. *Suffering Witness: The Quandary of Responsibility After the Irreparable*. Albany: State University of New York Press, 2000.

Hendelsman, Marceli. *Rozwój narodowości nowoczesnej [The Development of Modern Nationalism]*. Edited by Tadeusz Lepkowski, 9–10. Warsaw: Państwowy Instytut Wydawniczy, 1973.

Hoffman, Martin L. "Development of Prosocial Motivation: Empathy and Guilt." In *The Development of Prosocial Behavior*, edited by Nancy Eisenberg, 281–313. New York: Academic, 1982.

———. *Empathy and Moral Development: Implications for Caring and Justice*. Cambridge, Eng.: Cambridge University Press, 2000.

Hunt, Lynn. *Inventing Human Rights: A History*. New York: W. W. Norton, 2007.

Hutnikewicz, Artur. *Młoda Polska [Young Poland]*. Warsaw: Wydawnictwo Naukowe PWN, 2001.

Iwaszkiewicz, Jarosław. *Aleja Przyjaciół [The Alley of Friends]*. Warsaw: Czytelnik, 1984.

———. *Ciemne ścieżki [Dark Pathways]*. Warsaw: Czytelnik, 1982.

———. *Cztery Szkice Literackie [Four Literary Drawings]*. Warsaw: Czytelnik, 1953.

———. *Dzienniki: 1911–1955 I [Diaries: 1911–1955]*. Edited by Agnieszka and Robert Papiescy. Warsaw: Czytelnik, 2007.

———. *Książka moich wspomnień [The Book of My Reminiscences]*. Kraków: Wydawnictwo Literackie, 1957.

———. *Notatki 1939–1945 [Notes 1939–1945]*. Edited by Andrzej Zawada. Wrocław: Wydawnictwo Dolnośląskie, 1991.

———. "W Stawisku w czasie wojny" ["In Stawisko in the Time of War"]. In *Walka o dobra kultury: Warszawa 1939–1945. Tom I [The Struggle for Cultural Riches:*

Warsaw 1939–1945. Volume I], edited by Stanisław Lorentz, 162–75. Warsaw: Państwowy Instytut Wydawniczy, 1970.

———. *Wiersze Zebrane* [*Collected Poems*]. Warsaw: Czytelnik, 1968.

Iwaszkiewiczowa, Anna. *Dzienniki i wspomnienia* [*Diaries and Reminiscences*]. Warsaw: Czytelnik, 2000.

Iwaszkiewiczowie, Anna, and Jarosław Iwaszkiewiczowie. *Listy 1922–1926* [*Letters 1922–1926*]. Edited by Małgorzata Bojanowska and Ewa Cieślak. Warsaw: Czytelnik, 1998.

Janion, Maria, and Maria Żmigrodzka. *Romantyzm i historia* [*Romanticism and History*]. Warsaw: Państwowy Instytut Wydawniczy, 1978.

Jauss, Hans Robert. *Toward an Aesthetic of Reception.* Translated by Timothy Bahti. Minneapolis: University of Minnesota Press, 1982.

Kaczorowski, Aleksander. "Balada o Grodzisku" ["A Ballad About Grodzisko"]. *Gazeta Wyborcza,* February 26/27, 2000.

Kann, Maria. "Na oczach świata — 1943" ["In the Sight of the World — 1943"]. In Bartoszewski, *Tryptyk polsko-żydowski,* 57–109.

Kant, Immanuel. "What Is Enlightenment?" Translated by Lewis White Beck, Robert E. Anchor, and Emil L. Fackenheim. In *On History,* edited by Lewis White Beck, 3–11. Indianapolis, Ind.: Library of Liberal Arts, 1981.

Karski, Jan. "An Early Account of Polish Jewry Under Nazi and Soviet Occupation Presented to the Polish Government in Exile, February 1940." Translated by David Engel. In *Jews in Eastern Poland and the USSR, 1939–46,* edited by Norman Davis and Antony Polonsky, 256–74. New York: St. Martin's, 1991.

Kassov, Samuel D. *Who Will Write Our History? Emmanuel Ringenblum, the Warsaw Ghetto, and the Oyneg Shabbes Archive.* Bloomington: Indiana University Press, 2007.

Kirchner, Hanna. "Holocaust in the Diaries of Zofia Nałkowska and Maria Dąbrowska." In *Literatura polska wobec zagłady* [*Polish Literature vis-à-vis the Holocaust*], edited by Alina Brodzka-Wald et al., 105–23. Warsaw: Żydowski Instytut Historyczny, 2000.

———. *Nałkowska albo życie pisane* [*Nałkowska: A Written Life*]. Warsaw: Wydawnictwo AB, 2011.

Kögler, Hans Herbert, and Karsten R. Stueber, eds. *Empathy and Agency: The Problem of Understanding in Human Sciences.* Boulder, Colo.: Westview, 2000.

Kruk, Herman. *The Last Days of the Jerusalem of Lithuania.* Edited by Benjamin Harshav. New Haven, Conn.: Yale University Press, 2002.

Lalak, Mirosław. *Między historią a biografią: O prozie Stanisława Rembeka* [*Between History and Biography: About the Prose of Stanisław Rembek*]. Sczecin: Uniwersytet Szczeciński, 1991.

———. "Postać Żyda w prozie Stanisława Rembeka" ["Jewish Characters in Stanisław Rembek's Prose"]. In *Niepokojąca reszta:szkice krytyczne* [*Disquieting Remainders: Critical Sketches*], edited by Andrzej Skrendo, 30–39. Szczecin: Wydawnictwo 13 Muz, 2004.

Lehnstaedt, Stephen. "Who Will Write Their History? The Jewish Historical Institute in Warsaw and the Ringenblum Archives." *Yad Vashem Studies* 40, no. 1 (2012): 247–62.

Lejeune, Philippe. "The Practice of the Private Journal: Chronicle of an Investigation [1986–1998]." In *Marginal Voices, Marginal Forms: Diaries in European Literature and History*, edited by Rachel Langford and Russell West. 185–201. Amsterdam: Rodopi, 1999.

Leociak, Jacek. "O obecności *sacrum* w literaturze documentu osobistego okupowanej Warszawy" ["About the Presence of the Sacred in the Literature of Personal Documentation in Occupied Warsaw"]. *Łódzkie Studia Teologiczne* 3 (1994): 108–24.

——. *Text in the Face of Destruction: Accounts from the Warsaw Ghetto Reconsidered*. Translated by Emma Harris. Warsaw: Żydowski Instytut Historyczny, 2004.

Libera, Zdzisław. *Maria Dąbrowska*. Warsaw: Państwowe Zakłady Wydawnictw Szkolnych, 1975.

Lodge, David. *The Modes of Modern Writing: Metaphor, Metonymy, and the Typology of Modern Literature*. Chicago: University of Chicago Press, 1977.

Lucas, Richard C. *The Forgotten Holocaust: The Poles Under German Occupation 1939–1944*. New York: Hippocrene Books, 2005.

Lyotard, Jean-François. *Heidegger and "the jews."* Translated by Andreas Michel and Mark S. Roberts. Minneapolis: University of Minnesota Press, 1990.

Maciejewska, Irena. "Zagłada Żydów w twórczości Jarosława Iwaszkiewicza" ["The Holocaust in the Literary Writing of Jarosław Iwaszkiewicz"]. In *Stawisko: Almanach Iwaszkiewiczowski* [*Stawisko: The Iwaszkiewicz Almanac*], 119–36. Podkowa Leśna: Muzeum im. Anny i Jarosława Iwaszkiewicza, 1994.

Mandel, Barrett J. "Full of Life Now." In *Autobiography: Essays Theoretical and Critical*, edited by James Olney, 66–72. Princeton, N.J.: Princeton University Press, 1980.

Melzer, Emanuel. "Antisemitism in the Last Years of the Second Republic." In Gutman, Mendelsohn, Reinharz, and Shmeruk, *The Jews of Poland*, 126–41.

Mencweł, Andrzej. "Dąbrowska wobec Stalinizmu" ["Dąbrowska vis-à-vis Stalinism"]. *Twórczość* 8 (1997): 75–91.

Michlic, Joanna Beata. *Poland's Threatening Other: The Image of the Jew from 1880 to the Present*. Lincoln: University of Nebraska Press, 2006.

Nałkowska, Zofia. *Charaktery Medaliony* [*Characters Medallions*]. Warsaw: Państwowy Instytut Wydawniczy, 1995.

——. *Dzienniki II: 1909–1917* [*Diaries II: 1909–1917*]. Edited by Hanna Kirchner. Czytelnik: Warsaw, 1976.

——. *Dzienniki V: 1939–1944* [*Diaries V: 1939–1944*]. Edited by Hanna Kirchner. Czytelnik: Warsaw, 1996.

——. *Dzienniki VI: 1945–1954* [*Diaries VI: 1945–1954*]. Edited by Hanna Kirchner. Czytelnik: Warsaw, 2000.

Nathan, Leonard, and Arthur Quinn. *The Poet's Work: An Introduction to Czesław Miłosz*. Cambridge, Mass.: Harvard University Press, 1991.

Nowakowski, M. "O Wyroku na Franciszka Kłosa" ["About the Sentence of Franciszek Kłos"]. *Kultura* (Paris) 6 (1986): 30–32.

Nussbaum, Felicity A. "Toward Conceptualizing Diary." In *Studies in Autobiography*, edited by James Olney, 128–40. New York: Oxford University Press, 1988.

Oliner, Samuel P., and Pearl M. Oliner, eds. *The Altruistic Personality: Rescuers of Jews in Nazi Europe*. New York: Free, 1988.

Opalski, Magdalena. "The Holocaust in the Diaries of Zofia Nałkowska, Maria Dąbrowska, and Jarosław Iwaszkiewicz." In Shapiro, *Holocaust Chronicles*, 231–41.

Paczkowski, Andrzej. *The Spring Will Be Ours: Poland and the Poles from Occupation to Freedom.* Translated by Jane Cave. University Park: Penn State University, 2003.

Patterson, David. *Along the Edge of Annihilation: The Collapse and Recovery of Life in the Holocaust Diary.* Seattle: University of Washington Press, 1999.

Pease, Neal. *Rome's Most Faithful Daughter: The Catholic Church and Independent Poland, 1914–1939.* Athens: Ohio University Press, 2009.

Pieńkowska, Ewa. *Zofia Nałkowska.* Warsaw: Wydawnictwo Szkolne i Pedagogiczne, 1975.

Polak, Beata Anna, and Tomasz Polak. *Porzucić etyczną arogancję: ku reinterpretacji podstawowych pojęć humanistyki w świetle wydarzenia Szoa* [*To Abandon Ethical Arrogance: Toward a Reinterpretation of Basic Concepts of Humanistic Studies in Light of the Shoah*]. Poznań: Wydawnictwo Naukowe Wydziału Nauk Społecznych Uniwersytetu im. Adama Mickiewicza w Poznaniu, 2011.

Polonsky, Antony. "The Fate of the European Jews, 1939–1945: Continuity or Contingency?" *Studies in Contemporary Jewry* 13 (1997): 190–224.

———. "*My Brother's Keeper?*" *Recent Polish Debates on the Holocaust.* London: Routledge, 1990.

Próchnik, Adam. "Antysemitism." In *Polacy o Żydach: Zbiór artykułów z przedruku* [*The Poles About Jews: A Collection of Reprinted Articles*], 19–28. Warsaw: Wydawnictwo Polskiej Unii Zgody Narodów, 1937.

Radziwon, Marek. *Iwaszkiewicz: Pisarz po katastrofie* [*Iwaszkiewicz: A Writer After the Catastrophe*]. Warsaw: Wydawnictwo AB, 2010.

Rembek, Stanisław. *Cygaro Churchilla* [*Churchill's Cigar*]. Edited by Grzegorz Łatuszyński. Warsaw: Agawa, 2004.

———. *Dziennik Okupacyjny* [*The Diary of the Occupation*]. Edited by Marek Nowakowski. Warsaw: Agawa, 2000.

———. *Nagan* [*Revolver*]. Warsaw: Czytelnik, 1990.

———. *Wyrok na Franciszka Kłosa* [*The Sentence of Franciszek Kłos*]. Warsaw: Instytut Wydawniczy, 1977.

Ringelblum, Emanuel. *Polish-Jewish Relations During the Second World War.* Translated by Dafna Alon, Danuta Dabrowska, and Dana Keren. Evanston, Ill.: Northwestern University Press, 1992.

Rodak, Paweł. "Dziennik osobisty jako praktyka piśmienna: działanie, meterialność, tekst" ["Personal Diary as Writing Practice: Action, Materiality, Text"]. In *Antropologia pisma: Od terorii do Praktyki* [*Anthropology of Writing: From Theory to Practice*], edited by Philipe Artières and Paweł Rodak, 175–92. Warsaw: Wydawnictwo Uniwersytetu Warszawskiego, 2010.

Rudnicki, Adolf. *Żywe i martwe morze* [*An Alive and a Dead Sea*]. Warsaw: Polonia Publishing House, 1956.

Rudnicki, Szymon. *Równi, ale niezupełnie* [*Equal but Not Entirely*]. Warsaw: Biblioteka Midrasza, 2008.

Russell, Bertrand. *The Conquest of Happiness.* London: Allen and Unwin, 1930.

Sarnecki, Jerzy. "Z otchłani: Poezje" ["Out of the Abyss: Poems"]. In Bartoszewski, *Triptyk polsko-żydowski*, 115–53.

Scheler, Max. *Ressentiment.* Translated by Lewis B. Coser and William W. Holdheim. Milwaukee, Wis.: Marquette University Press, 2007.

Serejski, Marian H. *Naród a Państwo w polskiej myśli historycznej* [*Nation and State in Polish Historical Thought*]. Warsaw: Państwowy Instytut Wydawniczy, 1973.

Shallcross, Bożena. *The Holocaust Object in Polish and Polish-Jewish Culture.* Bloomington: Indiana University Press, 2011.

Shapiro, Robert Moses, ed. *Holocaust Chronicles: Individualizing the Holocaust Through Diaries and Other Contemporaneous Personal Accounts.* Hoboken, N.J.: Ktav, 1999.

Siedlecka, Janna. *Wypominki* [*Reminiscences*]. Łódź: ABC, 1996.

Smith, Adam. *The Theory of Moral Sentiments.* Cambridge, Eng.: Cambridge University Press, 2012.

Snyder, Timothy. *Sketches from Secret War: A Polish Artist's Mission to Liberate Soviet Ukraine.* New Haven, Conn.: Yale University Press, 2005.

Stein, Edith. *The Collected Works of Edith Stein, Volume Three.* Translated by Waltraut Stein. Washington, D.C.: ICS, 1989.

Steinlauf, Michael. *Bondage to the Dead: Poland and the Memory of the Holocaust.* New York: Syracuse University Press, 1997.

Sueber, Karsten R. *Rediscovering Empathy: Agency, Folk Psychology, and the Human Sciences.* Cambridge, Mass.: MIT Press, 2006.

Szapiro, Paweł. *Wojna żydowsko-niemiecka: Polska prasa konspiracyjna 1943–1944 o powstaniu w getcie Warszawy* [*The Jewish-German War: Polish Conspiratory Press 1943–1944 About the Warsaw Ghetto Uprising*]. London: Aneks, 1992.

Szarota, Tomasz. *Karuzela na placu Krasińskich: studia i szkice z lat wojny i okupacji* [*The Carousel on Krasińskich Square: Studies and Sketches from War Years and the Occupation*]. Warsaw: Oficyna Wydawnicza RYTM: Fundacja "Historia i Kultura," 2007.

Szlengel, Władysław. *Co czytałem umarłym: Wiersze z getta warszawskiego* [*What I Read to the Dead: Poems from the Warsaw Ghetto*]. Warsaw: Państowy Instytut Wydawniczy, 1979.

Szymanowski, Antoni. "Likwidacja getta warszawskiego — 1942" ["The Liquidation of the Warsaw Ghetto — 1942"]. In Bartoszewski, *Triptyk polsko-żydowski*, 16–19.

Taylor, Charles. "Responsibility for Self." In *The Identities of Persons*, edited by Amélie Oksenberg Rorty, 281–301. Berkeley: University of California Press, 1976.

———. *Sources of the Self: The Making of the Modern Identity.* Cambridge, Mass.: Harvard University Press, 1989.

Tec, Nechama. *When Light Pierced the Darkness: Christian Rescue of Jews in Nazi-Occupied Poland.* Oxford: Oxford University Press, 1986.

Thompson, Evan. "Empathy and Consciousness." *Journal of Consciousness Studies* 8, nos. 5–7 (2001): 1–32.

Todorov, Tzvetan. *Facing the Extreme: Moral Life in Concentration Camps.* Translated by Arthur Deuner and Abigail Pollak. New York: Henry Holt, 1996.

Tooms, S. Kay. "The Role of Empathy in Clinical Practice." *Journal of Consciousness Studies* 8, nos. 5–7 (2001): 247–58.

Tych, Feliks, and Lucyna Tych. "Świadkowie *Shoah*: Zagłada Żydów w polskich pamiętnikach i wspomnieniach" ["Witnesses of the Shoah: The Destruction of the Jews in Polish Diaries and Memoirs"]. In *Długi Cień Zagłady: Szkice Historyczne* [*The Long Shadow of the Holocaust: Historical Sketches*], edited by Feliks Tych, 9–55. Warsaw: Żydowski Instytut Historyczny, 1999.

Urynowicz, Marcin. "Stosunki Polsko-Żydowskie w Warszawie w okresie okupcji hit-lerowskiej" ["Polish-Jewish Relationships in Warsaw During the Hitlerian Oc-cupation"]. In *Polacy i Żydzi pod okupacją niemiecką, 1939–1945 (Studia i Materiały)* [*Poles and Jews Under German Occupation 1939–1945 (Studies and Materials)*], edited by Andrzej Żbikowski, 537–626. Warsaw: Instytut Pamięci Narodowej, 2006.

Vice, Sue. *Children Writing the Holocaust.* New York: Palgrave Macmillan, 2004.

Walicki, Andrzej. *The Enlightenment and the Birth of Modern Nationhood: Polish Political Thought from Noble Republicanism to Tadeusz Kościuszko.* Translated by Emma Harris. Notre Dame, Ind.: University of Notre Dame Press, 1989.

———. *Philosophy and Romantic Nationalism: The Case of Poland.* Oxford: Clarendon, 1982.

Weissman, Gary. *Fantasies of Witnessing: Postwar Efforts to Experience the Holocaust,* 5, 209, 211, 23. Ithaca, N.Y.: Cornell University Press, 2004.

Wellek, René. *Concepts of Criticism.* New Haven, Conn.: Yale University Press, 1963.

Woolf, Virginia. *A Writer's Diary.* New York: Harcourt, Brace, Jovanovich, 1953.

Zahavi, Dan. "Beyond Empathy: Phenomenological Approaches to Intersubjectivity." *Journal of Consciousness Studies* 8, nos. 5–7 (2001): 151–67.

Zapruder, Alexandra. *Salvaged Pages: Young Writers' Diaries of the Holocaust.* New Haven, Conn.: Yale University Press, 2002.

Zawada, Andrzej. *Jarosław Iwaszkiewicz.* Warsaw: Wiedza Powszechna, 1994.

Zimmerman, Joshua D., ed. *Contested Memories: Poles and Jews During the Holocaust and Its Aftermath.* New Brunswick, N.J.: Rutgers University Press, 2002.

INDEX

Abramowski, Edward, 46, 49–50, 51
aesthetics, 42, 72, 81
altruism, 81–88, 99–100; definitions, 87
Andrzejewski, Jerzy: "Holy Week," 41–42,
    111, 171n2
anti-Semitism, Polish, 177n35; as damaging
    Polish nation, 46–47, 55–57, 133–35,
    166; literary, 32, 79–80; prewar, 6, 9;
    publications, 53–54; *szmalcowniki*
    (Polish blackmailers), 64, 110; at
    universities, 46–47, 55–56; *Żydek*, 79
Armed Poland, 141
autonomy, 81–84, 99–100

Bashkirtseff, Marie, 13
Benda, Julien, 80–81
Bildung, 12, 14, 17, 27, 78, 89
Błoński, Jan, 5–6, 10
Blum, Lawrence A., 87
Blumenfeldowa, Stanisława, 59–62
Boener, Peter, 12
Borkowska, Grażyna, 48

Camus, Albert, 18
Catholic Church, 6
Christian self-identity: effects of Jewish
    genocide on, 6–8, 22, 151–54
Cohen, Stanley, 79

Dąbrowska, Maria, 3, 10
    attitudes toward Jews, 176n17; biases, 20,
        45, 47–48, 172n26; criticism of anti-
        Semitism at universities, 46–47, 55–56;
        during communist regime, 66–70; Jewish
        doctors, 57–58; personal relationships
        with Jews, 59–62; *ressentiment*, 55, 65,
        66–70; silences about atrocities, 3, 48, 65
    life events: birth, 45; marriage, 46;
        voluntary service in WWI, 51
    nationalism of, 8–9, 45–70, 48–49, 50;
        attachment to Polish countryside,

45–46, 52; ethical implications, 49–55;
    idealization of peasant, 52; influence
    of socialism, 46; Poland as model
    of universal friendship, 10; Polish
    underground work, 65; positivism, 52;
    privileging of Polish experience, 9, 59;
    romantic ideology of Polish destiny, 45,
    49, 51, 62–66
    relationships, 46; Abramowski, 46, 49–50,
        51; Blumenfeldowa, 59–62; marriage,
        46, 49; Stempowski, 46, 58
    social activism, 46, 48–49; moral authority,
        46, 55; moral revolution, 50
    works: *Adventures of a Thinking Person*, 61;
        "Annual Shame," 46, 55–56; *Diaries*,
        12, 47–48; *Life and Work of Edward
        Abramowski*, 50; *Night and Days*, 46;
        "Welcome to War and Freedom, A," 50
    writing life: diary keeping habits, 12;
        reviews, 117–18, 135–36; translations of
        Pepys, 13
Dąbrowski, Marian, 46, 49
death: death as heroic *vs.* death as ordinary,
    94–96; split of "dead and dead," 116
Dehlen, Maria, 136
deportations of 1942, 108, 149
diary: history of diary keeping, 12–14;
    compared to novel, 16, 92–93;
    definitions of diary, 78; influence of
    Holocaust on, 14; Romantic ideas, 12;
    self-education, 12
Drewnowski, Tadeusz, 47, 48
Drobniak, Piotr, 26

empathy, 15–23; breakdown of, 23, 88–92,
    97–100, 106–7; definitions, 16–17; what
    would I have done?, 97–98; "you as
    another I," 16, 21
Endecja (right-wing political movement), 11,
    46, 53–55, 58, 138, 144
Engelking-Boni, Barbara, 4

PAX, 136
PEN clubs, 102
Pepys, Samuel, 13
Pieńkowski, Stanisław, 53
Piłsudski, Józef, 6, 50, 51, 53
Podolia Governorate (Russian empire), 71
Poland
    historic events: agricultural reform,
        53; Communist regime, 66–70,
        136; deportations of 1942, 108, 149;
        economic crisis of 1930s, 53; failed
        Revolution of 1905, 46; Ghetto
        liquidation, 93–100 (see also Ghetto
        liquidation); Ghetto Uprising (1943),
        3, 5, 39, 68 (see also Ghetto Uprising
        (1943)); Holocaust, 9, 14, 17, 20–21,
        61, 79, 92, 133, 167–70, 171n6;
        independence (1918), 50, 53, 133;
        insurrection of 1831, 133; insurrection
        of 1863, 36–37, 50, 133; interwar
        period, 10–11, 134, 142–43, 177n35;
        Minorities Treaty (1919), 53, 177n28;
        Occupation, 3, 4, 17, 37, 62–66, 87,
        111, 133, 134, 143, 144–51, 171n4;
        Polish-Bolshevik war (1920), 133–34;
        Sanacja, 53; Warsaw Uprising (1944),
        63, 64, 68, 72; WWI, 51, 52
    historiography: Kraków school, 36–37, 52;
        Warsaw school, 36–37, 52
    nationalism: Christian destiny, 133, 134,
        141–44, 151–54, 182n19; as "Christ
        of nations," 10, 52; ethnic exclusivity,
        10–11; Europeanization of Poland, 54;
        heroic national myth, 10; independence
        (1918), 50, 53, 133; messianic destiny,
        10, 133, 134, 151–54; myth of
        invincibility, 134; Polish underground,
        64–65, 71–72, 144; sovereignty, 10
Poland Fights, 65
Poles about the Jews, The, 36–37, 55
Polish Christian diarists, 3–23
    ethical issues: empathy, 15–23;
        ethical crisis, 4; freedom from anti-
        Semitic socialization, 9; horizons of
        expectation, 19–21; metaphysical guilt,
        8; psychological effects of witnessing,
        4 (see also witnessing); relations with
        fellow Poles, 19–20, 21–22; relations
        with Jews, 19–21 (see also specific
        diarists); semblance of normalcy,
        10 (see also normalization); sense

of complicity, 8; xenophobic social
    climate, 9, 172n26
    humanism, 11; belief in, 3–4; collapse of
        faith in, 9; empathy, 15–23; protection
        of, 10
    influences: Holocaust, 17, 20–21;
        influence of European intellectualism,
        10, 17; self-identification as patriotic
        Poles, 10; xenophobic social climate, 9,
        172n26
    legacy of, 22–23, 169–70
    writing issues: criticisms of one another,
        11, 117–18; diary keeping habits,
        11–12; interactions with one another,
        11; publication, 169; writer-reader
        relationship, 12–13, 75
    See also specific diarists by name
Polish-Jewish relationships, 20, 53–54;
    breakdown of empathy, 23, 88–92,
    97–100, 106, 107; in communist Poland,
    66–70, 148; debate of Polish role in
    Final Solution, 6; doctors, 57–58;
    indifference to fate of Jews, 4–5, 72,
    79, 80, 91; Jewish question, 5, 54, 56,
    79; literary, 32, 79–80; moral failure of
    Polish society, 31–32, 41; rescuer-victim
    relationship, 81–100; rescuing Jews, 4,
    25, 40–42, 71, 82–100, 103–4, 174n1;
    szmalcowniki (Polish blackmailers), 64;
    at university, 36–37, 55–56
PPS (Polish Socialist Party), 49–50
Próchnik, Adam, 47
Professional Union of Polish Writers (ZZLP),
    102
Prosto z Mostu, 57

Rabska, Zuzanna, 84–85, 179n15
Radziwon, Marek, 32
Rajnfeld, Józef, 3, 171n1
Rembek, Stanisław, 3, 62, 133–70
    attitudes toward Jews: in diaries, 20, 133,
        137–51; in fiction, 133, 151–66; Jewish
        friendships, 138–39
    emotional life: depression, 136, 145–47
    life events: as correspondent in Algiers,
        136; as draftsman in Algiers, 136;
        education, 136; marriage, 136; military
        service, 136, 139–40; in Ministry of
        Culture, 136; prison camp experience,
        141; as teacher in Polish high schools,
        136; travel, 136

nationalism of, 8–9; "Literature and the Soldier" survey, 141–42, 151; nationalistic-religious Weltanschauung, 133, 141–44, 151–54; privileging Polish suffering, 9, 134, 148–50; realization of Poles' moral failure, 133, 134–35, 166 works: *A Ballad about a Disdainful Hanged Man*, 135, 136; *Churchill's Cigar*, 136–37, 180nn8–9; "A Delivered Relay," 135; *Diaries: 1920 and Thereabouts*, 137–39; *Diary of the Occupation*, 12, 134, 144–51, 165; *In the Field*, 135; film adaptations, 136; "A Letter to Churchill," 134, 154, 162–65; *Punitive Expedition, A*, 135; *Revolver*, 135, 138, 152–54; *Ripe Spikes*, 135, 152–54; *The Sentence of Franciszek Kłos*, 22, 134, 135, 136, 154–62; "September," 139–44; *Squadron* (film), 136; *Two January Tales*, 135
    writing life: diary keeping habits, 12; literary prizes, 135; themes of war, 135
Republic's Eastern Lands, The, 65
Righteous Among the Nations medals, 171n5, 172n20, 174n1
Ringelblum, Emanuel, 5
Romanticism, 12, 45, 49, 51, 62–66, 133; romantic ideology of Polish destiny, 45, 49, 51, 62–66; Romantic Polish poets, 10, 142, 143
Rozwój, 53–54
Rubinstein, Arthur, 33
Rudnicki, Adolf, 59, 67
Rusinek, Michał, 58–59
Russia, 67, 148
Russow, Poland, 45

Sanacja (Non-Party Block for Cooperation with the Government), 53
Schulz, Bruno, 103
Skamander group of poets, 16, 26, 34
Słonimski, Antoni, 16, 31–34
Smith, Adam, 14–15
Soviet Union, 67, 148
Stempowski, Stanisław, 46, 58
suffering, responses to: anxiety and, 90; breakdown of empathy, 88–92; ideology and, 69–70; indifference and, 4–5, 72, 79, 91; meaning of survival, 98–100
survival, 98–100
Szlengel, Wladyslaw, 116

szmalcowniki (Polish blackmailers), 64, 110
Sztejnbach, Bombardier, 138

Taylor, Charles, 14, 78
Tejchner, Maksymilian, 138–39
Todorov, Tzvetan, 94
Trade Union of Polish Writers, 57–58
Treblinka, 105, 109, 145, 149–50
Tuwim, Julian, 16, 31–34

Underground, 64–65, 71–72, 144
Union of Professional Polish Writers, 71
Untermenschen (German classification of Poles), 63
U.S. Holocaust Museum, 168

Valéry, Paul, 43–44

Wajda, Andrzej, 136
Walicki, Andrzej, 177n33
Warsaw, Poland, 71; Krasińskich Square, 5, 7, 39, 79, 110; during Occupation, 66–70 (*see also* Occupation)
Warsaw Uprising (1944), 63, 64, 68, 72
Weissman, Gary, 168
witnessing: empathy and, 17, 20, 98, 107, 109, 110–13, 116; the experience of witnessing, 167–70; ideology and, 8, 49; Jews as witness to Polish destiny, 151–66; non-witness witnessing, 168–70; poet as witness, 6, 8, 23, 44, 110, 115; psychological effects of, 4, 9, 14, 19, 80, 104, 109, 122; self-assessment and, 19–20, 25, 29, 44, 49, 92, 93, 130; silence, 104, 110, 111; silences about atrocities, 3, 48, 65; witness as Christian, 6, 8, 23, 145, 155, 165
Woolf, Virginia, 18
World War I, 51, 52
Wyleżyńska, Aurelia, 3, 62, 71–100
    attitudes toward Jews, 21–22; helper as hostage, 87; meaning of survival, 98–100; reaction to burning of Ghetto (1943), 8; rescue work, 71, 82–92
    emotional life: altruism, 81–88, 99–100; anxiety, 90; autonomy, 81–84, 99–100; breakdown of empathy, 88–92; guilt, 86; happiness, 81–84, 85, 87, 100; identity transformation, 88; influence of Huxley on, 82; influence of Russell on, 82–84; reaction of body to trauma, 95–96; sense of failure, 87

life events: birth, 71; death, 72; education, 71; move to Paris, 71; settlement in Warsaw, 71–72; travels, 71; volunteer in hospital, 71; work for Underground, 71–72

works, 178n2; "A Diamond in a Tooth," 76; "Germans in the Polish Mansion," 76

writing life: aesthetics linked with ethics, 72, 81; author-reader relation, 75; diary as moral corset, 81; diary as novel, 92–93; diary as testament, 73–75, 176n1; diary keeping habits, 12; experimentation, 75–78; influence of Benda on, 80–81; influence of Enlightenment on, 74, 78; influence of Gide on, 13, 18, 91–92; influence of Horace on, 73, 74, 179nn5–6; influence of Huxley on, 82; influence of Pushkin on, 73, 74; influence of Russell on, 82–84; organization of ideas, 74; preservation of diary, 71, 72, 73, 74; recorder of events, 75; self-analysis through writing, 77–81, 92–100

xenophobia, Polish, 5–6, 9, 11, 68, 79

Zawada, Andrzej, 28
Zaworska, Helena, 120
Żeromski, Stefan, 50
żydokomuna, 148